SILENT POLITICS:
POLLS AND THE AWARENESS OF PUBLIC OPINION

SILENT POLITICS:

POLLS AND THE AWARENESS OF PUBLIC OPINION

LEO BOGART

Wiley-Interscience, a Division of John Wiley & Sons, Inc.
New York · London · Sydney · Toronto

Library of Congress Catalog Card Number: 75-37430

ISBN 0-471-08520-0

Printed in the United States of America.

10 9 8 7 6 5 4 3 2 1

IN MEMORIAM
JACOB A. BOGART
1882-1970

PREFACE

We study people's opinions not only out of curiosity, but in the hope of influencing them. At a time in history when a few men walk on the moon while tens of millions hunger on earth, who can deny the urgent need to change men's minds, to change their ways? In our epoch humanity has attained the technological capacity to obliterate itself, while the forces of ignorance and evil run amok. Why should we not look to the arts of persuasion which might bring men to organize their private lives and public state to avoid self-destruction?

If men must be persuaded not to hate, to forgo immediate pleasure, self-interest, or the dictates of tradition in order to plan for their own eventual larger good, this can be done only with an understanding of what moves them. Here originates the study of public opinion.

The order of business that confronts government each week, the dominant subjects of popular conversation, and the lead stories in the newspapers and newscasts—all these taken together constitute the public issues which the tradition of democracy makes every man's concern.

In our time established institutions tremble, and the premises that underlie parliamentary democracy face serious challenge. The children of a revolutionary era no longer accept blindly the traditional American assumption that government is benign, rational, and a true expression of the people's will. They believe that the emergence of public issues need not be left to the haphazard processes of history; they can be contrived, and the attention of the public and the state can be deliberately redirected.

Our understanding of public opinion today is inseparable from our familiarity with opinion polls, which use the principle of sampling cross sections of the public to ask what they think of this or that. Feedback of some kind has always been part of the political process, for no ruler has ever occupied the seat of power without concern for the stability of his position, and without keeping a sharp ear cocked to the rumblings of dissatisfaction among those he governs. But before polling emerged in the twentieth century as a technique accepted by rulers and ruled, there had never been a means by which mere verbal expression of dissent could be used as a power in itself. Not only polling, but the publication and serious acceptance of polls by the public have introduced into the political process the notion of an independent criterion of legitimacy in the conduct of government.

The very fact that polls are widely accepted as a yardstick of public opinion makes them a target of state policy as well as a motivator and popularity index for politicians. Policies instituted to please, placate, or even follow public opinion have their counterpart in a public opinion which is not merely measured but manipulated through the "management" of news.

Feedback from polls leads to a deadly conformity· if it treats the majority wishes of the moment as immutable. The democratic ideal envisages a government whose leadership is strongly responsive to the public's wants and needs. But wants and needs are constantly changing, and what people at any moment want is generally different from what leaders think they need. The incongruity between wants and needs becomes more disparate as society becomes more complex and heterogeneous, and as different groups struggle to assert their separate interests.

Wants and needs tend toward congruity to the degree that the public is informed on the issues facing it, that leaders are attuned to public sentiment, and that they in turn have the capacity and will to communicate their intentions back to the people. I am concerned in this book with the forces that facilitate or hinder this process.

In an impersonal society it is easy for people to avoid disagreeable information, to conform to the group in their opinions, and to refuse to accept the unfortunate consequences to themselves and their descendants of actions which serve their short-run self-interest. There are realistic limits to the burden that any individual can shoulder on behalf of the entire human race. However, a democratic society can set intelligent priorities, and hold to them, only when public opinion is informed and imbued with a sense of collective responsibility.

The study of public opinion goes well beyond what surveys tell us. Much of what I have to say refers to their limitations, or dwells on aspects of opinion that elude measurement. Yet surveys are the only sensible means of describing the constant changes in what people know and hope for in a world beyond every man's full comprehension. Opinion research is a magnifying mirror of our collective ignorance and perplexities. It gives us cause for introspection.

New York, New York   Leo Bogart
October 1971

ACKNOWLEDGMENTS

The core ideas of this book, and much of the language, were originally voiced as a presidential address to the American Association for Public Opinion Research and were published in the *Public Opinion Quarterly,* Fall 1967, under the title "No Opinion, Don't Know, No Answer." The chapter, "Is There a World Public Opinion?" is adapted from an address to the World Association for Public Opinion Research, published under the same title in *Polls,* Spring 1966. I appreciate the permission given by the editors of both publications to use this material. Portions of the manuscript were read in draft form by my wife Agnes Bogart and by Charles M. Kinsolving, Jr., Max Ralis, Joseph Spigelman, and Frederick W. Williams. I am grateful for their comments. I received particular encouragement from Richard Baxter. Marie Thornton relentlessly typed this book through several transformations and deserves special thanks, though she seems unscathed.

L. B.

CONTENTS

xiii

SILENT POLITICS:
POLLS AND THE AWARENESS OF PUBLIC OPINION

Part One

POLLS AND POLITICS

SHOULD POLLS MAKE POLICY?

Public opinion is everything. . . . With it nothing can fail. Without it nothing can succeed.

Abraham Lincoln

In July 1945 General Leslie Groves, head of the Manhattan Project, asked Arthur Compton, a nuclear physicist, to do "an opinion poll among those who know what is going on."[1] The resulting survey was conducted among 150 staff members of the Chicago laboratory that had produced the first atomic weapon. They may have had private thoughts about what to do with the bomb, but they had not been involved in the discussions at higher levels. To many of them the poll was their first encounter with the problem. According to the atomic scientist Eugene Rabinowich, "We were not given more than a few minutes to answer. . . . The man distributing [the questionnaires] said, 'Put your mark in one of the places reflecting your opinion.' "

Compton's analysis of the poll results was that "there were a few who preferred not to use the bomb at all, but 87 percent voted for its military use, at least if after other means were tried this was found necessary to bring surrender." The term "military use" in retrospect carries unmistakable and horrifying implications. But included in the 87 percent were 46 percent who said, "Give a military demonstration in Japan to be followed by a renewed opportunity for surrender before full use of the weapons is employed," and an additional 26 percent who said, "Give an experimental demonstration in this country with representatives of Japan present, followed by a new opportunity for surrender before full use of the weapon is employed."

The poll results were turned over to War Secretary Henry L. Stimson five days before the bomb burst over Hiroshima. It seems unlikely that this survey could have had much influence on Harry Truman. Of more than passing interest are both the use of the opinion polling method in arriving at so momentous a decision and the vulnerability of that method to debatable and perhaps distorted interpretations of the results.

A survey among American colonists in 1774 might well have shown a majority satisfied with the existing system and opposed to taking up arms for independence as Noel Perrin suggests:[2] "422 did ask, 'What system?' These last included many frontiersmen." Perrin goes on: "Concerning the Quartering Act, the response was in no wise expected. Thirty-one of 32 men questioned in Augusta, Georgia, did say they wished there were more British troops among us. All of eight maidservants in New York City felt the same way. It was even so throughout the colonies, save only nests of eggheads in Boston, among tutors in colleges, and among those on whom the troops are actually quartered."

Today, opinion surveys, professional and amateur, are an integral part of decision-making in politics as well as business. Presidents John F. Kennedy and Lyndon B. Johnson both took particularly strong interest in the polls. Johnson once told a Gridiron Dinner that Patrick Henry had conducted a poll before he made his "Give Me Liberty or Give Me Death" speech. (The results: 46 percent for liberty, 29 percent for death, and the rest "didn't know.") This show of cynicism masked an extraordinary sensitivity to surveys. Johnson kept in his pocket a chart of his Gallup Poll popularity standing and drew it forth often to impress visitors.

"Why did Johnson retire, do you think?" asks political analyst Walter Lippmann. "He knew that he was beaten. And where did he get that? He got it from polls, a little bit, but mostly he just knew, as a public man very well trained in public affairs—he assumed it. I don't think you can measure everything."

"I don't need any poll," says Franz Xaver Unertl, a German politician. "When I want to know what people are thinking, I go to the toilet during the intermission at a meeting and listen to what they say." Reliance on intuition in preference to measurement is reminiscent of the argument advanced by dictators who discredit election results on the grounds that they fail to express the "true" will of the people. In January 1970 a general election in the African country of Lesotho was declared invalid by the prime minister, Chief Leabua Jonathan, when the ballotting went the wrong way. After arresting the winner, the Chief announced, "It may appear to be undemocratic in other circles, but in my conscience I know that the majority of the people are behind me."[3]

Few political figures in contemporary America would publicly contest the findings of opinion polls by insisting on the superiority of their own insights. "I stay so close to my constituents that I don't have to run a poll," said former Congresswoman Edna F. Kelley. In point of fact, there is only very slight (.19) correlation between the foreign policy attitudes of a congressional constituency and the congressman's perception of these attitudes.[4] But a growing number of public officials are using polls of their own to find out what is on the voters' minds.

A congressman's ability to use the franking privilege permits him to poll his constituents at minimal expense; thereby he may become more visible to the voters and gain a laudable reputation for concern with their interests. Many, if not most, congressional polls use questionnaires that are unprofessionally constructed and elicit returns from only a tiny and unrepresentative sampling of the electorate. Consider this question from a "poll" that one congressman addressed to the 180,000 voters of his district: "Do you feel demonstrators who block U.S. troop trains, burn draft cards, and send gifts and blood plasma to North Vietnam should be fined and imprisoned when such acts would be considered treasonous if we were in a declared state of war?" What red-blooded American would dare answer nay to such an inquiry?

Electioneering rather than research is often the paramount interest in this sort of survey. Former Congressman Theodore Kupferman of New York argued in response to a query that his purpose was "not only to give me an idea of what my constituents are thinking, it is also to allow them to participate. Please tell me how you would cover 400,000 people unless you had a questionnaire delivered to each person in the District."[5]

Another congressman remarked, "Polling your people with questionnaires is a greater gimmick than mailing out free flower seeds . . . . Everyone is flattered to be asked his opinion on great issues. You get credit for putting 'democracy' into action; you advertise yourself. By releasing the compiled results to newspapers you can live off the publicity for weeks. You can use your poll to justify questionable votes later, or even to beg off a dangerous commitment when the House leadership is twisting your arm. And the beautiful thing is you can mail your poll out free!"[6]

A voter poll made by New Jersey Congressman Peter H. B. Frelinghuysen yielded a questionnaire returned by his mother. She wrote, "I can't answer these questions. Why do you think we sent *you* to Washington?" Mothers aside, an official who says or does something that is disapproved by a plurality of respondents in a survey risks the pragmatic political hazard of defending a minority position. He also faces the accusation that he has "defied" public opinion, even though the very exercise of his leadership can shift opinion toward the course of action he supports.

Opinion research sharpens this apposition, because it has introduced a new element of self-consciousness into the relationship between leaders and peoples. During the period 1939–1941, President Franklin D. Roosevelt took a number of actions designed to help the Western Allies without bringing America into the war. These measures were taken with cautious awareness of what public opinion polls showed about the complex feelings of the American people toward the European conflict. Roosevelt's actions, like any strong executive behavior, had important consequences in the evolution of public sentiment. It is of interest to compare this feedback process with the decisions taken by President Lincoln at the outset of the Civil War, when the real condition of public opinion in the Northern states could be evaluated only by judgment and not by poll statistics. How different would Roosevelt's actions have been if he had not had opinion survey data, or Lincoln's if he had?[7]

Compare the starting points in presidential popularity as measured by the Gallup Poll: Nixon, 59 percent approving of "the way he is handling his job" shortly after he assumed office; Eisenhower with 68 percent; Johnson, 69 percent; Kennedy, 77 percent; and Truman, 86 percent. With the exception of Harry Truman, who dropped steadily in public approval during his first year in office, all of the postwar presidents ended their first year within a range of about ten percentage points from where they started, but they also had considerable ups and downs in popularity within that time.

Pollster Burns W. Roper notes that "when a President takes office he has nowhere to go but down. A winning candidate has been successful in building voters' support and starts his term with something approaching a consensus. As he takes office, he is the focus of the nation's hopes."[8]

This becomes all the more evident at difficult moments. Roosevelt had 86 percent approval after Pearl Harbor; Truman was at the same level after Roosevelt's death; Kennedy had 83 percent following the Bay of Pigs invasion of Cuba; Johnson, 80 percent directly after Kennedy's assassination. Roper concludes, "Clearly, the public gives its most solid support, not in triumph, but in tragedy." Lesser "highs" have come about during international crises following strong action by the President, for example, at the start of the Korean War, the U-2 incident, the Cuban missile crisis, the Dominican crisis. Presidential popularity also rises after a success in international relations.

A study of the presidential "lows" leads Roper to conclude that "while a crisis in the international arena is likely to elicit approval, a crisis on the domestic scene is more likely to reflect discredit on the President. . . . Domestic events tend to hurt the President, whatever he does about them."

Irving Crespi, Vice President of the Gallup organization, refers to presidential popularity polls as "continuing elections," because of which "the politically ambitious must mature and develop under the pitiless glare of unending public assessment. . . . The incumbents of such offices (as the presidency) must take into account, as they seek to develop and marshal support for policies and legislation, that their prospects for reelection are continually being appraised in a way that is accepted by many as highly reliable. The effect of all this upon the electoral process is to make it an endless event, with elections as periodic climaxes."[9]

Crespi warns, "A long-term effect of the saliency given to the majority opinion by polls is likely to be the enhancement of the political appeal of candidates who manage effectively to compromise issues rather than to offer partisan choices. This in turn is likely to counteract any movements toward ideological party alignments and to strengthen the tendency for our two party system to offer choices between candidates who differ only moderately from each other."[10] A not dissimilar viewpoint is voiced by Richard Scammon and Ben Wattenberg,[11] who point out that both parties must compete for the favors of the same middle-aged, middle-income majority who constitute the core of the electorate.

When polls make politicians self-conscious about the views they express, they constrict the areas of public debate. Polls must always be conservative in their effects, since at best they deal in yesterday's opinions and never tomorrow's. To the most artful political practitioner, polls are far less of a guide to action than they are an instrument in the struggle for power.

What bearing *should* the answers given to opinion surveys, amateur *or* professional, have on legislative or administrative action? In the domain of consumer research, it is easy enough to say that a manufacturer should give his toothpaste the flavor preferred by a majority of his customers. But the tendency to regard policy as a commodity that should obey the laws of supply and demand becomes scandalous when it is extended from the realm of marketing to the realm of politics. A leader who does what is popular, even when it does not make sense, does his

constituents no service, yet this kind of accommodation goes on continually. Chancellor Kurt Kiesinger vetoed a proposed revaluation of the
German mark, though it was supported strongly by all the fiscal experts.
To justify his act, he cited the findings of an opinion poll which showed
that 87 percent of the public was opposed. (The mark was eventually
devaluated anyway.)

It is only a step from the argument that public officials should follow
the polls to the theory that they should be picked by the pollsters to
meet marketing specifications. In Los Angeles, Hal Every, who runs two
affiliated organizations, the Public Relations Center and the Western
Opinion Research Center, advertises: "You can be elected state senator;
leading public relations firm with top flight experience in statewide
campaigns wants a senator candidate." Every envisions that "in the
world of 1984 voters . . . will first be polled as to what type of candidate
they want, even on physical and personal characteristics. The information
will be fed into a computer and the candidate most closely reflecting the
voters' choice will be selected to run for office. "In the presidential race,"
he says, "the government will sample the nation to find 1,000 typical
voters and they will make the final selection."[12]

Vladimir K. Zworykin, a renowned electronics expert, suggests that
"modern technology makes it possible to give the people the ability to
communicate their wishes and opinions to the government with a
directness and immediacy comparable with that realized at present only
in the opposite direction."[13] He foresees a system in which every telephone
is provided with simple auxiliary equipment that can convert it into a
voting station. Registered voters will express their preferences on specific
questions submitted over broadcast channels in much the same manner
as citizens today use the voting machines to express their opinions in a
referendum. According to Zworykin, "Government leaders would be
able to align their policies more closely with the popular will, which
would be known rather than a subject for speculation." Zworykin fails
to mention that a "feedback" computerized home communications system
applied to opinion polling carries with it the further interesting and
sinister possibility of being used to maintain a permanent file of each
individual's recorded opinions on various subjects, along with his income tax dossier, census data, parking violation record and F.B.I. checks.

Zworykin echoes a widely held view that in a democracy those in
authority should respond directly to public opinion. Even the Yippies
demonstrating at the 1968 Democratic National Convention in Chicago
called for "a national referendum system conducted via television or a
telephone voting system." This assumes that the right questions can

be asked and that everybody's responses are equally valid. It also assumes that opinions can be regarded atomistically, one by one, without regard to the context in which they come into play with each other, and without regard to the intensity with which they are held. As we shall see, neither of these assumptions is correct.

To the extent that public officials are persuaded that they must follow what polls show to be public opinion, there must inevitably be efforts to produce survey results that support a particular course of action. One example was a nationwide survey conducted by administration supporters and introduced into the tense and protracted Senate debate over President Nixon's nomination of Judge Clement Haynsworth to the Supreme Court in November 1969. The questions began with a one-sided pre-amble: "President Nixon has strongly defended this nomination." The answers reported, predictably, 46 percent in favor and 24 percent opposed, with the remainder undecided. It later turned out that only 66 percent of those questioned were aware of the Haynsworth nomination, which meant that only three persons in ten supported it, even with the aid of a loaded question.

At about the same time, Nixon contrasted the "vocal minority"—those critical of his administration's policy in Southeast Asia—with the "silent majority"—who supported him. Advertisements in the press exhorted the public to send in coupons or letters to counter the huge antiwar "Moratorium" demonstration, which brought several hundreds of thousands of people to Washington on November 15, 1969.

A film prepared by the U.S. Information Agency for overseas showings began with a scene of the crowd identified as probable members of the "silent majority," watching the antiwar demonstrators. The principal performer in the film was George Gallup, Jr., who was described as "a researcher respected for his objective approach." (He was not identified as the *son* of the well-known research pioneer with whom many in the audience of the film must surely have confused him.) Gallup Jr. announced that 77 percent of those who had watched the President's speech on television were in favor of his Vietnam position. This reflected not only the persuasive power of the Presidency and of the speech, but the preponderance of administration supporters in the viewing audience. A few days later the Harris Poll found only a bare plurality out of sympathy with the Moratorium Day marchers and 81 percent who agreed that "the anti-war demonstrations may not be entirely right, but they are raising real questions which ought to be discussed and answered." In short, public reactions were not as simple as the Administration might have wished.

A great many of the major policy issues that confront the body politic are impenetrable to any sensible polling by conventional methods, because of the specialized knowledge required to render intelligent judgment. One such issue was the debate on the creation of a new antiballistic missile defense system.

According to one account, President Nixon's support of the ABM was "the clincher" in assuring him of Senator Strom Thurmond's support at a time when it was wavering, before the 1968 convention ballot.[14] The Republican administration moved rapidly to execute the ABM program after it took office.

The technical complexities and military and political assumptions involved in the decisions on how to cope with Soviet or Chinese nuclear attack capabilities were of an order of sophistication few members of the electorate could grasp and on which even the best informed were in profound disagreement. The public showed confusion on the basic facts of the issue; a majority mistakenly thought that the United States already had some antiballistic missiles ready for action in 1968. How could one possibly expect the population at large to hold reasoned opinions on a matter so difficult to understand, and how could one evaluate any opinions expressed in response to a poll?

In April 1969 Gallup found that 69 percent of the public claimed to have heard or read discussions about the ABM program; 40 percent had an opinion on it, 25 percent in favor and 15 percent opposed. Obviously the same evidence could be interpreted to mean either that ABM was favored by five out of every eight people who had thought about it, or that only one person in four was a supporter.

At the same time, the Harris Survey found 47 percent approving Nixon's decision to go ahead with the antimissile system at the $7 billion level, while 26 percent disapproved and 27 percent were not sure. Majorities agreed with a series of pro-ABM statements presented for their scrutiny, such as that it is "better to be overprepared than to be caught short"; and "the Russians are developing super-nuclear missiles; we need to defend against them." However, in an illustration of the familiar principle that people answer questions in context, a substantial plurality (49 percent) *also* agreed with the argument that the country "could have used $7 billion better for education, health, housing, poverty needs at home" (31 percent disagreed). The findings of these published polls must be kept in mind as we consider the private poll that was used by the Nixon administration in its narrowly successful effort to get the ABM bill through the Senate.

On June 13, 1969, at the height of Senate debate over the Safeguard

ABM system, leading newspapers carried a full-page advertisement signed by the "Citizens Committee for Peace with Security," a group which included well-known sports and show business figures—Vince Lombardi, Roy Campanella, Hildegarde, and "Murray the K" (a disc jockey), as well as fifty-five individuals later identified as being associated with corporations with large Defense Department contracts.[15] The headline read, "84% of All Americans Support an ABM System," and the text went on to say, "A nationwide opinion poll representing adults through the continental United States reveals overwhelming support for a U.S. anti-ballistic missile defense system. Only 8% believe that no ABM system is needed . . . Now for the first time we are hearing the real voice of America . . . and not what the noisy 10 percent, opposed to the plan, would like Congress and the country to believe! The overwhelming support of the ABM proposal and the desire of the voters to have Congress enact such legislation have been obscured by the clamor of a minority. An organized campaign of letter writing to Congress, directed by a small group of militant opponents, has created an erroneous impression. The real voice of America is not being heard! Largely through the activities of these organizations, representing the attitudes of the 10 per cent opposed to the plan, Congressional mail is running against the Safeguard program. . . . Now you know the facts—become an active member of the 84% majority—let your voice be heard!"

In properly conducted polls, questions on obscure or complicated matters are normally preceded by others which establish whether the respondent is familiar with the subject. No such attempt was made in the instance of the poll cited.

The three questions quoted in the advertisement were among eight questions on the ABM included in a much larger study commissioned by David R. Derge, a political scientist from the University of Indiana. (Derge had been hired by campaign chairman John Mitchell in 1968 to supervise election campaign research for Nixon.) The survey's sponsors refused permission to release data from the five other questions.

There was a preamble before the first question in the interview sequence: "The kinds of weapons that could be used against enemy missiles are called anti-ballistic missiles or ABM's for short. These ABM's are intended to meet and destroy incoming enemy missiles." The positive wording of this preamble, which presented the accepted military function of ABM, without referring to the risks that might raise opposition, imposed a predetermined perspective upon the following question and influenced the results.

The first question in the advertisement was, "Do you think the United

States should have some sort of ABM defense system, or should not?"
Since no alternatives were proposed, the respondent had the option of
being either for "defense" or opposed to it. The next question cited
was even more directive, since it stated only one side of the issue under
debate and used the highest governmental authority to support it: "President Nixon has come out for a limited ABM system—called the Safeguard
System—which is supposed to protect our ability to strike back at an
attacker. Do you think Congress should approve this system, or should
not?" The response: 73 percent, yes; 10 percent, no; 3 percent, "it depends"; and 14 percent expressed no opinion, which is remarkable considering that the phrasing of the question made opposition seem virtually
treasonable.

Opinion Research Corporation, which conducted the survey, subsequently repudiated its use in the advertisement after leading opinion
research practitioners protested. The research executive responsible for
the study was offered a major post in the Nixon administration but
declined for reasons of health.

The promoter of the advertisement, William J. Casey, was later named
by President Nixon to the General Advisory Committee of the U.S.
Arms Control and Disarmament Agency, and early in 1971 he was
selected by Nixon as chairman of the Securities and Exchange Commission, to superintend the integrity of the nation's financial markets.
The factual statements in the advertisement came under attack by some
senators at the hearing on the President's nomination of Casey, who
acknowledged that the advertisement was "a little fuzzy" in alleging
that the Russians were developing an ABM system. Senator William
Fulbright called this "a complete misrepresentation." Queried about
the ABM advertisement, Casey argued, "The use of headlines to drama-
tize a point is an accepted practice in communications."

David Derge came into prominence again at the time of the public
furor that followed President Nixon's dispatch of United States troops
to Cambodia. Derge's question in a Chilton Research telephone survey
was reminiscent of the one asked in the ABM study; it read, "President
Nixon has decided to assist South Vietnam with American support in
actions against North Vietnamese Communist forces in Cambodia. Do
you approve or disapprove of this decision?" Predictably, 53 percent approved and 31 percent disapproved. At about the same time a Harris
poll found 50 percent supporting the President and 43 percent with
"serious doubts" about his action.[16]

The pseudopoll has been employed as a tactical weapon by local
political pressure groups as well as on the national scene. When Negro

militants occupied a construction site in Harlem which had been cleared for a New York State office building, a committee of their supporters polled 6000 passers-by and offered the results (reportedly only 4 percent wanted the building) as evidence of what "the Harlem community" really wanted.[17]

In the midst of the discussion involving the restructuring of admissions policy at New York's City University, a history professor conducted a "survey" by standing on a street corner in Harlem and asking 48 persons what they thought of the student demands. (He found that 19 agreed with them, 14 opposed them, 12 had mixed feelings, and 3 had no opinion.) This was duly reported to the press as evidence of opinion in "the black community."[18] Although no one may have taken these findings seriously, their use is indicative of the inevitable recourse to public opinion as arbiter of public policy.

Misleading uses of such surveys and pseudosurveys as those just cited are efforts to manipulate public opinion by creating an impression of overwhelming support for a debatable and debated course of action. Such misuses are perhaps the inevitable outgrowth of the naive assumption that surveys may be taken as literal descriptions of public opinion and the equally naive proposition that a democracy should be ruled by the public will as surveys describe it. Presidents of television networks gauge the success of their policies by their ratings. It is no less fatuous but much more serious when Presidents of the United States follow the same philosophy. From here it is only a small step for zealous aides to make certain that ratings are to the President's satisfaction.

POLLING AND THE CONCEPT OF OPINION

Must I drink the whole bottle in order to judge the quality of the wine?

Adolphe Quetelet

Messrs. Darwin and Galton have set the example of circulars of questions sent out by the hundreds to those able to reply. The custom has spread, and it will be well for us in the next generation if such circulars be not ranked among the common pests of life.

William James, *Principles of Psychology*

No doubt the character and quality of public opinion have changed over the years with the growth of literacy and mass communications. Such change has been subtle, gradual, and continuous, whereas in the academic discussion of public opinion there is a sharp discontinuity between the periods before and after the development of the systematic opinion survey. The world of public opinion in today's sense really began with the Gallup Polls of the mid-1930s, and it is impossible for us to retreat to the meaning of public opinion as it was understood by Thomas Jefferson in the eighteenth century, by Alexis de Tocqueville and Lord Bryce in the nineteenth,—or even by Walter Lippmann in 1922.[19]

The term "public opinion" as used in polling is quite distinct from

14

the historical concept of public opinion as a state of mind, diffuse, shapeless, and shifting as a cloud. For many years, philosophers and political scientists dealt with public opinion as though it represented a natural force, constrained perhaps by certain regularities and laws, but as capricious and unpredictable as human nature itself. It was one force among many in the complex flux of politics. These forces were like currents of the air or ocean, constantly changing in their contours and directions. The public opinion survey method requires that these elusive currents be treated as though they were static, that we define and measure what was formerly undefinable and unmeasurable. Once this is done, and done over and over again, it is easy to succumb to the illusion that the measurements represent reality rather than a distorted, dim, approximate reflection of a reality that alters its shape when seen from different angles.

In recent years, and to an increasing degree, public opinion surveys have become an important part of the process by which newsmen and political leaders appraise the public's sense of social priorities. This may happen even when the results are kept secret, as in the case of some polls conducted for political candidates in the United States or for party functionaries in Communist countries.

Opinion surveys have become a mechanism through which the public becomes sensitized to its own needs and self-conscious about its own collective stance. For this to take place (that is, for the public to be aware of public opinion) the communications media must take poll results seriously, not only as news items but as guidelines for news judgments and as subjects of editorial comment.

An entire generation of Americans now has grown up accepting polling as a commonplace institution and poll findings as part of the normal daily flow of expected information. Awareness of the statistical measurements of survey findings coexists with the individual's own intuitive assessment of what people are thinking and saying, but it seems to occupy a different psychological space, so that two incompatible conclusions may not be perceived as contradictory.

The marvelous vagueness of the French expressions *on dit* and *on pense* expresses perfectly the ambiguity of generalizing from one's personal experience or impressions to what may be described as impersonal and objective truth. The professional journalist has never been immune from this same kind of generalization, although his perceptions may be sharper than the layman's and his contacts more widespread.

It is likely that writers have always written of the popular mood as being one thing or another in the same way that one may observe in casual conversation that "people think this" or "people think that." In the past the climate of opinion has usually been described in terms of mood or feeling—an emotional state not susceptible to measurement. The journalist who assesses the popular temper has been much like the artist who translates his own personal experiences and observations into intuitions of a deeper and more generalized truth.

Outcroppings of this tradition are common: On one occasion (May 2, 1969) *Time Magazine* reported that the American public's reaction to campus demonstrators could be summed up in a single word, "Enough!" Perhaps, but how did *Time* know? In a single issue of *The New York Times* (March 9, 1969) one could find an article reporting that Rumanian General Secretary Nicolae Ceausescu's popularity was gaining to the point where he could now win a free election and another reporting a "marked change" in the past six months in the Israeli public's attitude toward Arab guerillas. A third dispatch reported an "anti-American mood" in Pakistan. The authority in all three cases was not a systematic opinion survey but the judgment of the reporter.

Polling, through its adherence to scientific method and its use of statistics, gives form and the appearance of measured precision to what was formerly visceral in origin and nebulous in shape. Polling presents public opinion not as a disembodied collective expression but as a sum of individuals' opinions. In this respect, of course, there lies room for error, since matters of public discussion reflect something more than—and different from—the arithmetic average of people's individual beliefs.

Too often, the polling method gets people to answer questions on matters they have not thought about and for which they feel no sense of responsibility. We are likely to answer questions differently when we know the decision is really up to us, but it is more difficult to have this feeling when we are told who is going to win an election before we have decided whom to vote for, or who has won before we have voted. "Don't know" in response to a survey question often means "Don't want to know," which is another way of saying, "I don't want to get involved."

The Founding Fathers of the American Republic equated the workings of democracy with a rational exchange of views: "When men exert their reason coolly and freely on a variety of distinct questions," wrote James Madison in *The Federalist,* "they inevitably fall into different opinions on some of them. When they are governed by a common passion, their opinions, if they are so to be called, will be the same."[20]

The answers to questions in surveys should never be confused with the fluid changing expression of public opinion as a "common passion." Consider the vague and ephemeral nature of many verbal expressions of attitude, their sensitivity to changes in question wordings, question sequence, and the authority of the questioner. There is a vast difference between the reality of public opinion and the polls that measure shadows cast, as in Plato's myth, upon the wall of the cave.

The prevailing model underlying the discipline of survey research is that of the single opinion. A person holds an opinion, which he communicates to an interviewer. When he is influenced to change his mind, he replaces his former opinion with another one. This model has the virtue of great simplicity, but it makes no sense, because conflicting and contradictory opinions may be held simultaneously and because they constantly jostle one another for dominance.

The mechanics of survey research, like any other human enterprise, are subject to a substantial range of error, which has been amply discussed in many treatises and explored in many diagnostic experiments. Bad interviewing, unrepresentative cross sections, poor questionnaire construction, and slips in data processing can all contribute to make the final results unreliable, apart from the statistical tolerances with which the laws of probability surround all samplings. A great deal of survey research makes excessive demands on respondents, with long interviews on dull subjects and questions that may be inappropriate, too sensitive, or overly personal. One market survey asked, "How often do you have a bowel movement?"

The answers given to less intimate questions may still be inaccurate indicators of how people really feel. When verbal responses to questions are compared with involuntary physiological responses like the heartbeat rate and pulse pressure, it appears that people understate their negative emotional reactions on racial matters and overstate them on matters related to political authoritarianism and to civil disorder. Different people show widely varying levels of unconscious emotional response even when they report themselves verbally at the same point on an attitude scale. Verbal neutrality means emotional apathy for some and agonizing uncertainty for others.[21]

The distortions and inaccuracies of reported data have little to do with the essential misuses of research. Human nature is too subtle, fragile, and complex to be measured by a question which asks, "Do you agree or disagree?" Opinions are contradictory and illogical, subject to constant shifting and change. They are amenable to influence and evolution; they are swayed by crass material interest, but they are also swayed by poetry.

Opinion surveys are often dubious indicators of actual behavior because they do not, and perhaps cannot, measure the seething, changing character of the public temper. They generally fail to embody the rich context of motivation and cross-communication out of which opinions arise and activate people in the mass. When a working committee arrives at a consensus after a prolonged, many-sided discussion, it may do so as a matter of voting and majority rule. More commonly, when there is intense feeling on the part of some individual members of a committee and comparative indifference on the part of others, this finds expression in the decision that is eventually reached. The process by which a group comes to take a position is not amenable to study by a technique that approaches people one by one.

The paradox of scientific method is that we change phenomena by measuring them. An interview acts as a catalyst. The confrontation of interviewer and respondent forces the crystallization and expression of opinions where there were no more than chaotic swirls of thought. The respondent's statements themselves represent a form of behavior; they are commitments. A question asked by an interviewer changes an abstract and perhaps irrelevant matter into a genuine subject of action; the respondent confronts a voting decision, exactly as he might on a choice of candidates or on a proposition in a plebiscite. The conventional poll forces expression into predetermined channels, by presenting clear-cut and mutually exclusive choices. To accommodate one's thoughts to these channels represents for the respondent an arousal of interest, an affirmative act.

Pollsters can elicit "opinions" on imaginary issues as well as on genuine ones. A classic case was a question asked in 1948 about a non-existent "Metallic Metals Act," on which only 30 percent ventured no opinion; of the remainder, 59 percent agreed that "it would be a good thing but should be left to individual states," whereas 16 percent thought "it is all right for foreign countries but should not be required here."

Surveys can also elicit the expression of quick responses of a kind that most people would reconsider if confronted with the consequences. A 1970 poll by CBS found majorities of the public ready to express opposition to basic provisions of the Bill of Rights: over half would deny the universal right to criticize the government if this were harmful to the national interest; a majority would deny the media the right to report such criticism if the government considered this against the national interest; three-fourths would deny extremists the right to demonstrate against the government, even when there was no danger of violence.

When in 1969 the Supreme Court began to require immediate compliance with its earlier decision ending school desegregation, Governor John McKeithen of Louisiana challenged the federal government to conduct a poll of the local citizenry before it integrated the schools in his state. There was no reason to doubt that such a poll would have shown an anti-integration majority.

North Carolina segregationists actually did introduce opinion polls as evidence in lawsuits which sought to prevent the bussing of school children, but a 1970 U.S. District Court decision excluded their use, although acknowledging that "a judge would ordinarily like to decide cases to suit his neighbors."

The might of dominant opinion does not make right, though this point is not always readily appreciated. When 80 percent of the students at a Japanese university failed an examination, some of them protested that their answers were correct because they were in the majority.[22]

Majorities might have been summoned at certain critical times to support almost any sinister and antidemocratic forces in history and many idiotic proposals.

In the Spring of 1954, Gallup reported that nearly two out of every three Americans (62 percent) would favor using atomic artillery shells on the Chinese Communists, and one out of three would favor dropping hydrogen-bombs on the Chinese mainland. It would be unwise to equate these numbers, representing fast and sometimes perhaps flippant responses to an anonymous interviewer, with any high degree of considered resolve to face the horrendous consequences of nuclear war.

Minorities as well as majorities can be dangerous. In a 1964 NORC survey, 7 percent of American adults agreed that Hitler was (wholly or "partly") right to try to kill all the Jews.[23] We attribute no particular importance to this 7 percent (which projected to some 8 million individuals, each one a potential mass murderer) because the sentiments they expressed to an interviewer were made individually without awareness of their collective strength. By contrast, we may feel enormous concern about the similarly small percentage of people who now vote for the neo-Nazi party in Germany, precisely because they have already demonstrated a willingness to practice what they preach. In short, opinions must always be evaluated in relation to the likelihood that they will lead to action, and to the context in which they are expressed.

An opinion stated spontaneously in speech or writing is different in quality from one offered in answer to a structured questionnaire. The process of setting words down on paper forces a writer to eliminate the inconsistencies in his position. The public relations man who writes speeches for a corporate president learns that his boss rapidly comes to imagine that the ideas were his own. He begins to believe the words he reads simply because he has uttered them. This kind of commitment is the basis for Leon Festinger's theory of cognitive dissonance, which applies to situations in which an individual "takes a stand" and shifts his views to reduce incongruities.[24] But a large proportion of the ideas that float through our minds do *not* represent "commitments" in which the ego is involved. They are ideas that are part of the common currency of the mass media with which we have a passive familiarity.

A great many questions asked in public opinion surveys are actually designed to measure the public's information on issues of the day rather than the public's thoughts about what should be done about those issues. Fundamental values tend to be more homogeneous, in any given country, than opinions about the tactics of ways and means. Typically, the opinions measured in polls deal with the means to be used to achieve ends that are taken for granted, or assumed to be held in common, rather than with differences of value judgments with regard to the ends that are sought.

We think of public opinion as polarized on great issues; we think of it as intense, because polarized opinions must be intense almost by definition. Because of the identification of public opinion with the measurements of surveys, the illusion is easily conveyed of a public which is "opinionated"—which is committed to strongly held views. The publication of poll results undoubtedly acts as a reinforcing agent in support of the public's consciousness of its own collective opinions as a definable, describable force. These data may become reference points by which the individual formulates and expresses his "personal" beliefs. When polls are published and widely discussed, what people say they want is likely to be what they are told they want by the polls. Thus yesterday's perceptions govern tomorrow's expressions of the public mood.

The student of public opinion knows that his descriptive measurements of the moment do not represent the "real thing." His primary task is to understand how opinions come to be held at all, and how they evolve and change.

E. M. Forster has drawn a distinction between "flat" and "round" characterizations in fiction.[25] Most opinion studies, like most works of fiction, employ flat, abbreviated treatments of their subjects. We reject the reality of comic-book characters who are predictably heroes or villains, yet we too often settle for comic-book statistics on infinitely complex matters of reflection and debate. It is the rare poll that allows us to see opinion as multifaceted, multilayered, and intricate.

REPORTING THE POLLS

We know the figures are wrong, but we want to give them to you anyway.

A Television Pollster

An understanding of the subtleties of public opinion may come slowly to a social scientist poring over tabulations and retabulations of survey statistics long after the responses they represent have entered the realm of history. But to those who pay for research, fast crude reports carry greater impact, both in the guidance they give the political strategist and in their direct feedback effect on the further evolution of opinion.

The politician's sensitivity to polls reflects their high and growing visibility. Polls are a form of mass entertainment, with large and steadily increasing amounts of attention devoted to them in the press and on television.

Newspapers and magazines have for many years used syndicated columns by professional pollsters like George Gallup, the late Elmo Roper, Archibald Crossley, Louis Harris, and Daniel Yankelovich or by such regional organizations as the California, Texas, Iowa, and Minnesota polls (the latter two run by newspapers). The television networks, especially the Columbia Broadcasting System, have commissioned research to provide news background, and have also put pollsters on the air as political commentators.

Political polling builds public awareness of a research organization and thereby brings it the commercial clients that are the mainstay of its business. Most of its skills and resources are devoted to marketing matters rather than politics. Published public opinion surveys are not significant sources of profit when they lack commercial sponsorship. The biggest weekly fee that George Gallup received for his syndicated service in 1968 was $350 from the *Philadelphia Bulletin*. Most of his subscribing newspapers pay far less, some as little as $10 a week. Newspaper subscriptions to syndicated poll columns decline sharply after presidential elections, making it even more difficult for the researcher to make ends meet on the conventional political opinion surveys he does for publication.

Both the American Association for Public Opinion Research and the National Council on Public Polls have devoted strenuous efforts to establishing proper standards for political surveys and to making the press and public officials aware that such standards exist. Press coverage of opinion surveys has often shown a total absence of professional judgment as to their significance or adequacy. Bad surveys and good surveys are commonly given equal space as though they were to be equated in the reader's judgment, and their failure to agree may be cited as evidence of polls' inherent limitations.[26]

The newsman is accustomed to a confrontation of opposing viewpoints in the interpretation of events. It is therefore quite logical for him to assume that a similar clash of opposing viewpoints on the part of different "polls" also represents merely a difference of interpretations. The newsman who considers political analysis to be his own particular specialty may feel gleeful at the polls' occasional failures. The objection that the polls are inaccurate as well as presumptuous is all the easier to maintain when the newsman is himself ignorant of the criteria by which valid polls can be distinguished from phony ones. Polls that are run by journalists themselves, without professional help, are sometimes notoriously amateurish and unreliable, and can even degenerate into utter nonsense: An "opinion poll" conducted among 95 daily newspaper editors found Jesus Christ outscoring Winston Churchill 280 to 175 in a contest for the title of "most admired man in history." Franklin D. Roosevelt, however, pulled in narrowly ahead of Moses, 21 to 20.[27]

Reporters eliciting opinions generally are unsystematic, both with respect to whom they talk to and to the questions they ask. Yet the words "poll" and "survey" are commonly applied to this practice. One newspaper sent *four* reporters out to interview a "scientifically selected" sample of 600 voters in 33 counties in the span of a single week.

In the fall of 1965, the American Association for Public Opinion Research formally objected to the use of street-corner interviewing by a newspaper which devoted enormous attention to a preelection survey, giving percentage figures on a district-by-district basis. The editors defended themselves by pointing out that this was not a scientific public opinion survey but merely a "straw poll"—as though the ordinary reader would make a distinction.

On February 3, 1966, *The New York Times* ran a front-page story, continued over an entire inside page, headed, "Wide Support Found in Nation for Renewed Vietnam Bombing." The authority for this was a "spot check" in which ten staff correspondents interviewed state and local officials, professionals and businessmen, editors, students, and others on opinion in their communities. "The results reflect a broad trend although they do not purport to be scientific," the article says, leaving the reader to wonder how a broad trend can be detected by unscientific means.[28]

Another story in *The New York Times* carried the headline, "Johnson Policies Disenchant Iowa." The subheadline read, "Bellwether County Shows He Would Lose Election Now." In fact, the "survey" was based on interviews by a reporter with "the first fifty people of voting age willing to give their views" in a single precinct.[29]

Broadcasters have also used pseudopolls as a way to involve their audience and build station loyalty and interest in news programs. By May 1968, 71 television stations were using an "instant poll" first developed by WFIL-TV in Philadelphia. The procedure is to ask such a question as "Should the United States withdraw from Vietnam immediately?" on an early evening news program. Telephone votes are counted during the evening, with continuing reminders to the viewers, and the results are announced on the late news. Such programs have the names "Public Poll," "Viewer Interest Poll," "Tonight's Big Question," and even "The Nut Poll." WFLA-TV averages 2000 phone calls a night on its "Pulse Poll." The people who are eager to have their "votes" counted are, of course, no representative cross section of anything. A broadcaster in Springfield, Massachusetts, urged his viewers, "If you feel strongly enough, you can call several times."

Public misunderstanding of opinion surveys can be expected to continue as long as the mass media ignore or belittle their technical intricacies. This attitude may be the inevitable result of regarding the raw percentages of yes and no votes, rather than the interpretation of their meaning, as the essential product of polling. Inevitably the news media must show greater interest not just in the results of opinion surveys, but in the broader application of social research and social theory to the large and complex subjects out of which specific news stories emerge each day.

   This kind of study moves slowly, and sometimes up blind alleys; it is expensive, and it requires special skills which are in short supply. The chief inhibition to such research, however, is that it is often lacking in the element of political drama that media and the public have come to expect of opinion surveys, and that is most visibly evident in the periodic effort to divine the outcome of elections.

ON PREDICTING ELECTIONS

It's like trying to measure a gaseous body with a rubber band.

Paul Cherrington

Polling is associated in most people's minds with the prediction of election results.[30] It is at election time that polls become a dominant subject in the popular culture—a favorite butt of newspaper cartoonists and television comedians. Yet for all their acceptance as part of the American scene, and for all the general recognition of their power, polls remain for many people a suspect form of activity—for some an occult and perhaps sinister art, for others a hoax that requires restriction.

The fundamental principle of statistical sampling, the basis of polling, seems to be hard for many people to understand. Indeed, 45 percent of the public (in Minnesota, at least) does not think a survey based on 2000 interviews can be accurate. But since this information itself comes from a survey, and since only a comparative handful of the public refuses to answer pollsters' questions, it is evident that most of the skeptics are still willing to accept polls as part of the current political scene.

Many of the limitations of opinion research do not apply to election surveys. The interviewer soliciting a choice of candidates is indeed provoking a meaningful answer; the respondent must choose, much as he would in the voting booth. Preelection polls are closer to consumer studies than are most kinds of opinion surveys. Voting intentions and brand preferences alike represent opinions that are directly linked to

25

actions. Hence they reflect a different order of phenomena than opinions on matters of state, on which the decisions are understood to be in more powerful hands. A market researcher may ask about brand preference, but he usually also goes on to find out from the record of past purchases whether or not the respondent is a likely prospect for the product. By the same token, since 1948 it has been accepted that it is not enough in political polls to determine which candidate the people favor; their past voting record is also needed to assess the likelihood that they will act on their preferences on Election Day. Voting intentions, like brand preferences, may change, but votes, like purchases, are irrevocable.

Formal training as a statistician is not a prerequisite for successful performance as an election pollster. Among those who have taken on the augur's mantle are a roach and rodent exterminator in Portland, Oregon, and a Kansas City miller. The miller, in 1948, allowed his customers to select chicken feed decorated with either a donkey or an elephant. He discontinued his "poll" because the Democratic majority (54 percent) ran contrary to the national expectations based on the results of scientific election surveys.

The failure of the 1948 polls was the occasion for intensive self-appraisal on the part of the public opinion research profession.[31] It brought about two major changes in technique: (1) a shift from the less accurate method of "quota" sampling (which gave wide latitude of choice to the interviewer in deciding whom to question) to "probability" sampling (in which interviewers received explicit instructions in order to yield a representative cross section of the public) and (2) a continuation of polling until almost the very eve of the election, in order to take into account the possibility of a last-minute shift in preference (such as seems to have occurred in the case of President Truman).[32]

A week before the election, on October 26, 1948, Truman evoked the ghostly memory of the *Literary Digest:* "In 1936 the Republicans had a poll that told them they had a sure thing. And they did. They met a sure defeat in 1936 . . . . These polls that the Republican candidate is putting out are like sleeping pills designed to lull the voter into sleeping on Election Day. You might call them sleeping polls . . . . An overdose could be fatal—can so affect your mind that your body will be too lazy to go to the polls on Election Day. . . . These Republican polls are no accident. They are part of a design to prevent a big vote, to keep you at home on November 2 by convincing you that it makes no difference whether you vote or not."[33]

Truman's charges found an echo on election day, 1968, when *Pravda* alleged that the American polls were made to "influence voters. It is as if they are saying to the voter: 'Why are you suffering from doubts when the election has been predetermined?' "

Although allegations of collusion may be dismissed as propaganda or as campaign oratory, it is unquestionably true that preelection surveys are no longer used merely as a way of informing the public on the latest state of the race, but as a means of influencing the outcome. This is done in several ways:

1. They provide candidates for office with intelligence about where they are strong and where they are weak.

2. They offer guidelines as to what candidates should and shouldn't say to win voter approval.

3. More questionable use of preelection research is the carefully timed, last-minute release of polls to influence convention delegates with demonstrations that Candidate X couldn't possibly win, whereas Candidate Y might.

4. A less guileful but more important effect of polls as an influence on elections comes about when they create the impression that the outcome is a sure thing three or four months before the election itself. What this does to demoralize party workers and to drive away potential contributors to party funds represents a grim example of self-fulfilling prophecy.

If there is reason for concern over the role of preelection surveys, it should not be about their accuracy as a measurement of opinion at the time they are taken, but about the greater question of whether polls that are taken today are in any sense a reliable predictor of the future.

In Britain, the United States pollsters' debacle of 1948 was repeated in the election of June 1970 which unseated Harold Wilson's Labor government in spite of the predictions of four out of the five national polls. The pollsters blamed the low turnout and a last-minute trend to the Conservatives in the few days after their final surveys. Pollster Mark Abrams' post mortem concluded that the biggest factor was abstention from voting.[34] Another after-the-fact analysis demonstrated that polls with impeccably correct samples could still produce the wrong results in a simulated election.[35]

Whatever the excuses, Wilson noted glumly that the pollsters "have not distinguished themselves." This lack of distinction was particularly galling for him because the timing of the election itself, well before the expiration of the normal five-year parliamentary term, was set by the

Labor Party's political analysts on the basis of earlier polls which showed a steady upswing in the Prime Minister's popularity.

Predicting election returns from polls is hazardous because of the difficulty of determining who will cast a ballot on Election Day.[36] (One of the reasons for the failure of the 1936 *Literary Digest* poll was that 6 million more voters cast ballots that year than in 1932.) In the 1960 election, one-fourth of the people who in August told the Opinion Research Corporation that they did not intend to vote reported later that they actually did vote, most of them for Kennedy.[37]

In 1968, 60 percent of the 120,000,000 Americans of voting age (or about 80 percent of the registered voters) voted. (This compares with 62 percent of the eligible voters in 1964 and 64 percent in 1960.) Since 1948, the polling organizations have become more and more sophisticated in their ability to screen out probable nonvoters by asking questions on the respondent's certainty in his voting intentions and on his past record of voting or not voting. The prediction of turnout is especially difficult in primary elections, where fewer go to the polls. A pollster might make different assumptions about the subsequent voting behavior of the undecided voters he interviews and come up with substantially different projections of the same survey results.[38] Among survey respondents who said they were "undecided" in the elections of 1960, 1962, 1964, and 1966, 46 percent eventually voted, compared with 76 percent who said they had made up their minds and expressed a definite preference in the original interview.[39]

Predicting state-by-state results under the American Electoral College system presents added complications. The inexorable laws of statistics require that a state or local survey use a sample of the same size as a national sample to produce results of comparable accuracy. This makes state-by-state polls fifty times as expensive as national polls, and the margin of error still makes predictions difficult in a close contest. In 1948, Dewey would have won the presidency if there had been a swing of 0.001 percent of the voters in Ohio, 0.002 percent in California, or 0.004 percent in Illinois.[40]

In 1968, for the first time in a national election, the leading polling organizations (acting in response to pressures brought within professional circles in previous years) included, in their releases to subscribing newspapers, the number of interviews conducted in each survey. Such information gave specialists, though not the general public, an indication of the margin of error in the survey results. With a sample of 1000 the chances are 19 to 1 that the survey projections obtained for two evenly matched candidates would be within $3\frac{1}{2}$ percentage points above *or* below the true proportions. With a sample of 1500 this margin of error decreases, but only to 3 percentage points, and with 2000 interviews the margin of error is diminished to $2\frac{1}{2}$ percentage points plus or minus. Most presidential elections are decided well within this range of tolerance.

The syndicated pollsters who release their results for publication generally abstain from private polling on behalf of candidates, since this would represent an obvious conflict of interest.[41] (Private polling is generally a much more profitable proposition.) Louis Harris won national attention in 1960 as John F. Kennedy's private pollster and election night companion. (A few years earlier he had managed Franklin D. Roosevelt, Jr.'s, unsuccessful campaign for the New York gubernatorial nomination.) He gave up his political counselling in order to set up his publicly syndicated poll. Samuel Lubell, who had published newspaper columns in many elections as an independent political analyst, worked privately for Governor Nelson A. Rockefeller in the 1970 New York election. Opinion Research Corporation worked privately for Richard Nixon in the 1968 campaign, at the same time that it also (through a different group of research analysts in the same building) ran public surveys on the same subject for the Columbia Broadcasting System. Don Muchmore, a California pollster, worked for both Ronald Reagan and his opponent Governor Pat Brown, in the same election and has cited this as evidence of his objectivity.

Pollster Oliver Quayle reports that one week before Election Day a midwestern Senator for whom he was doing surveys asked him to do one last "quickie" poll. When Quayle protested that it was a waste of his money, the Senator said, "Do it anyway. I just want to know." But most preelection polling is sponsored with more immediate political aims in mind.

In 1966 Robert P. Griffin, the Republican candidate for the Senate in Michigan, sought to raise funds around the United States using, in support of his appeal, a public opinion poll published in the *Detroit News* which showed him moving slightly ahead of his opponent, G. Mennen Williams. According to the accompanying letter, the poll indicated "that he can win, but only if he is financially able to wage an even stronger campaign in these final hours." Griffin *did* win. The use of such surveys for fund-raising purposes is particularly helpful when the race is contested by a narrow margin. When the polls show a wide gap between the candidates, obviously they are no help to either side, since the apparent winner obviously does not need help and the apparent loser is beyond help.

In the California senatorial primary of 1968, polls showing a drop in the popularity of Senator Thomas H Kuchel helped his opponent, Max Rafferty, get financial support from conservative backers who originally assumed that he had little chance to beat the incumbent.[42]

In the same year, Paul O'Dwyer, the Democratic contender for the Senate in New York, accused his incumbent Republican rival, Jacob Javits, of trying to create a bandwagon effect to influence the *Daily News* poll, which was starting that day. This was being done, said O'Dwyer, by the release of yet another poll made by the Republican organization, which showed Javits ahead. O'Dwyer commented, "I am in a much better position to judge political trends than any poll taken by amateurs from an undisclosed 1500 people." Javits' victory was as monumental as the polls indicated. However, O'Dwyer had some reason to be skeptical. When he ran again in the 1970 Senate primary a poll "leaked" by one of his opponents and duly reported in the *New York Post* of June 2, 1970, later turned out never to have been done at all.

Perhaps the most dangerous misuse of private preelection polls has been not for fund-raising or to create a bandwagon effect among voters, but to manipulate a candidate's public stance on public issues. It has now become quite common for candidates cynically to adapt their campaign utterances to what their private polls show to be publicly acceptable.

A firm of Los Angeles opinion analysts, Decision Making Information, Inc., provides computerized advice to candidates on the acceptability of alternative policy positions to voters, classified into 21 different demographic groups. It also proffers media recommendations based on the known reading and viewing propensities of these different kinds of people. The firms's head, Richard B. Wirthlin, admits, "We haven't refined this enough yet to tell a candidate he should put his television spot in 'Bonanza' rather than 'The Newlywed Game' but with enough polling, there's no reason why we can't."[43] D.M.I.'s polls have guided clients like Governor Ronald Reagan in determining whether or not to intervene in a teacher's strike. In the words of William E. Roberts of D.M.I.'s parent company, Spencer-Roberts, "A well regulated survey can give a candidate a line on what the public wants, and that's a wonderful thing."

During the 1966 Senate campaign in Massachusetts, polls by Opinion Research Corporation indicated that Republican candidate Edward Brooke's silence on the race issue was hurting him. Brooke repositioned himself as a moderate opposed to extremists of both races and he won.[44]

In the same year, political promoter Joseph Napolitan told Democratic Representative Henry Helstoski of New Jersey that 70 percent of his constituents opposed his stand against the bombing of North Vietnam. Helstoski dropped the point from his campaign speeches and managed to win narrowly.

Napolitan used surveys similarly to guide his planning for Hubert Humphrey in the 1968 presidential campaign. In the words of a disaffected advertising agency man, "The polls supposedly said that the majority of the country thinks the Negro has had too many handouts. So Napolitan advised Humphrey to stop talking about the Marshall Plan for the cities and switch to law and order stuff. We were told, 'Do not show a black man in any commercial.' "[45] Essentially Napolitan was using research as it is traditionally used in testing advertising copy for consumer products: to emphasize strengths and eliminate weaknesses.

In his management of Milton Shapp's (first and unsuccessful) 1966 campaign for the Governorship of Pennsylvania, Napolitan used advertising which cited the findings of his polls. In Catholic areas Shapp spoke out for legalized bingo. In Protestant areas he did not take the opposite view, but merely remained silent on the subject. According to his manager, "He hasn't changed his position. He's for it, but he just doesn't mention it where there is strong opposition to it."[46]

Richard M. Nixon commented on the practice in the course of the 1968 campaign: "I don't think that any political man who has any sense of responsibility at all can change his position every time he takes a poll." But he used many of them himself, for a variety of purposes.

The Nixon-for-President Committee sent out a fund-raising appeal in an envelop stamped "Opinion Survey" on the cover. The enclosure began with a letter which spoke of Nixon and then said, "Do you share his views? If so, here is how you can help. First, you can give us your opinions on the problems facing America. For this purpose a questionnaire is enclosed. Please study it carefully, fill it in, and return it to us. Second, you can make a contribution to Mr. Nixon's campaign." The questionnaire itself, which included a curious assortment of multiple choices on six major issues, concluded with the appeal, "Do you want to see a man in the White House who values your opinion? Then be sure to return this survey promptly. . . . (Please send your personal check made payable to Nixon Finance Committee.)" The accompanying letter was signed by Maurice H. Stans, whom Nixon subsequently appointed to head the Commerce Department.

The Nixon organization ran a private poll in seven key states "to determine which of seven potential vice presidential candidates would be most popular with the voters."[47] In New Hampshire Nixon's surveys showed that he would get two-thirds of the vote. He said publicly that he would be happy with 35 percent. Actually he got 79 percent and acted "surprised."

At another point in the campaign, after the assassination of Robert Kennedy, Nixon's supporters released a poll showing him running ahead of the field in New Jersey. The poll had actually been taken before Senator Kennedy's death, which radically changed the competitive picture.

The 1968 national election campaign represented a high point in the use of polls by political candidates for their private counsel and in their maneuverings to win the support of convention delegates. More surveys were made in 1968 (by some 200 different polling organizations) than in any other previous campaign, at a cost of some 4 million dollars. The findings were front-page news in newspapers across the country between spring and Election Day.

Early in the year, pollster Archibald Crossley was hired by an anonymous client to conduct a survey of political preferences in New York, Pennsylvania, California, and (at the client's insistence) Stratford County, New Hampshire, which Crossley observes "is not typical of New Hampshire. There were very few interviews there. It is a Democratic County, running 4 to 7 points more Democratic than the State." Crossley agreed to make the survey on the condition that the results not be released without his approval. The study showed President Johnson trailing Nixon by a single percentage point but ahead of other Republicans. The results were leaked by Drew Pearson who said they "proved that Johnson was ahead of Republicans in New York and Pennsylvania and leading them in an unnamed 'bellwether county' in New Hampshire." Crossley commented angrily, "It was supposed to be a confidential relationship, and I have kept my part of the confidence." The client later turned out to be Johnson's close friend and political supporter, Arthur B. Krim, a movie mogul. This inauspicious episode set the keynote for the cynical misuse of polls as an instrument of political manipulation in 1968.

POLLS AND THE CAMPAIGN OF 1968

They lie when they poll. They are trying to rig an election.

George Wallace

Polling of voter presidential preferences for the 1972 election began in the spring of 1971, and there was every indication that research would play an important part in the campaign. In 1968, polls, private and public, guided the maneuverings of presidential candidates from the start. Their uses and misuses are worthy of study as an illustration of how intimate a part they play in American politics.

Eugene McCarthy did surprisingly well in the New Hampshire Democratic primary on March 12, 1968. Four days later Robert Kennedy announced his candidacy after a John Kraft poll found he might do well in the California primary. Private poll results determined Hubert Humphrey's decision *not* to enter the same primary, after President Johnson withdrew from the race on March 31. (It was perhaps symptomatic of the pollsters' growing involvement with election campaign strategy that in California the regular Democratic organization hired a market research firm to assist with the difficult task of collecting the requisite number of signatures for the pro-Administration slate to get on the ballot.)

Michigan's Governor George Romney dropped out of the New Hampshire primary race two weeks before the election (and after making a campaign investment of 1 million dollars) because his polls showed him

33

trailing Nixon 70 percent to 11 percent. The *San Francisco Chronicle* commented, "Romney's retirement from the campaign before its first primary shows more vividly than any previous political event we can recall how political polls have largely taken over the making of decisions in modern politics."

The 1968 campaign was complicated by the fact that there were a number of leading contenders for the nomination of both parties. It was further complicated by the third-party candidate, George Wallace, who drew his support from adherents of both major parties and whose influence on the outcome was therefore particularly difficult to predict.

Press reports of the polls compared the standings of the various candidates among Democratic, Republican, and Independent voters. Within each of these groupings, findings were further reported by sex, age, education, and region. Since an original sampling of 1500 adults could hardly have included more than 600 or 700 Republicans, it is apparent that many of the subgroupings reported in the press reflected a comparative handful of individuals (for example, Republicans in the age group 21 to 29). A professional survey analyst would immediately be able to discern how much weight to give to the reported differences in outlook or preferences between different groups in the population. But the average reader, and even the average politician, was in no position to make this kind of critical assessment.

From early April until the time of the Republican Convention, Gallup queried voters on four possible three-way electoral slates. Before the assassination of Robert Kennedy in June, Nixon and McCarthy were fairly evenly matched.[48] An untrained layman looking at the figures might have considered that the campaign was actually seesawing back and forth, though many of the differences were well within the bounds of statistical tolerance. By mid-June McCarthy led Nixon by a slender margin and also led Rockefeller by a single percentage point. This faint edge, completely nonsignificant to a statistician, was played in newspaper headlines as "McCarthy leads two Republicans" and provided his cause a tremendous psychological boost.

Nixon entered the Republican convention with a commanding lead in delegates. The Rockefeller strategy was to convince enough uncommitted or pro-Nixon delegates that their candidate could not win and that only Rockefeller could defeat either Humphrey or McCarthy.

To win his objective, Rockefeller spent about 5 million dollars on advertising. The media plan prepared by Jack Tinker and Partners, Rockefeller's agency, was aimed, in its own words, "at effective influence on the national public opinion polls," and it did just that—it "moved" them—

in the agency's opinion.[49] As early as May 27 Rockefeller was quoting polls from California, Ohio, and Minnesota as "the hard facts of the situation today" which showed him to be the Republican candidate with the best chance of success. Leonard Hall, Rockefeller's adviser, declared in July, "We stand or fall on public opinion. Rockefeller is campaigning as though the whole country were one big primary, with the results to be made known through the polls on or about August 1."

While Rockefeller sought to influence the polls in order to be taken seriously as a candidate, Ronald Reagan sought by every means to deny his candidacy in order to avoid being listed in the national polls, since the results would clearly document his unpopularity. (A private Rockefeller poll that demonstrated Reagan's low standing was held in reserve and never released.)

Pollster Albert Sindlinger reported in mid-July that Rockefeller was the favorite candidate of 41 percent of the electorate, compared with 37 percent who favored Nixon, 35 percent McCarthy, and 30 percent Humphrey. At the same time, 61 percent expected Nixon to get the Republican nomination and 62 percent expected Humphrey to get the Democratic nomination. The implication was that voters were pessimistic or cynical about the likelihood that the conventions would pick the candidate they themselves favored.

On the eve of the Republican Convention, Monday, July 29, the Miami *Herald* leaked the fact (ahead of the scheduled July 31 release date) that the Gallup Poll showed Nixon ahead. Nixon's spokesman, Herbert Klein, hailed the results as clear evidence of Nixon's strength and as "a breakthrough." Rockefeller discounted the findings as not indicative of a trend and observed wittily that "one Gallup doesn't make a race." Meanwhile his supporters reanalyzed the Gallup results to demonstrate that their man was leading both Democratic contenders in all parts of the country except the South, and that he was strongest in the industrial states with the big electoral votes.

Two days later, on Wednesday, July 31, the Harris poll, scheduled for August 1 release, was also leaked to the press ahead of time. It showed Rockefeller running ahead of both Humphrey and McCarthy, while Nixon ran behind. On the same day, Archibald Crossley revealed that he was using Gallup's interviewers and samples to conduct private polls for Rockefeller but reported that he had found distinctly less pro-Nixon sentiment. During this critical preconvention week, George Gallup was traveling in Europe. His son, George Gallup Jr., recognized that the discrepancy between his results and Harris' was being used as evidence by the inveterate critics of the polls. Harris insisted that there was a definite trend in the data and Gallup, Jr., acknowledged that his poll might have "caught a transitory peak" in Nixon's popularity and a corresponding dip in Rockefeller's.

After a series of telephone conferences, the two men issued a joint statement. Its point was that the surveys "are not as dissimilar as might appear to the public at first glance" and that the differences could be explained by the time element and by normal sampling fluctuations. "Public opinion changed over time, and each [survey] was an accurate reflection of opinion at the time it was made." The statement went on to say, "If these polls are plotted out sequentially, as though they were conducted by a single organization, using the same sampling techniques and the same question-asking techniques, then the following conclusions can be firmly reached: (1) A Nixon-Humphrey-Wallace race today would be extremely close, hovering around the 50-50 mark, with Wallace perhaps holding the balance; (2) Rockefeller has now moved to an open lead over both his possible Democratic opponents, Humphrey and McCarthy; (3) The McCarthy vote has shown and continues to show the greatest amount of volatility among the four leading candidates." Attached to the statement was a series of tables showing that a shift of a single percentage point in the results of each of the last four polls could have produced a highly consistent trend.

Herbert Klein called the Harris Poll "incredible" and greeted the joint statement dourly: "It looks like there's a pollsters' protective society being organized." He added, "After backing away from a vote of the people in primary elections. Rockefeller declared a new set of ground rules based on the notion of nomination by polls."

The Rockefeller camp, in the meanwhile, hailed the statement. Two days later another force entered the picture—Burns Roper, also the son and successor of a pioneer pollster (Elmo Roper). In a press release the younger Roper noted that the 13-point difference (on a Nixon-McCarthy contest) between Gallup and Harris would represent a shift of about 10 million votes in a single week.

Gallup had asked questions with Nixon first in the sequence and showed him the winner, whereas Harris had apparently asked about Humphrey first, and showed *him* in the lead. Moreover, Harris had combined the reinterviews of an earlier sample with another group of new interviews from a fresh sample. Roper referred skeptically to Harris' reported achievement in reinterviewing 1127 of the 1346 original respondents in mid-June as a "phenomenal reinterview rate."

Once Nixon had the Republican nomination in hand, the attention of press and public alike turned to the Democrats. Gallup reported that

Nixon had a two to one lead over either Humphrey or McCarthy as the man who "can do a better job of dealing with the Vietnam war"—an ambiguously worded question that permitted hawks and doves to be lumped together.[50]

On the eve of the Chicago convention, Johnson still harbored the thought of reversing his decision not to run and sought an advance report on the last preconvention Harris Poll results. These showed him trailing Nixon by six percentage points, the same as Humphrey and McCarthy. This killed any thought of a last-minute Johnson boom.[51]

The Harris survey showed a gain for Nixon, but it had been preceded by sensational false rumors (duly reported in the press) that it would show him leading Humphrey two to one. Harris, in an interview, expressed his strong concern with security against leaks, and remarked that he had "personally gathered the information from the computers."

The published polls which showed McCarthy's strength were a source of optimism for his youthful supporters on the eve of a convention known to be dominated by the Humphrey forces. A dispatcher in McCarthy's chauffeur service told a reporter, "I just can't believe that they'll ignore the polls and the petitions and the primary results. I can't believe that so many people who want something so badly can lose." McCarthy's people launched a telephone campaign "to create a mountain of public opinion that not even the most cynical delegate can climb over. . . . Respected accounting and research firms will certify your call and verify the strength of our numbers."

McCarthy's staff was less adept at the use of systematic research. Pollster Oliver Quayle conducted seven private state polls for them and shipped them off special delivery to meet the assigned deadline. Although he was paid $6000 for each poll, two of the reports were returned by the Post Office Department months later marked "undeliverable." Nobody at McCarthy headquarters had ever raised any questions as to where they were.[52]

Fifty-three percent of the public watched the nomination of Humphrey at the Democratic Convention, but 71 percent saw the televised scenes of rioting which most viewers identified as an organized attempt to disrupt the proceedings. A majority sided with the forces of Mayor Richard Daley, and thought that the disturbances would have a negative effect for the Democrats.[53]

During the critical postconvention weeks, when fund-raising and the organization of volunteers customarily reaches its peak, the Humphrey forces retreated into a state of hopeless demoralization. Their candidate appeared to be much too far behind to be able to catch up. It was the polls that created this impression, and thereby enormously exacerbated the depressing effects of the violence and disorder at the convention itself. In the wake of the debacle at Chicago, both Gallup and Harris found Nixon in a commanding lead over Humphrey. The lead widened as September passed on.[54]

Nixon ran as a winner. Sindlinger polls found that Humphrey was close behind Nixon in voters' own preferences, but that Nixon ran nearly two to one ahead of Humphrey as the candidate people *thought* would be elected.

The polls conducted by Opinion Research Corporation for Nixon cost $250,000. Opinion Research Corporation set up panels of 500 voters in 13 states and reinterviewed them periodically. Nixon personally contributed "semantic differential" scale items (shifty/direct, sincere/insincere) to compare his "image" with Humphrey's. According to O.R.C., over half the Wallace voters preferred Nixon to Humphrey and a majority acknowledged they might switch choices before the election. This guided Nixon's strategy of appealing to the Wallace vote on the grounds that Wallace was a lost cause rather than by a direct attack on his principles.[55]

Both Wallace and Nixon had made "law and order" a major issue in the election, and Humphrey was forced to follow suit, although he proposed to solve the problem of "crime in the streets" by building "schools not jails." The "law and order" issue was itself in part a product of the polls, which brought the subject to the attention of politicians a year or more before the election. Gallup, asking the public what it was most concerned about, had long before this found crime emerging as a subject of growing popular concern. Many of the responses to his open-ended questions really reflected public disturbance over the urban riots of 1967 and early 1968 rather than a concern about crime in the traditional sense. Since all crime was reported under the same heading, the subject appeared larger in public consciousness than it might otherwise have seemed, and the consequent discussion of it may have had a further reinforcing effect.[56]

Although Wallace's candidacy had originally provoked great anxiety in both major parties, the surveys showed it to be a diminishing factor on the electoral scene. There were substantial differences from region to region in the social-class sources of the Wallace vote. The Democratic losses benefited Wallace in some parts of the country and Nixon in others.[57] The Wallace vote outside the South was twice as heavy among those under 35 as the Goldwater vote had been in 1964. A postelection analysis concluded that Nixon would probably have won even if Wallace were not in the race.[58]

Wallace's problem, from the very outset of his campaign, was to be taken seriously as a national contender, rather than as a purely sectional candidate. He managed to achieve an astonishing degree of broad public acceptance. Given the fact that Wallace *was* treated by the news media as a major candidate, most people evidently found it difficult to reject him altogether as a man on the fringe rather than one in the democratic mainstream.[59]

Wallace's declining position in the polls was in striking contrast to his ability to fill large convention halls in cities all around the country and to arouse a revivalist fervor among those who came to hear him. At one such rally in Scranton, Pennsylvania, on October 9, Wallace, forgetting the part of the country he was in, accused the pollsters of being part of the "Eastern Establishment moneyed interests," and repeated that they were "part of this Eastern crowd with Eastern money." He charged that the polls were rigged, and that Gallup gave Nixon advance knowledge of his poll releases, but also acknowledged to a reporter that he too got advance copies of the same releases before they were published.

Wallace made these charges part of his standard speech throughout October. He aroused crowds by asking his supporters, "Have any of you-all ever been asked about this here election by Mr. Harris or Mr. Gallup?" to be rewarded by shouts of, "No" and "Never."[60]

Richard Kutzleb, the Humphrey press officer for New York, summed up the typical politician's attitude toward polls in his comment, "Any poll that shows us gaining or slightly ahead is accurate." The polls did, in fact, show gains for Humphrey as the campaign went into its final stages.

Gallup's last national poll, taken October 31-November 2 and released two days before the election, found Nixon leading by a hair.[61] The last word was had by Harris, who on the eve of the election released the findings of his weekend survey which found Humphrey ahead, also by a hair. Nixon won the actual election by a mere half million votes. Had they been distributed somewhat differently, state by state, the correct prediction would have been Harris' rather than Gallup's. Such are the uncertainties of election forecasting!

Every major election in recent years has brought forth inquests on the political effects of polls. Minor as well as major politicians have called for direct restrictions on the pollsters. Mayor R. W. Grady of Rockledge, Florida (a city of 14,000 on the Banana River), and a Romney supporter, persuaded his city council to draft an ordinance forbidding national pollsters to quiz residents about their politics. Grady complained of Romney's withdrawal from the New Hampshire primary: "It was just a crime for a man to withdraw from a race on the basis of a poll, before the people had a chance to vote for or against him."

Representative Lucian Nedzi of Detroit introduced a bill requiring that poll data be filed in the Library of Congress within 72 hours after it had been made public, with particulars regarding the sampling specifications also placed on file. (A somewhat similar bill had been vetoed by the Governor of Texas after passing the State legislature.)

Martin Steadman, Mario Procaccino's manager in his 1969 New York mayoralty race, accused the *Daly News* poll of "doing in" his candidate. (The *News* poll showed a 20-point lead for Mayor John Lindsay, while in the actual vote Lindsay was only 7 points ahead.) The other defeated candidate in the same race, State Senator John J. Marchi, asserted that "the money stopped" after the *Daily News* poll showed incumbent Mayor John Lindsay leading decisively. Marchi introduced a bill in the state legislature which would set up licensing requirements to establish the "good character, competence, and integrity" of pollsters.

In the United Kingdom an influential Parliamentary committee suggested in May 1966 that poll results should be banned from publication for 72 hours before elections. In West Germany, the leading research organizations announced on July 3, 1969, that they would discontinue political polling immediately before the Bundestag elections, because they believed the outcome could be influenced by the published poll results.

Are such restrictions justified? The most significant "bandwagon" effect of polls is probably on party workers and contributors, rather than on voters flocking to back a sure winner. Voters in most elections are faced with a long roster of offices to be filled, of which only a few have been the topics of preelection forecasts. Normally, therefore, they would have an incentive to vote, regardless of whether they considered the major race predetermined. People may be attracted to a winner, but they are also likely to assume that the candidate they favor is a winner. A meticulous study of the evidence by Joseph Klapper's Office of Social Research at the Columbia Broadcasting System led to the conclusion that "there is no absolutely conclusive evidence that . . . the publication of poll results does or does not affect the subsequent vote." A poll on polls, made after the 1960 elections by the Opinion Research Corporation, found that two people in three could not remember the preelection forecasts. Nixon and Kennedy voters gave identical answers, suggesting that neither group had been influenced by the pollsters' estimates of a Kennedy victory.[62]

George Gallup regarded the 1948 election results as disproof of the theory that polls cause people to jump on the bandwagon, but the possibility remains that Truman might have won by an even bigger margin if some of his supporters failed to vote for what they thought was a hopeless cause.

There is some very limited experimental evidence that supports the commonsense supposition that when a poll report shows a candidate or position favored by the majority, there is a corresponding change in voting intention and opinion.[63] But Mervin D. Field, head of California's best-known statewide poll, argues that polls can produce not only a bandwagon effect but also a "reverse bandwagon."[64] "The poll results lead voters to support the trailing candidate—creating an 'underdog effect.' They do this by convincing potential supporters of the underdog that their vote is useless, or by reducing the potential majority of the winning candidate by convincing supporters of the leading candidate that their vote is unnecessary. As a result either or both groups do not vote on election day. . . . If the bandwagon theory were valid it would require that leading candidates' margins, as reported in well publicized polls, should generally tend to become greater as the campaigns progress." Field points out that there have been many cases where this has not happened. The fact remains that no politician welcomes a preelection survey that shows him running substantially behind.

Agitation to have polls investigated generally starts from the premise that there are terrible secrets to be uncovered, when in fact the pollsters' perennial problems of theory, method, and technique are familiar to their own fraternity and can be communicated to others with little difficulty. Incompetence and bias in polling characteristically are encountered outside the ranks of the survey research profession, which can only enforce its code of ethics within its own membership. The troubles with the public polls are essentially the troubles with the news media, which too often cannot distinguish between good and bad surveys, which interpret or on occasion misinterpret them, which give them prominence and invest their findings with oracular portent. But any investigation of press handling of the polls would merely uncover evidence of the larger and more significant ineptitude or disinterest with which the media too often report expert findings in the domain of social science.

Any move to curtail the pollster's freedom to study election preferences and trends must inevitably be linked to a curtailment of his right, or any citizen's right to investigate, through appropriate inquiry, the state of the public temper on any issue of the day, or even nonissues like the taste of toothpaste or magazine reading preferences. A restriction of the right to question people's opinions is a threat to their right to hold them.

Part Two

OPINION RESEARCH AND PUBLIC POLICY

LEADERSHIP AND PUBLIC OPINION

To be turned from one's course by men's opinions, by blame, and by misrepresentation, shows a man unfit to hold an office.

Plutarch

The limitations and abuses of opinion surveys offer more reason to urge that they be better understood than to argue that they should be restricted. Although election polls are most visible and most widely criticized, far more interesting questions can be raised about the broader kind of political opinion research and its proper place in the formation of public policy. We can take up these questions under several headings, beginning with the long-standing concern of political theorists over the proper relationship of government and public opinion. The responsiveness of official leaders to opinion is expressed in a willingness to reexamine and reorder social priorities in order to meet changing public demands. Priorities in a diversified country reflect a balance of forces among the interests of distinct and often opposing constituencies. The exercise of effective leadership requires an understanding of not only what these constituencies want but how badly they want it.

Such observations could have been made at any previous point in history, but the practice of survey research has given the old discussions new meanings. Polls are commonly used as political weapons either to support state policies or to insist on changes in those policies and in priorities. Such citations of survey data ignore the proper target. Polls can best be used not to make decisions but to provide useful intelligence for policy makers, who must always have access to other kinds of information, and to other criteria of judgment.

Public opinion is strongly responsive to leadership, and poll results must be interpreted accordingly. The sense of deference to authority is deeply instilled in all human infants by the basic condition of their biological dependence. This is what often makes the source of information so important to credibility. In polls and research experiments, controversial statements arouse wide swings of agreement or disagreement, depending on whether they are attributed to one source or to another.

Under dictatorships and democracies alike, major political events occur at such a distance and on so vast a scale that the average person regards them as abstractions. It is difficult to translate their implications into the homely terms of our own daily lives. By accepting authority (whether embodied in important individuals or in the beliefs of our peers), we are provided with convenient and reassuring explanations for the complex phenomena of the political universe. The mass media tend to simplify great public debates into a clash of wills between powerful men. It is far easier to visualize matters of great complexity in terms of a clear-cut choice of personalities than to cope with the technicalities and conjectures that surround any significant legislative argument.

A leader is in a position to define a situation in a way that brings his followers to act as he desires. But there are usually limits to his powers. When his directives appear to conflict with an accepted norm—for instance, the ideals of equality, fair play, and justice—not only may his specific orders be ignored; his fundamental authority may be questioned. But fewer of his followers protest than think protest is called for, and a substantial minority can be subverted into acts which they themselves acknowledge to be improper and illegitimate.[1]

A leader can lead only up to a point without coercion, penalties, or terror. It is the rare figure whose leadership is absolute, who enjoys the wholehearted voluntary acceptance and enthusiasm of his entire constituency. More commonly, he must secure the support of the majority and hope that dissident elements will provide him with at least the tacit permissiveness of their silence. When opposition becomes vocal or finds expression in rebellious acts, the direct threat of subversion may be small compared with the hidden dangers of widespread but unspoken popular unrest. The leader's supremacy in the eyes of the majority depends on the assumption that he embodies the consensus. Overt opposition raises doubts as to whether this is truly the case.

Opinion polls introduce a new element into the relationship of leaders and the public, for they create on the part of all concerned—the leader, his supporters, and his opponents—a heightened awareness of dissension, and thus can lead to a questioning of the leader's legitimacy as a spokesman for the body politic.

Albert Einstein once advised a young man uncertain about his career: "Become a public opinion pollster. There you will never be unemployed. We know, after all, that people are ruled by being told tall stories—so the rulers must constantly test and see what they can get away with."[2]

Any political leader, whether he seeks office or holds it, balances the need to be true to his principles and the need to maintain a power base from which his ideals can be realized. Harry Truman said, "They talk about the power of the president, how I can just push a button to get things done. Why, I spend most of my time kissing somebody's behind."[3]

As he articulates beliefs into programs, a leader can mobilize public support. But his power or influence may also arise from his ability to anticipate and act on a change in the public mood, as did the French Socialist leader who proclaimed, "My followers are on the barricades. I must go and lead them."

If a legislator is to represent public views rather than vote his private conscience, whose views should he follow? Realistically, his career may depend most on his "party faithful" and active supporters. Should he follow them, *all* his local constituents, or the national trend of opinion?

Edmund Burke, in his speech to the electors of Bristol on November 3, 1774, said, "It ought to be the happiness and glory of a representative to live in the strictest union, the closest correspondence, and the most unreserved communication with his constituents. Their wishes ought to have great weight with him; their opinion high respect; their business unremitted attention. . . ." But, Burke went on to say, "Your representative owes you, not his industry only, but his judgment; and he betrays instead of serving you if he sacrifices it to your opinion."

Winston Churchill reiterated the same sentiments two centuries later when he said, "Nothing is more dangerous than to live in the temperamental atmosphere of a Gallup poll, always feeling one's pulse and taking one's temperature. . . . There is only one duty, only one safe course, and that is to try to be right and not to fear to do or say what you believe to be right."

Leadership entails a type of responsibility different from that which accompanies the expression of opinion from the sidelines or a participation in decisions which others must execute. A leader cannot please everyone; his inactions appear like actions in their consequences. The standards others use in judging him can never be the same as the standards he must impose upon himself. There is a perpetual state of tension between what the public wants its leaders to do and what in their heart of hearts they know they would do in their place as leaders.

At a news conference on September 26, 1969, President Nixon told a questioner that he would "under no circumstances" be affected by campus protests in opposition to the Vietnam war. In a subsequent statement, the President drew a "clear distinction between public opinion and public demonstrations. To listen to public opinion is one thing; to be swayed by public demonstrations is another. A demonstration—in whatever cause—is an organized expression of one particular set of opinions, which may or may not be shared by the majority of the people. If a President—any President—allowed his course to be set by those who demonstrate, he would betray the trust of all the rest. Whatever the issues, to allow Government policy to be made in the streets would destroy the democratic process. It would give the decision, not to the majority, and not to those with the strongest arguments, but to those with the loudest voices. It would reduce statecraft to slogans. It would invite anarchy. It would allow every group to test its strength not at the ballot box but through confrontation in the streets. The planned demonstration will tell us that a great many Americans are deeply concerned about the war; that some of these consider U.S. participation immoral; that many want U.S. troops withdrawn immediately and unconditionally. But all of us in the Administration are already well aware of this sentiment. We are already aware that it is widespread. . . . The policies we are now following reflect our own best judgment, based on exhaustive study of all the available evidence, of how to achieve that goal. To abandon that policy merely because of public demonstrations would therefore be an act of gross irresponsibility on my part."[4]

Critics of Nixon's Vietnam policies accused him of being a "dissenter from the policy of the public-at-large"[5] and argued that his failure to follow the shift of public opinion in the direction of immediate troop withdrawal was leading to alienation and disillusionment with the democratic process.

On March 31, 1971, Nixon told a television audience, "When Presidents begin to worry about images, when they begin to be concerned about polls, when they begin to read their press clippings, they become like athletes who are so concerned about what is written about them, and what is said about them, that they don't play the game well." Nixon also told *The New York Times'* columnist Cyrus Sulzberger, "I am certain a Gallup Poll would show that a great majority of the people would want to pull out of Vietnam. But a Gallup Poll would also show that a great majority of the people would want to pull three or more divisions out of Europe. And it would also show that a great majority of the people would cut our defense budget. Polls are not the answer. You must also look at the facts."

In conversations with intellectuals in *his* administration, President Johnson expressed himself as "puzzled by the alienation and protests of thoughtful men," citing intellectuals with whom he had had good relations on most questions until the Vietnam War tore them apart. "Since most of his critics agreed that he had to carry on the War and not turn tail and run, what was it that they really wanted him to do, he asked [in a quotation paraphrased by a reporter]. Perhaps, the President is said to have remarked, intellectuals really wanted him to do something he did not think a President could do and something that most other citizens would not want him to do: to agonize about his problems in public."[6]

Indeed, leaders must live privately with the consequences of their own difficult private decisions, and precisely because they cannot "agonize" in public, they may appear aloof and callous. Former Secretary of State Dean Acheson recently recalled that he had brought Robert Oppenheimer, "the father of the atomic bomb," into President Truman's office "wringing his hands, and [Oppenheimer] said, 'I have blood on my hands.' 'Don't ever bring that damn fool in here again,' Truman told me afterward. 'He didn't set that bomb off. I did. This kind of sniveling makes me sick.' "[7]

The issues are further complicated because leaders themselves can, up to a point, control the facts that the public has at its disposal, especially on military matters. The publication in 1971 of the secret Pentagon study on Vietnam placed on the record information that might have influenced the continuing debate over Indochina policy during the 1960s if it had been reported as it occurred.

When governments engage in secret diplomacy, propaganda, and military actions, public opinion can be based only on what the public knows. If, as is often the case, a substantial part of the population is uninformed about and uninterested in a subject, then actions contrary to the apparent will of the polled majority may nonetheless fall within the latitude that a compliant body politic permits its leaders. How sensitive should a leader be to opinion formed without knowledge of important information? And yet how easy it is for public opinion to be flouted on the grounds that the public lacks the essential facts in possession of its leaders!

Governments deal with contingencies and possibilities, as well as with the known facts of the moment, to which public opinion responds. Even if the public had access to all the intelligence and expert advice upon which a ruler can draw in formulating policy, it would be impossible for him to govern by the dictates of polled opinion. Government policies must be consistent in all the domains that concern government. Public opinion is not. Government policies are meant to be carried out over an extended period of time. Public opinion shifts with events and with the rise and fall of political personalities. The social philosopher Jacques Ellul writes, "No sooner would government begin to pursue certain aims favored in an opinion poll, than opinion would turn against it. To the degree that opinion changes are rapid, policy changes would have to be equally rapid; to the extent that opinion is irrational, political action would have to be equally irrational. . . . The government cannot postpone actions and decisions until vague images and myths eventually coalesce into opinion. In the present world of politics, action must at all times be the forerunner of opinion. Even where public opinion is already formed, it can be disastrous to follow it."[8]

Dean Rusk, as Secretary of State, referred to the importance of leadership in establishing foreign policy: "We cannot test public opinion until the President and the leaders of the country have gone to the public to explain what is required and have asked them for support for the necessary action. I doubt, for example, that three months before the leadership began to talk about what came to be the Marshall Plan, any public opinion expert would have said that the country would have accepted such proposals."[9]

Franklin Roosevelt wrote a friend, "My problem is to get the American people to think of conceivable consequences without scaring the American people into thinking that they are going to be dragged into this war."[10] Historians have suggested that Roosevelt was not expecting the United States to intervene directly in Europe, but wanted to build up American military power as an arsenal for the Allies without provoking too much public controversy.[11] In this he was largely successful. Even though he progressively increased aid to Britain during the summer and fall of 1941, his policies continued to draw a constant measure of public support in the polls.[12] However, before the Japanese bombing of Pearl Harbor, the polls made it seem doubtful that there would be any popular or congressional support for any war that might appear to have the aim of protecting European colonies in Asia or the Pacific.

Roosevelt used American public opinion effectively as an instrument of diplomatic negotiation. At the Yalta Conference, Stalin complained that whenever he made a proposal Churchill and Roosevelt rejected it, using the excuse that it would be opposed by public opinion at home.[13]

George Kennan reports an incident that occurred during the Dumbarton Oaks Conference when the Russian delegates' obduracy produced a suggestion that the Americans "should in effect, throw ourselves on Stalin's mercy, pointing out the domestic political embarrassment he was causing to the administration." Kennan thought it "unwise for American statesmen to plead domestic political pressures, or the pressures of public opinion, as an argument to support their positions vis-à-vis other governments."[14]

The hands of a diplomat are always strengthened by strong domestic support, even when he starts with a decided disadvantage. Joseph Smrkovsky, president of the Czechoslovakian National Assembly, reported that during his negotiations in Moscow after the 1968 Soviet invasion of his country, the solution "became apparent when the clear and unanimous position of the Czech and Slovak peoples was demonstrated, and this influenced the attitude of our interlocutors and our personal attitude."

According to sociologist Amitai Etzioni, "In democratic societies . . . one of the most outstanding features is that the national leadership is confronted with the public opinion it helped to crystallize at earlier points in time . . . . Thus at various points American administrations have felt they could ill afford politically to support the admission of Communist China to the United Nations, because the American public was educated against it, and the administration believed that no amount of short run explanation could change public opinion to make the political costs low enough."[15] What Etzioni has called "the Kennedy experiment" was an attempt to reduce Soviet-American tensions by gestures that would produce reciprocal measures from the other side to which a further accommodating response could be made. Etzioni sees this as an attempt to influence American public opinion rather than the Soviet rulers: "Its primary purpose, it seems, was not to affect international relations directly but to increase the range of options the Kennedy administration could take up without running high political risks from a public steeped in cold war psychology."

A democratic ruler must be concerned with public opinion not because he feels impelled to follow its dictates, but to more shrewdly and effectively manage himself, his associates, and the news he controls so as to swing opinion behind the policies he advocates.

Opinion can be changed suddenly both by events which are unex-

pected and by staged events, such as a direct appeal by a political figure
or the announcement of a new policy by an incumbent administration.
Public support for a president inevitably arises after a public speech or
statement, as Franklin Roosevelt well knew when he initiated his fireside
chats. Polls taken before and after televised Presidential speeches inevitably find a switch in public sentiment in support of the administration. Favorable opinion went up from 42 percent to 72 percent after
Johnson's speech on the Tonkin Gulf Resolution, from 49 percent to
69 percent after Nixon's speech announcing plans for a phased withdrawal from Vietnam, and from 7 percent to 50 percent after his speech
announcing the invasion of Cambodia.[16]

Not only Presidential speeches, but planted questions at Presidential
press conferences have been used to push administration policies, often
of issues remote from public concern. Hence the following obliging
query for President Eisenhower, at a press conference on April 29, 1959:
"Mr. Hagerty [the press secretary] indicated yesterday that you might
have some comments that you would like to make about the labor bill
which was passed by the Senate and is now going to the House. Would
you care to, at this time?"[17]

There are obviously serious limitations to any overuse of Presidential
prerogatives to assert leadership by means of public appeals through the
mass media. When President Nixon granted an exclusive television interview to Howard K. Smith of ABC in March 1971, he drew only 11
percent of the viewing audience in metropolitan New York, while a new
movie on another station got a 42 percent share.

The passage of legislation or a court decision, like the enunciation of
executive policy, legitimizes a position that was previously in the realm of
debate, and thereby pulls opinion in the direction it has indicated.

When the institutions of representative government operate without
interference or strain, a head of state need not be excessively concerned
about the popularity of his policies. The demands of political succession
must always provide realistic restraints on his capacities to take actions
that the public will not support, since he, his protégés, and his party will
always be up for a vote in the next election. Constitutional government
has built into its structure checks that limit the options open to rulers.
Yet democratic rulers, knowing full well both the extents and limits of
their powers, have a sharp interest in those expressions of public thinking
that go beyond legislative debate or newspaper editorials. Presidents have
always watched their mail carefully, even though most of them are shrewd
enough politically to know that letter-writers are not a cross section of
the electorate.

Letters addressed to public officials are generally understood to emanate from a highly unrepresentative minority of the public, including eccentrics as well as people with axes to grind. A handful of individuals, writing letters under a variety of assumed names to public officials, or to the press, can generate an impression of a mass movement in support of a cause on which no public opinion has previously existed.[18]

The number of spontaneous reactions to a public communication goes up in relation to the strength of the feelings it arouses. Only 27 people of every 10,000 in the audience of a popular television program writes a letter after the typical broadcast, but Edward R. Murrow's exposé of Senator Joe McCarthy drew 50,000 letters, wires, and calls—one from every 100 viewers. McCarthy's rebuttal program drew half as many communications from an audience twice the size).[19]

Though the flow of mail on controversial matters is easily manipulated by pressure groups, there is an emotional response to it, arising from the awareness that it represents a good deal of individual effort. Mail, like poll results, can be presented as evidence of support for a leader's position, and thus be helpful in creating a bandwagon effect for the policies he favors. But since it is the recipient of the letters who does the counting, a preponderance of critical mail can be written off as the work of the lobbies and special interests, while a few favorable letters can be cited verbatim to indicate popular support.

Franklin Roosevelt insisted on getting a careful tabulation of the opinions expressed in his mail and sometimes referred to these in his press conferences.[20] Richard Nixon received half a million pieces of mail at the White House within his first four months in office. Twice a week the President was shown "a random sampling of twenty to thirty letters." All letters were answered, although no systematic analysis was made of their content. A man writing in opposition to the antiballistic missile system received a form letter in reply from the Adjutant General of the Army. After Nixon's 1970 decision to send American armed forces into Cambodia, the White House announced that telephone calls were running six to one in favor and telegrams two to one. Such statistics were perhaps not completely accurate: A college professor who called the White House and said he wanted to record an opinion on Cambodia was asked how he was voting and was cut off when he said he was against the President's policy. When he called back and said he supported the policy "the voice on the other end said, 'Oh, fine, and how many are in your family? Four—well, that's four votes then, right?' "[21]

At the same time, wires addressed to the Senate Foreign Relations Committee were eight to one in *opposition*. People who want to give vent to their opinions apparently find it easier to give support to someone who shares their views than to voice opposition to those who do not.[22]

It is essential for rulers to retain some direct channels of access to ideas and information that might otherwise be kept from them by their own palace guards. Polls provide public officials with a more accurate reading on the divisions of sentiment on important issues than do mail counts or newspaper editorials. But surveys are incapable of generating or passing on original ideas, uniquely framed propositions, and images that reflect the interplay of personal experience and feeling with abstract political principles.

DEFINING PRIORITIES

It isn't just the election. Should we put more money in the market or leave it in savings bonds; is public or private school better for the children; shall we take a winter vacation or leave it 'til spring; shall we have the house painted first or the inside redecorated? We're undecided about everything!

Lady being interviewed by a
pollster (caption for a
New Yorker cartoon by Chon Day)

"What is to be done?" asked Lenin, but it was a rhetorical question. He *knew* what was to be done, and his successors have shown similar certainty in their pronouncements at Communist Party Congresses through half a century.

A young couple getting married in the Soviet Union must wait a long time to get an apartment. One Russian spoke of this problem cheerfully: "You know, we have very powerful bosses. When they want to get something done they give the orders and it gets done. When they wanted atomic weapons and space rockets, the money was found to get these things. Now they have given the word to solve the housing shortage, and it'll be solved."

This optimistic prediction was somewhat premature, but its real interest is not in the speaker's touching faith that his country's leaders were finally ready to turn their attention to a matter of uppermost concern to him and to other ordinary people.[23] The point is rather the implicit premise that in an authoritarian society, national goals can be decided in committee and placed in rank order—1, 2, 3, 4. The decision makers present a united front—whatever the preceding discussion and debate—and the agreed-upon priorities are clearly understood and largely accepted by a docile population which understands who is in charge.

In the United States, and in the West generally, we are accustomed to a continuing public competition for economic priorities, on the part of various groups which reflect different definitions of social need as well as their own different and particular interests. All decisions on priorities are reversible, so the debate never ceases.

What has high priority for an individual reflects what he identifies with his own group interests. But people are often mistaken in the social role or group identity they assume as most expressive of their interests and loyalties. They are prone to fall back on the symbolic reference points of the past, rather than to recognize what is best for them in the future. A survey of 1,000 Boston homeowners, many of them with incomes at the poverty level, found that only 9 percent defined "the urban crisis" in terms of jobs, and only 18 percent raised such issues as housing, transportation, pollution, and urban renewal. Instead the phrase was identified primarily with crime, violence, youthful rebellion, and racial tension.[24]

One price of the democratic freedom that makes possible a continuing competition for attention, money, and action is a considerable amount of confusion, among all concerned, as to what public priorities actually are at any given moment. To the social critic this confusion and clash of interests is evidence of the Establishment's insensitivity to human suffering. To the social revolutionary it suggests a total absence of national goals and plans to achieve them. It lends credence to the charge that our social system is equipped to carry us only from day to day, from crisis to crisis.

There is indeed a constant shifting in the public's definition of urgent problems. The percentage naming the Vietnam War as the country's "most important problem" rose from 42 percent in the May 1968 Gallup Poll to 52 percent in July. The percentage mentioning crime, lawlessness, riots, and delinquency rose from 15 percent to 29 percent in the same period, while the percentage mentioning race relations fell from 25 percent to 13 percent. There is also a shifting in the urgency with which *subgroups* of the population regard various problems. The war was mentioned by twice as many Negroes as mentioned race relations as the number one problem in 1968, but a year later the war and race relations were named by an equal number.

In February 1969, public opinion ran 49 percent to 39 percent against putting a man on the moon. On the actual eve of the Apollo 11 launching in July 1969, opinion had turned around in favor of the moon landing, 51 percent to 41 percent. However, 56 percent (about the same as in February) still did not believe that the space program was worth a $4 billion a year investment; 37 percent thought it was.

Except in wartime and in the Great Depression, we seldom see our national priorities radically altered all at once. The President may closet himself with his advisors over the weekend to work on his budget message, but the resulting document is merely a stage in the long painful process of budgetary review which goes on within each federal agency and in Congress.

The old "guns versus butter" debate is more relevant than ever to a society juggling the costs of armaments and the space program in relation to pressing demands for the solution of social problems in the fields of race relations, poverty and urban decay, air and water pollution, transportation, education, and public health.[25]

Asking people what they want government to do inevitably yields answers different from what they themselves want to pay for. Individual responsibility for social action is attenuated and remote when that action is to be taken by society as a whole. Among the American public at large, 92 percent agree that cities "must be made better places to work and live in," and 60 percent report a sense of urgency about the urban problem. But opinion runs 69 percent to 25 percent against paying higher taxes for urban improvement.

Similarly, 56 percent of Americans feel there is considerable air pollution where they live, and the proportion rises to 72 percent in the cities and 75 percent in the suburbs. But only 44 percent are willing to pay $15 more in taxes each year to alleviate the problem.[26]

The taxes people least resist paying are the local ones that take care of the activities whose tangible benefits they see close at hand; schools, police, sanitation, and the like.[27] Most activities of the federal government are more remote than those of the states, but the federal government is probably more vivid and real to most people because of its prominence in the mass media, which are part of everyone's close life experience.

President Nixon's 1971 proposal for a massive program of federal revenue-sharing with states and localities brought into the spotlight of discussion the incongruities in perceived value and direct importance to the citizen of what he receives from spending programs at different levels of government.

Although there has already been a great expansion of federal aid programs to states and municipalities, there is never a *direct* confrontation between the pressure groups that represent the most intimate public concerns at the level of personal contact with local institutions like schools, hospitals, the police—and those pressure groups that function at the more diffuse, impersonal level of public concern like the military or space programs. Only in the mass media do these competing social demands float into a common level of attention and discourse.

A public issue may grow out of a major news event, but it may also arise from a mounting tide of minor incidents. The news media define public issues and sometimes create them where none existed before. The press has always been a source of ideas for the legislative agenda and also a source of pressure on politicians, telling them what is presumably on the public mind. What is on the public mind—what people are thinking and talking about—is commonly equated with what the news media make available.

When a story is featured on the front page of a newspaper or on television, the public, newsmen, and politicians alike are wont to regard it as a matter of public interest. But a subject which is big in the news is not necessarily big in private discussion. Matters of obviously great importance to those in the know may strike most readers or viewers as dull. Others are nasty subjects from which people deflect their attention. Still others (for example, the population crisis) are too complex, too remote, or too abstract to warrant any expenditure of energy by the average person, even when he recognizes their importance.

As newsmen seek to differentiate each day's trivia from the minor manifestations of major and continuing stories, they sort out priorities for public discussion and action; at the same time their own sense of what is trivial and what is significant is shaped by what opinion surveys tell them about public interests, preferences, and concerns.

Priorities for discussion rarely relate directly to the amount of money or manpower which a society expends upon different social tasks or functions. The routine activities necessary to maintain an institution seldom receive the attention of its leaders unless something occurs to upset their normal flow. The reform of the mammoth American postal system was of low priority compared to such pressing problems as the Vietnam War, inflation, and racial tension, until the 1970 strike of postal employees thrust it high upon the national agenda. Matters assume social priority according to the amount of drama they generate, the uncertainties that surround them, or the threats they represent for the smooth functioning of routine. A problem which the experts consider to have very high priority may arouse only apathy from the public at large and from decision-makers, until some symbolically significant critical incident occurs.

The management of a business is only incidentally concerned with the continuing work flow of production, sales, or administration. Instead it is likely to be preoccupied with conditions that interfere with the normal state of affairs as a result of competitive activities, acts of nature, and government restrictions, or else it is itself engaged in upsetting the equilibrium in an effort to expand the firm's profits, scope of operations, and market position.

When an agenda is made up for a business meeting it is customary to provide a place both for the routine and the extraordinary. A well-structured agenda rearranges the traditional sequence of topics in order to permit an expansion of debate and reflection on the matters which seem to be most urgent—in the judgment of the Chairman or the Steering Committee.

How does a chairman decide what is important to talk about and what is not? He may apply no more than his own personal wisdom or insight, or that of his close advisors. More likely, he responds to what he senses people *want* to talk about, as reflected in earlier correspondence and conversation.

Setting priorities for attention, discussion, and action therefore seems to involve three elements:

1. A real set of problems or objective needs on the part of the constituency. Many of these may be unarticulated or even unperceived. Many of them may be the special needs of particular segments or subgroups. They may contradict, compete, or conflict with each other.

2. A leadership which imposes its own judgment, assumptions, or biases to organize these needs into a program or agenda.

3. A communication system through which the needs may be expressed, considered, debated, and eventually ranked and handled by the constituency or its representatives.

High priority goes to things that are changing and highest priority goes to those with the fastest rate of change, particularly those that show a propensity to get out of hand. Rapid social change brings rising expectations, impatient demands, and angry actions which accelerate the very forces that have already brought about change. The historic disadvantages of the Negro minority acquire greater poignancy as those disadvantages are reduced. Poverty becomes a subject of greater concern to national policy-makers as poverty decreases. Its visibility is a function of the drama of its transformation and not of its original extent.

Officials in a position of public accountability necessarily view priorities differently than does the public. The issues which preoccupy journalists and politicians are not necessarily salient in public interest.[28]

It has been argued that the most urgent social needs are precisely those which affect specific sectors of society and to which most other people are indifferent. For example, Robert Heilbroner maintains that "our own national goal of racial equality . . . has been seriously impeded by the democratic process of consulting the will of the majority. How fast can one bring equality when large numbers—perhaps even majorities—do not wish to have it brought? So, too, our ability to raze and rebuild the slums is crippled by our insistence on relying on a market mechanism and on deferring to prerogatives of private property, with the result that urban renewal has come to a virtual halt."[29]

There is, however, a profound difference between a majority that stands in aggressive opposition to social action that benefits a subgroup and a majority that merely fails to move in support of goals to which that subgroup assigns high urgency. Revolutionary tactics on the part of the minority may be an act of desperation in the first instance and of expediency in the second. But in either case the attitude of the majority is never immovable.

In a democracy, the changing of public priorities should not have to come about through the use of the club and the firebomb. Yet these instruments have been used successfully to shift the social agenda, because the normal machinery of state has not moved quickly enough to anticipate changing public needs.

What function can survey research perform to sensitize the media and the government to the intensity of demand for solution of problems which seem on the surface to lack any urgency? In a society facing many complex choices, poll questions often tend to limit the options. Poll results tend to be conservative, because responses gravitate toward what the public knows and feels comfortable with. Thus poll findings published in the press offer reassurance to statesmen and public alike.

A great bulwark of democracy is the tradition of investigative reporting in journalism, which stems from the initiative of the news-gathering organization. The essence of this kind of reporting is that it is done in depth, that it digs below the surface of events, that it deals with them not as incidents but as evidences of a deeper and more significant pattern.

For the pollster to become an investigative reporter it is essential that he too tackle his problems in depth, that he take the initiative. In polling, as in journalism, this means that the investigator must be given his head; that he must be in a position to size up problems *before* they become a subject of public concern.

Social problems that seem remote and abstract because they have been around for a long time can become immediate if individual news items are perceived by journalists as part of a larger continuing story. Such a linkage is apt to occur much sooner if the story line is defined for them by the pollsters, if the problem is given a name, say, "student unrest," "crime in the streets," or "pollution of the environment." As soon as polls start to ask people's opinions about something, that subject becomes a matter of public debate.

The effort expended to gauge people's perceptions of national problems and goals is pitiful in relation to their significance and size. A greater variety of polls, more often, more localized, would tell what people are talking about as well as what they think the priorities are.

Who will provide the funds required to study great problems and report on them with the speed required to make them subjects of active public discussion? The government is certainly neither a likely nor a proper source. Only the news media are in a position to give the pollster both support and attention. It is in their own uneasy grappling with the question of their professionalism that newsmen turn increasingly from their intuitions to the methods and theories of social science.

Public opinion polls make it difficult for the media to categorize bloc opinions in sharp and rigid terms, to classify people into bins with all others of the same arbitrarily selected characteristics. Polls make it impossible to describe the state of mind of the many on the basis of the dramatic actions of the few.

In a time of revolutionary crisis and counterrevolutionary threat, polls can make a major contribution to democracy. They threaten complacency if they alert us to the social needs which have not yet found their voices. But they also serve a stabilizing purpose. By reminding us of the majority's opinion, even of its apathetic neutrality, they help to assure that majority of its rights.

THE OPINION CONSTITUENCY

I know more about Kamchatka than I do about Georgia.

James Madison

One of the functions of opinion research is to distinguish the views of different constituencies within a population. The pollsters—and the media that report their findings—face the difficult task of judging what the relevant constituencies are. Here public opinion research can have an important influence on the formation of public opinion. For the pollster's definition of the constituency, like the journalists's, helps to create role identifications and, as a consequence, the affirmation of opinions appropriate to those roles.

A legitimate constituency of government must have some objective common reference point, in geography, ethnic origins, or occupational interests. A constituency must have an accepted identity for its members; it is not merely a political unit. It represents a body of people who share certain characteristics and burdens, who think of themselves as "we." Because of this, it makes sense to generalize about their opinions under a single heading. Different constituencies may be presumed to have different values, different sets of priorities, different degrees of willingness to mortgage the future for the sake of present needs.

In most nations taxpayers in prosperous communities carry the burden of providing social services to those in impoverished areas. This is not done out of kindness; it is taken for granted as part of the political system. When there is a flood or cyclone in one part of the United States, it is understood that the President will declare it a disaster area and provide federal aid to the victims, paid for out of the national treasury. By contrast, aid to victims of catastrophe abroad can never be given on the same scale; they are not part of our national constituency.

Under the anachronistic structure of American government, state and municipal boundaries set by surveyors long since dead still cut crazily through the live tissue of the metropolitan regions in which most of the people live and work. Central cities have been cut off by these arbitrary dividing lines from proper sources of tax support and civic involvement in their own growing hinterlands. The well-known result is decay in the cities and insipidity in the suburbs. An incidental by-product is the loss of civic conscience, an ambiguity of identity with the geographic and economic reference points that make for common experience and concern.

An intelligent, politically active Mt. Kisco, New York, matron said indignantly, "For every ten dollars in state taxes that we pay in Westchester County, we get back only three." She was defining her constituency as Westchester rather than as the New York metropolitan area or as that of American families with over $50,000 yearly income. In our mobile, complex society there are many such signs of confusion about primary loyalties and responsibilities, on the part of institutions as well as of individuals. Great intellectual and cultural institutions in our urban centers cannot shut their eyes to the misery and social ills of the slums that so often adjoin them when they stand fast as the city deteriorates. But a response to these demands may mean surrender of their primary mission of service to the wider area which represents their real constituency. Unless there is public recognition that urban universities, museums, and hospitals belong to a wider body politic than that of the people next door, they can decay into parochialism and be destroyed in the process. The leadership of many such institutions has acted on the opposite premise, as though there really were a self-conscious local constituency actively and legitimately concerned with the affairs of the universities, hospitals, and museums that sit on their borders. (In elections held among "the poor" to select representatives to community councils, votes ranged from 0.7 to 5 percent of those eligible.[30] Thus the way is open for a militant, organized minority to capture control of offices which provide them with an appearance of legitimacy in the eyes of the public and of the mass media.)

The word "community" has lately come into uses so casual that it is applied to nonfunctional, accidental, or arbitrary aggregations of individuals. (Vice President Spiro Agnew, for instance, has directed his ire at what he has termed "the liberal community." An organization of Philadelphia homosexuals issues statements on behalf of "the gay community.")

In its original sociological sense the term community applies to people living in a particular place who are tied together by bonds of intimate acquaintance and family feeling. Significant communities of interest among people in modern society are increasingly based on occupational or avocational identity rather than on geographic propinquity. This trend is nourished by the anonymity of life in large metropolitan centers, along with the ready accessibility of transportation. There has been a rise in voluntary associations based on work or leisure interests rather than on residence. These new "communities" function almost invisibly to those not part of them. Mike Nichols, the film director, has given an insider's view: "The danger in Hollywood is to think this is the world. To me there's safety in thinking that this is just one of many different places. I used to have a friend who edited 'The Dry Cleaner's Monthly,' and its the same thing in the dry cleaner's world. In that world there are leaders, too—dry cleaners whose names are magic, up and coming young dry cleaners. There are many worlds."[31]

A true community acts by consensus, since its basic beliefs are shared by all. A community shows solidarity in the same way that members of a family present a common front to the outside world regardless of internal differences. Community opinion *can* be described in broad generalizations, whether it deals with the wearing of breechclouts or of bikinis, with the eating of pork or the smoking of pot. In a preliterate folk society of simple structure and commonly held values, collective "opinion" fades into the mores—the deeply ingrained, taken-for-granted ground rules of daily existence.

Public opinion arises not from agreement but from conflicts in values. Opinion implies the articulation of a point of view which can be recorded and measured. Consensus is simply not measurable in the same terms as opinion. Only those subjects on which there is no consensus are controversial, raising divergent answers to the same questions. (According to a Gallup Poll, 96 percent of the American people believe in God and 61 percent believe in the Devil. God's existence is a matter of consensus; that of the Devil evidently is a matter of opinion.)

The clash of ideas characterizes a society composed of diverse elements, a mobile society with a rapid rate of change. Industrial society is by definition a complex order full of internal contradictions and conflicts among antagonistic groups and social classes. It devours information on many subjects from many sources.

Differences of individual opinion are bound to exist between men in any culture, however insular and unchanging it may be, but in folk society differences of opinion must really be differences of judgment, which arise despite an identity of outlook and values. Such differences can easily be ascribed to personal eccentricities, rather than to expressions of conflicting social interests. As traditional preliterate societies become more complex in their economic and political organization, they are subject to a factionalism in which diverging opinions may come into play—a peace party and a war party, supporters of one or the other of rival pretenders to a throne, secularists and theocrats.

Often what appears to be dissension within a single homogeneous society, in the eyes of contemporary European visitors, or in the view of historians, is actually no more than an eruption of tribal conflict after a period of subjugation or domination by one group over another. Today we see a resurgence of tribalism in the African states carved out of the map by nineteenth-century colonialists. But it strikes a false note to speak of the clash of Ibos and Yorubas as though it represented a difference of "opinion." The perceptions of group identity and allegiance are too sharp and too deep; the sense that the individual's own fate is tied to that of the group is too intense; the conflict of perceived values and interests is too implacable for the term "opinion" to apply in any meaningful way.

The nationalism of modern states occasionally reaches the same emotional pitch of inherent cat-and-dog incompatibility. The tribal rivalry of primitive Israelites and Canaanites is only a hair's breadth removed from the national rivalry of Israelis and Arabs. Historical antipathies like those of Slavs and Germans, Hindus and Moslems, Orangemen and Irish Catholics are qualitatively different from those national conflicts in which (whatever the real motives or grounds) each side appeals to universal values which at least some of those on the other side presumably share. When ideological appeals are made to freedom, justice, equality, order, morality, or whatever, we leave the realm of purely communal loyalties and are again back in the realm of opinion.

In the Age of Enlightenment (at least, so it seems, in retrospect) differences of opinion were discussed in reasoned and personal terms—like the agreement to disagree on the part of well-informed and well-intentioned gentlemen. (In fact, one had to be a gentleman to have an opinion.)

During the class struggles of the Victorian era, differences of opinion were seen in a different light—as the characteristic expressions of different segments of the population. Divergent opinions could be linked to groups marked by a sense of their own identity and by social class, ethnic, regional, or other special concerns. It was understood that a conflict in the real interests of groups or social classes is bound to be reflected in differences of opinion between their respective members.

The assumption that people's opinions are linked to their origins or social station proceeds from the premise that they know their rightful place and where their interests truly lie. In point of fact, people are subject to many conflicts of interest, loyalty, and motivation in our mobile and complex society, and this is reflected in the confusion and ambiguity of their beliefs.

Rarely do we find near-unanimity within any one segment of the public, even on questions that run close to the group's own vital interests, or to its proclaimed tenets. Two-thirds of a national cross section of high school students queried by Purdue University as recently as 1964 were opposed to a lowering of the voting age to 18. In mid-1970, a Gilbert Youth study found that 38 percent of the 17- and 18-year-olds still opposed it. Even after the Supreme Court lowered the voting age to 18 for national elections, in December of the same year, Gallup found 14 percent of those aged 18 to 20 still against an extension of the rule to state and local elections.

A majority of those in labor union families favor compulsory strike arbitration.[32] A majority of American Catholics (including the most devout in their observances) confess to interviewers that they favor and use contraceptives in spite of the Papal ban. (The reason for such inconsistencies is obvious: No one is *just* a Catholic; he is a Catholic Negro 18-year-old labor union member who is many other things besides.)

A survey in Buffalo, New York, shows how divided the views of different groups can be even on matters directly linked to those differences that define group identity. Take the question, "Do you feel that Negroes have been receiving as good an education as whites in this community?" Here 82 percent of the city whites, 70 percent of the suburbanites, and only 37 percent of the Negroes answered, "Yes." (While there was obviously a strong disagreement here, not *all* the whites were lined up on one side, nor were *all* the Negroes on the other).[33]

To the extent that a group is considered to represent a unitary bloc of opinion, its views acquire disproportionate political force, since consensus is self-reinforcing, while internal divisions are debilitating and inhibit social action. Those who are assumed to speak for a community carry its full political weight behind them, as long as their voices are unchallenged. They are unlikely to be challenged if the notion of a single-minded community is accepted as "the real thing" by the mass media.

In spite of the general prevalence of polls which reveal the diversity of opinion within every segment of the public, it is still customary, in the news media as well as in private conversation, to refer to groups as though their opinions were homogeneous. The views of farmers, Negroes, New Yorkers, or labor union members are commonly characterized as though they exhibited a consensus of thought, when in fact these views inevitably mirror the internal divisions and diversified nature of the groups themselves.

When the word "community" is applied, as it very commonly is, to large sectors of the population distinguished by common ethnic or racial origins, the term has obviously changed its meaning to become synonymous with the diffuse word "group." Yet it continues to carry its original overtones of meaning.

The term "the black community" in the mouth of a politician or pamphleteer suggests a true consensus of feeling on the part of those thus characterized. But how much unanimity of outlook can we expect from people who have few unique channels of common communication, who are geographically dispersed, whose relationships with each other are as impersonal as any others in urban society and whose day-by-day concerns and allegiances stem from many points of orientation—job, social class, avocational interests, or neighborhood—as well as race?

Martin Mayer describes a meeting of the Community School Board in Ocean Hill, a predominantly Negro neighborhood in Brooklyn: "The door to the meeting room burst open and fifteen to twenty militants rushed in and ranged themselves against the wall. This was a Community Board, they said, and they were the community, and they were there to see that the Board did what the community wanted. ('At this point,' the minutes of the meeting say gallantly and rather glumly, 'the community entered the room.')"[34]

The controversy over "community control" of the Ocean Hill schools precipitated a city wide teachers' strike which left deep scars in the body politic of New York. During the crisis a city official commented, "The community itself can't muster enough people to make a decent show because most people in the district don't give a damn."[35] (More than half of those in the area were on welfare, many of them comparatively new arrivals in the city.) The demonstrators included many individuals from outside the local area who were familiar figures at demonstrations all around New York. The term "community" applied to this arbitrarily defined school district was a political fiction.

In this specific case there *was* evidence, from a Harris Poll, of what the parents of the Ocean Hill area thought: 29 percent supported the local board which had ousted a group of teachers who were backed by their union; 24 percent supported the teachers; and the remaining 47 percent were unsure. Opinion was preponderantly unfavorable toward *all* the parties in the struggle: the local board and its administrator, the teachers, the principals, and (in particular) the City Board of Education.[36]

Stereotyping as a social psychological concept originally related to the majority of the public's perception of a minority in terms which assume uniformity rather than the heterogeneity of real human beings. In the new form of stereotyping, the *opinion* rather than the *character* of minorities is presumed to have a unitary and predictable form. Stereotyping destroys the unique individuality of each person by reducing him to the mere expression of a bloc. Its effect is just as damaging in the domain of opinions as in that of prejudice.

Growing manifestations of Negro impatience have been reflected not only in urban disorders but in opinion surveys, as we shall see in the next chapter. But impatience with the iniquities of the white-dominated political order has by no means implied a wholesale rejection. Opinion among Negroes has not only shown great political diversity, but it has shown it spread across a spectrum far more similar to that of whites than might have been supposed.

Among whites identifying their political allegiances in a Harris survey conducted in December 1968, 43 percent classed themselves as conservatives, 37 percent as middle-of-the-road, 17 percent as liberal, and 2 percent as radical. Among Negroes, the proportions were 37 percent conservative, 26 percent middle-of-the-road, and 37 percent liberal (with none interviewed admitting to a radical persuasion). Negroes had a somewhat more liberal orientation, but hardly a dramatically leftist one! (Of course, terms like "conservative" and "middle-of-the-road" might have quite different reference points for Negroes and whites.) While 38 percent of the public at large felt that the United States is a better place to live in than it was ten years earlier, 58 percent of the Negroes agreed with this.

There was misperception also in the domain of nomenclature. In 1969, 38 percent liked the term "Negro" most, while 11 percent liked it least.[37] Twenty percent most liked the term "colored people"; 31 percent liked it least. And 19 percent most liked the term "black," while 25 percent liked it least. However, young, urban Negroes leaned toward the term "black" with its militant and nationalist connotations, and their sympathizers in the mass media and in politics gave this term increasing currency in spite of the preference of the Negro-colored-black (in order of preference) majority. [A 1970 Roper survey in Louisville also found that while only a small minority (8 percent) of Negroes preferred the term "black," and 51 percent preferred "Negro," almost as many whites (25 percent) used the term "black" as "Negro" (27 percent). Other local studies in Detroit and Minneapolis showed similar results.]

In spite of its comparative unacceptability to the majority, the term "black" gained ever more common usage in the mass media and in the language of government and politics. To the militant minority, the word "Negro" carried a bitter historical burden which had to be cast off in the search for a proud new identity. This minority was concentrated within the spirited elements of urban youth who were not only more assertive and visible than their elders in contacts with authority, but also more likely to supply the Negro newsmen whom big city newspapers, television networks, and magazines were belatedly eager to recruit. White media practitioners in many instances fell in line with the terminology preferred by their own young Negro reporters, either in ignorance of what the Negro majority preferred or out of indifference to the whole matter. And since the term "black" was daily reiterated by white reporters in the newscasts and in the press, it was also adopted by Negro publications, and entered the consciousness and usage of those to whom the term applied.

Television has in many ways become an important force in the developing political consciousness of the Negro public. The Report of the National Advisory Commission on Civil Disorders, while absolving television of the charge of having caused urban riots, found that it did have an effect, especially in conveying the impression that disturbances in all-Negro areas were actually a Negro-white confrontation. (In fact, an analysis of the television coverage of racial incidents found that actual scenes of violence were kept to a minimum.) The Commission declared that ghetto residents distrusted the media, and cited as evidence a master's thesis by Thomas H. Allen conducted among 100 Negroes in a Pittsburgh neighborhood. Although some of the figures cited in this small study are in manifest contradiction to more solid data from large national surveys, the Commission's authority has given them wide prominence.

The Negro public's sense of group identity and of political potency underwent rapid evolution in the late 1960s, with nationalist, separatist, radical and antiwhite sentiment especially evident among young people in the urban slums. We shall come back to the subject of this change, which has been well-documented by research. But research also makes it possible to place such attitudes in proper focus. Three out of ten big-city Negroes polled in a fifteen-city survey made in 1968 for the Kerner Commission said that they themselves had been refused a job because of racial discrimination, but seven out of ten agreed that many or some Negroes suffer for this reason.[38] What is extraordinary, of course, is that the belief is not unanimous! Half of those questioned gave no particular indication that racial discrimination was a salient issue in their personal lives. Two-thirds said that there had been "a lot of progress in getting rid of racial discrimination" in the past ten or fifteen years.

A mere 6 percent thought close friendship between Negroes and whites to be "impossible." Eight percent said they wanted to live in an all-Negro neighborhood. Six percent favored creation of a separate black nation. In the same year, the Columbia Broadcasting System, in a national sample, found that 3 percent of Negroes thought it would be a "good idea" for a completely separate country to be carved out of some American states. But among white Americans the proportion who thought this was a good idea was much higher—23 percent—and the motives that underlay this opinion were unquestionably segregationist and anti-Negro rather than New Left sympathy for black aspirations.

Only 6 percent of a national cross section of Negroes interviewed by Opinion Research Corporation in the spring of 1968 agreed with the views of separatist Stokely Carmichael and 5 percent with those of radical H. Rap Brown. By contrast, over half aligned themselves with Ralph Abernathy, Martin Luther King's successor in nonviolent protest. Nine out of ten opposed violent action to achieve equal rights and only one in thirty-three said he would participate in demonstrations that might lead to riots. (This must be put into perspective: In a sample of white Americans interviewed at the same time, about half indicated some attitude of opposition to equality or integration, and one-third overtly expressed anti-Negro feelings.)

Misperceptions about racial attitudes exist on both sides. For many years, white Southerners almost unanimously accepted the myth of Negro acquiescence in the practices of segregation, in spite of the bitter opposition which almost all Negroes felt, but rarely demonstrated. The Supreme Court's landmark school desegregation decision in 1954 was traumatic for the South, not merely because it directed that past practices be changed, but because it unleashed a full revelation to Southern whites of what Southern Negroes really thought.

A curious subvariety of the stereotyping of racial attitudes was exemplified by the extensive publicity given to reports of "rampant" Negro anti-

Semitism, reaching a climax with a *Time* cover story on January 31, 1969. A sociologist, Robert B. Hill, observed that such reports in the media completely ignored the numerous studies that demonstrate that most Negroes are actually less anti-Semitic than most whites, and that black nationalism has not appreciably influenced their attitude.[39]

As I noted earlier, all of the survey results cited are transitory reflections of a rapidly changing state of mind on the part of people caught up in a profound social upheaval. Complex explanations of the internal divisions and inconsistencies in group opinions do not lend themselves to the space or time requirements of news media, to the time pressures of news reporting, or, for that matter, to the sampling size limitations and analytical budgets of opinion polling organizations.

The 5 or 6 percent of Negroes who consistently give separatist or radical answers (to Negro interviewers) in surveys represent a far more articulate and visible force than their numbers suggest. The emergence of a black militant minority into the forefront of the news is easily translated into the media image of a Negro public suffused with "black rage." This image is projected larger than life by the machinery of the popular culture. The new stereotype becomes the subject of museum exhibits, television documentaries, newspaper editorials, interviews, and polls. Is it any wonder that many Negroes themselves are therefore impelled to accept it as a proper model of behavior?

As the media rushed to redress their past neglect of racial minority talent and interests they sometimes became vulnerable to political minority talent and interests. One illustration of this was a "Black Heritage" lecture series of 108 half-hour television programs intended to be widely reproduced, syndicated, and adapted for school use. They came under attack from the NAACP's Roy Wilkins for ". . . the emphasis given to periods which were only incidental to Negro-American history but which were given wholly disproportionate attention and time simply because they fitted the Black Revolution thesis."[40]

What is described often enough as though it were the real thing has a way of becoming such in the eyes of those who are told repeatedly that they are part of it. This is less likely to happen if there is on the part of the media, the public, and the authorities, an understanding of the *variety* of opinions, motives, temperaments, and aspirations which characterize any group, and almost any political constituency. How, except through the systematic study of people's changing beliefs, can such an understanding be achieved?

Part Three

THE MOVEMENT OF OPINION

PUBLIC OPINION TRENDS

The dissenting opinions of one generation become the prevailing interpretations of the next.

Burton J. Hendricks

The collective opinions of a complex society emerge from a mosaic of the beliefs held by its component elements, with each element reflecting some of the diversity of the larger society itself. Because different groups, special interests, and schools of thought coexist and interact, opinion on most significant matters is in a constant state of flux and ferment. Just as surveys illuminate the differences of belief that characterize Negroes and whites, or farm hands and corporate executives, so do they provide what is now indispensable historical evidence of how public opinion evolves through time.

Shifts in public opinion are of three kinds: broad secular trends, responses to major ongoing political developments, and short-run reactions to what is in the news of the moment.

The broad secular trends in opinion really reflect the inexorable currents of history. They are one aspect of what by hindsight we term a historical force. Such trends represent the processes of social change in technology, productivity, life-style, work organization, the movements of population, and the shape of the population age pyramid. These processes can be arrested or swerved by wars or economic depressions, but essentially they continue with compelling force, and they are reflected

75

in certain inevitable tendencies of opinion, for example, a more cosmopolitan view of the world, growing acceptance of racial and sexual equality, declining religious sentiment.

Even a static assessment of public opinion at any moment in time provides indications of this movement. The survey analyst who finds differences of outlook between the young and the old, the well-educated and the ignorant, the rich and the poor, the metropolitan and rural sectors, can usually guess with fair accuracy the direction public opinion will take.

Such differences are of greater predictive value when they concern broad aspects of human relations than when they involve responses to specific events and notions on the strategy of handling them. On the great current issues of domestic or international politics, opinion swings with the news of the day; it responds to drama, it heeds the appeals of respected leaders, it cringes at the prospect of disaster, it is bored by the repetitive and the inconclusive. All these responses are apt to vary from group to group, and from subject to subject. The short-term trends of opinion may therefore be very hard to predict; they are bound to reflect the personalities and institutions involved and the manner in which events are dramatized or reduced to manageable human scale through the interpretation of the mass media.

Shifts in public perception of an issue's importance, in information about it, and in notions of what should be done about it can all be traced easily through conventional opinion surveys, in which the same questions are repeated to observe a trend. These broad collective changes are merely reflections of the transformations in individual outlook that occur as people interact with each other and with information and ideas from the media. Changes in collective opinion may reflect a shift on the part of individuals from one position to a different one on a particular issue; more often they mean simply that people who were formerly uninterested, uninformed, or indifferent on the matter have now come to regard it as deserving of their serious attention.

Perhaps the most clear-cut demonstration of predictable opinion change is that which occurs among human beings as they mature, as their perceptions of the wider world take on a sharper focus and as their roles and responsibilities alter. The changes of attitude that children (and adults) undergo as they grow older are typical of the substantial differences of opinion that may and do occur between population groups with distinct and definable characteristics. But there is invariably a core of individual differences of outlook which cannot be explained by position in society or in the life cycle. These differences reflect idiosyncrasies of personality, upbringing, and information, as well as subtle interactions among the innumerable social forces that propel people's thought into conformity with those of their sex, age group, and social class. At any age level, the more intelligent and better informed child has more opinions on more subjects. In any case, the interplay of individuals within the family leaves its own impression on the child's evolving view of the world. The father is the conventional source of political authority. In those cases in which the child perceives the mother as the dominant parent, his interest in politics is likely to develop later and to be weaker.[1]

As children get older they are less likely to accept government (best represented by the face of the president or that of George Washington), its leaders, and its laws uncritically. By the eighth grade, government is best represented by an abstraction like the act of voting or a session of Congress.[2]

As they get older children develop more of an identification with one political party or the other. In fact, a child of nine is just as likely to accept a party label as is a young adult. By that age, social class origins are clearly reflected in political allegiances, with working-class children leaning toward the Democrats as their parents do. Below the age of nine, however, those party preferences children express are not related to their parents' social class. The acceptance of a party represents part of the discovery of individual identity, and the system of opinions appropriate to that party is acquired in the process of affirming this symbolic identification.

The primary role played by parents in maintaining continuity of political thinking is not necessarily recognized by those who are themselves undergoing this kind of socialization. A 1969 survey of 8000 Phoenix high school students found that only one-third of the lower classmen and less than one-fourth of the juniors and seniors said their parents had had the most influence on the development of their political opinions. Three in ten mentioned the news media, but only 8 percent at any grade level mentioned their friends. The proportion who said they took an active interest in politics by speaking out and reading on the subject rose from 23 percent of the freshmen to 40 percent of the seniors.

It is commonplace to observe that the rebelliousness of adolescence is reflected in a political liberalism which gives way to the growing conservatism of middle age, with its responsibilities and vested interests. This truth may be based on the inevitable consequences of the life cycle. (Jack Weinberg, a University of California rebel in the disruptions of 1964, who coined the slogan, "Don't Trust Anyone over 30," turned 30

himself on April 4, 1970.) But it would be silly to assume that generational differences of opinion can all be explained on the grounds that
everybody becomes conservative with age. The times *do* change. Each
generation faces its own characteristic historical experience, and its
divergences of outlook from its predecessors may presage a genuine bend
in the long-term trend of opinion and not merely reflect the inevitable
cleavage between young and old. A generation reared in the era of
nuclear weapons, with easy access to contraception, is bound to have
unique attitudes toward self, society, and others, as well as unique forms
of expressing them.

Among a national sample of tenth-grade high school boys questioned
in 1966, only 7 percent named Vietnam as one of the "problems young
men your age worry about most." Four years later 75 percent of the
same boys gave this answer. How much of this difference was due to the
change in the salience of the war itself as a subject of national concern
and how much of it reflected the maturation of this age group to the
point of direct vulnerability to the draft? It is hard to separate one from
the other.[3]

The late 1960s saw the coming of age of an unusually large cohort of
young people born in the "baby boom" that followed marriages post-
poned by the Depression and World War II. The bulge in the population
pyramid created extraordinary pressures on schools, colleges, and the
teen-age job market, and added to the special problems of this group.
At the same time, the postwar period saw startling increases in the levels
of educational attainment and aspiration, in affluence, and in the pace
of population movement. These forces sharpened the discontinuities in
life experience between young people and their parents. Hence the
visibility of the "youth culture," with its swinging dress and hair styles,
its new musical tastes, its alienation from the square world of its elders,
its susceptibility to drugs, and its propensity for expressive forms of
political action.

The cultural discontinuities are dramatized by the findings of a 1971
survey, which found that the "crow's foot" peace symbol was familiar to
56 percent of those between 18 and 24 but to only 13 percent of those 55
and over.[4] Two out of three young people interviewed in a national
survey in 1970 agreed that there was a "generation gap," but the proportion rose to 84 percent among a more sophisticated sample in metropolitan areas. Among this group, three out of four considered middle-aged
and older people prejudiced against new ideas; 71 percent described
their parents as part of the "silent majority," but only 45 percent characterized themselves this way.[5]

The polls do not tell us what is inherent in the "generation gap" and what is a continuing process of opinion change, but they make the differences of outlook between age groups very clear. People in their twenties are Democratic two to one over Republican, while people in their seventies are evenly split between the two parties.[6]

Among those aged 18, 19, and 20, the proportion of Democrats (42 percent) is not very different from that among people of 21 and over (45 percent), but there are far fewer Republicans (16 percent) among the new younger voters compared to those over 20 (28 percent) and correspondingly more independents (42 percent compared to 27 percent). Older voters are most likely to vote a straight party ticket. Younger people are not only far more likely than older ones to describe their party identification as "independent"; they are also substantially more likely, whether Democrats or Republicans, to describe their party identity as "weak" rather than as "strong."

Young people of voting age are least likely to be registered, or to vote, or to work in political campaigns. In 1968, four states (Georgia, Kentucky, Alaska, and Hawaii) permitted people under 21 to vote. Of those eligible in the 18 to 20-year-old group, the Census Bureau found that 33 percent voted. This compared with 51 percent of those aged 21 to 24, and with 61 percent of all eligible voters. This should not be too surprising. People are apt to develop a keener sense of political responsibility as they acquire other responsibilities: at work, raising a family, owning a home, and setting down roots. For most individuals this phase of life gets under way in the middle and late twenties.

Youthful political activism, in spite of its high public visibility, is largely confined to the elite of university students. In 1970, 61 percent of college students classed themselves as liberal and 26 percent as conservative, while 34 percent of the general public described itself as liberal and 52 percent as conservative.[7] In 1969, 28 percent of college students said they had "participated in a demonstration of some kind."[8] Another survey that year classified 3 percent of college students as revolutionaries, 10 percent as radical dissidents, and 39 percent as reformers.[9]

Among 1542 recent graduates of a wide variety of colleges covered by a 1970 University of California survey, 99 percent agreed that some form of confrontation was "necessary and effective" to change the country's direction. College youth are left of center compared with their noncollege peers as well as the population at large. The higher the academic quality of the university, the more radical the sentiment.

But the differences between young people and their elders are generally a matter of degree rather than of polarities.[10] Consider attitudes toward the militant Students for a Democratic Society at the peak time of its activity and influence: among college students 6 percent declared themselves highly favorable and 37 percent highly unfavorable. Among the general public the proportions were 7 percent highly favorable to the S.D.S. and 42 percent highly unfavorable.[11] (Studies made in specific colleges would have found many more adherents to S.D.S., of course, just as studies made among specific subgroups of the general public might have found a much higher level of disapproval).

The intensely political atmosphere on the campuses of major colleges has a liberalizing effect not only on the students, but on their conservative parents. A poll of top corporate executives from *Fortune*'s 500 biggest companies was conducted in 1971 by Ruth Clark, who analyzed the opinions of those who had sons and daughters in college. They proved to be consistently more liberal than their colleagues in their views on social issues, and more opposed to the Vietnam War. Since their social position, education, and other characteristics were almost identical, the only plausible explanation was that they had been converted through discussion with their children.

The children of the well-to-do largely attend precisely the kind of institutions in which political discussion is most active and in which radical ideas have the greatest following. This is not the climate of political experience in which most Americans are raised.

A variety of studies documents not only the lower level of political participation among young people in the American mainstream but the strong currents of conservatism among them. A 1970 University of Michigan survey of 2200 high school seniors found that 40 percent supported the government's Vietnam policy, while only 20 percent clearly disagreed. Shortly after the Kent State killings of May 1970, a survey of 1100 Ohio high school students found that 18 percent considered the troops at fault, while 58 percent blamed the students "for gathering and throwing rocks at the troops."[12]

The shallowness of political involvement may be seen in young people's attitudes toward Eugene McCarthy, widely regarded as the idol of the nation's youth during the early stages of the 1968 Presidential campaign. A study of Wisconsin high school students during the 1968 election campaign found that while three-fourths could identify him as a Democrat in May, in the heat of the primary races, only a third could do so in November.[13]

As Philip Converse and his colleagues commented in their analysis of the 1968 election, "Although privileged young college students angry at Vietnam and the shabby treatment of the Negro saw themselves as sallying forth to do battle against a corrupted and cynical older generation, a more head-on confrontation at the polls, if a less apparent one, was with their own agemates who had gone from high school off to the factory instead of college, and who were appalled by the collapse of patriotism and respect for the law that they saw around them.[14]

In 1970, half of those aged 14 to 25 said their "main career achievement goal" was to make money. The proportion was even higher among young people from low-income families.[15] Among a cross section of high school students, 55 percent rated "getting a secure steady job" as an "extremely important" life goal, while 34 percent gave this rating to "working for a better society." Four out of five expect to own their own cars, and two in three their own homes, in a matter of ten years.[16] In short, the values of American society have not undergone sharp or sudden transformations within a single generation.

However, it is not impossible to forecast changes in fundamental attitudes. In fact, they sometimes can be predicted from a single survey. Consider a Gallup Poll of July 1969, which found that the proportion of Americans who think premarital sex is wrong was half of those in their twenties, two-thirds of those in their thirties and forties, and four-fifths of those fifty and over. Some of the differences may reflect the inherent stodginess of older people, but can there be any doubt that the generation now in its twenties will carry over some of its distinctive permissiveness as it moves along in life?

The rate of change in public opinion is braked by the stability of basic social values and selfish interests and accelerated by the continual flow of new information through the mass media. Trend studies made over the years document many instances of long-term changes in public opinion as well as occasions of dramatic shifts over the short run. These can be traced in trivial but indicative matters, like fashion and style. A majority opposed women's wearing bikini bathing suits when these were a novelty; a few years later a majority favored it.

In 1957, 14 percent of those questioned by the Gallup Poll thought religion was losing influence and 69 percent thought it was gaining. In 1969, 70 percent said that religion was losing, and 14 percent believed it was gaining.[17] Such sharp reversals in response mirror the growth of cynicism perhaps more than of secularism, but the data are better indicators than the figures on church attendance.

Even in life's most intimate sphere, changes of outlook and behavior sometimes occur very rapidly as a product of revolutionary social or political change. In 1950, 55 percent of the Japanese told the *Mainichi* surveys that they wanted to depend on their children in their old age.

Nine years later this number had dropped to 39 percent. At the same time, among those Japanese with two living children there was a startling increase in acceptance of the idea of limiting family size. In 1950 30 percent said they wanted no more children. In 1959 the proportion was 58 percent. This change in attitude was reflected in the declining birth rate of postwar Japan.[18]

Heroes change, not only from one generation to the next, but within generations. A cross section of West Germans were asked in 1950 what great men had contributed the most valuable achievements for their country. Thirty-five percent named Bismarck and ten percent named Hitler. (None named Adenauer, who was not at that time a known public figure.) By 1967 Bismarck had dropped to 13 percent, Hitler to 2 percent, and Adenauer was named as the greatest German by 44 percent. In 1972, the proportions would surely be different again.

Racial attitudes in the United States have undergone remarkable transformations since World War II, reflecting not merely the changes in American society and in the American population structure, but also the effects of court and administrative actions and the rising political consciousness of Negroes.

In 1958, less than two out of five people told the Gallup Poll they were willing to vote for a well-qualified Negro of their own party for president. When the question was repeated in 1971, seven out of ten said they would.[19] The proportion who say Negroes are as intelligent as whites went from two in five in 1942 to four in five in 1956. (It has stabilized since).[20] In 1963, three out of five Southern white parents said they would object to sending their children to a school with even a few Negro pupils. By 1970 the proportion had dropped to one in six.[21]

Each successive age group since World War II has had a higher average level of schooling, and this, too, has important consequences in this domain. The individual who goes on from grade school to high school, or from high school to college, or from college to graduate school, is not merely extending his education, but he is changing his orientation, his friends and models, his values, and his sense of who he is. The growing acceptability of school integration may be discerned in the high proportion of college-educated persons (40 percent, compared with 19 percent who have not gone beyond high school and 15 percent of the grade-school educated) who told the Gallup Poll in July 1969 that school integration was not moving fast enough.[22]

Educational and generational differences may be interrelated in very complex ways. Among white residents of big cities racial attitudes in 1968 were unrelated to educational levels among persons over 40, while among people under 40, those who had been to college were significantly more liberal.[23] In such findings we can see the shape of the future.

Not all changes in public opinion are reflections of gradual long-term social trends. Social movements that take the form of organized group activities have a catalytic effect on attitudes. People involved in political meetings, listening to speeches, and reading the literature of a cause with which they identify are brought to a heightened awareness of political issues and are provided with ready-made explanations to support the policies of their group. People whose behavior reflects the contagious emotions of a crowd respond otherwise when they are confronted as individuals or placed in a crowd with a different reason for gathering. A year after the burning of Watts, that Los Angeles neighborhood staged a summer festival with Sargent Shriver as Grand Marshal. He was greeted with enthusiasm where whites had been angrily attacked twelve months earlier.

Such a sudden shift in expressed mass sentiment and mass action is not necessarily amenable to measurement by public opinion research. Polls may, however, reveal the symptoms of euphoria which accompany peace and prosperity or the malaise of a society in turmoil.

History is made up both of the accretion of small happenings that add up to a transformation as well as of major events that produce crashing discontinuities with the past.[24] Opinion polls record the reactions to both kinds of change.

The West German currency reform in June 1949 produced a drastic reduction in the proportion of Germans who named food and clothing as their greatest cares and worries. (At the end of April, two out of five named clothing and over half mentioned food. By July, the level was about one in ten.)[25] However, it is not always possible to predict easily when opinion will be swayed by major political events and when it will remain firm. To illustrate, at the end of 1945 over half the people in West Germany described Nazism as "a good idea badly carried out." The proportion was not essentially different in 1948 in spite of the Nuremberg trials, the Berlin air lift, and all the other events of the occupation period.[26] Similarly, there was little change in the proportion (two out of five) who agreed that "some races of people are more fit to rule than others."[27]

Critical episodes in individual relations bring radical re-evaluations of other people's character and motives. Similarly, moments of international tension or crisis can produce rapid changes. At the end of 1945, one-third of the American public expected another world war within 25 years; by the spring of 1948, the proportion had risen to three out of four.[28] Public sentiment switched from a ratio of five to three "optimistic" over the possibility of a settlement with the Soviet Union to five to three "pessimistic" immediately after the Russian invasion of Czechoslovakia in 1968.[29]

In Israel, public concern over Arab terrorism following the Six Day War rose massively *after* the first major Israeli reprisal raid into Jordan. This official action provided the catalyst as well as the rationale by which a series of news items became transformed into a national problem.[30] Similarly, the response of American Jews to the European Jewish holocaust began to crystallize not during the war itself (when there was a sense of futility about the prospects of ending the Nazi murders except through an Allied victory), but several years after the war's end, when the Zionist struggle to form the State of Israel became a rallying point for constructive energies.

The transformation of information into changed opinions, and of opinion into changed behavior, is well exemplified by the reduction of cigarette smoking following the Surgeon General's report and the subsequent information campaign. Not only did per capita consumption begin to drop, but opinion surveys revealed that many smokers were trying to reduce their consumption, and that three out of five (compared, however, to four out of five nonsmokers) accepted the idea that cigarette smoking was a cause of lung cancer.

After Senate hearings in 1970 on the birth control pill, the same proportion of women (67 percent) thought it was an effective contraceptive as had three years earlier, but the proportion who would recommend the pill to other women dropped from 53 to 37 percent. Opinion shifted from two to one that the pill was not dangerous to health to two to one that it was. (The hearings represented the only significant force to shift opinion in an unfavorable direction since the benchmark survey.)

Public opinion sometimes shows an extraordinary imperturbability in the face of revelations that might be expected to produce a vehement reaction. An illustration of this occurred at the time of congressional hearings on television quiz shows, in November 1959. The first of a series of national surveys was made before the hearings began, and parallel samples were interviewed every evening for a week. During this period the hearings, with their revelations about the "fixing" of well-remembered and popular contestants, were the principal headline news.

At the start of the week, one-third of the public reported talking about the hearings; the proportion doubled by the end of the week. In spite of this very high level of discussion, and although there was a rapid growth in public awareness of the personalities involved in the scandal, there was almost *no* change in opinions about the motivations of the contestants and the "fixers," or in opinions about the seriousness of the offense. The average viewer apparently felt that the fixing of quiz shows was part of "the System." There was nothing he personally could do about them, and in spite of all his indignant conversation his moral sense was not offended to the point where he felt he *ought* to do anything about them.

How does the public respond to a major but unanticipated event, for example, the outbreak of a war or an assassination? The reactions may be intense, yet they may not entail a *change* of opinion so much as the sudden intensification of opinions or values already held. The murder of President Kennedy stirred profound feelings of shock, grief, guilt, and patriotism, along with grave anxieties about the political state of the nation, but there were no changes in the basic beliefs and values of the American people on such matters as communism, civil rights, or the assessment of human nature.[31]

Yet as the assassination itself became another item in history, opinions about its perpetrator, meaning, and consequences became increasingly diverse, as the public discussion of the Warren Commission report best indicates.[32] As people reflected on the assassination and discussed it with others, they tended to reinterpret what had happened in terms of their own predispositions, with different kinds of attitude shift occurring among different population groups. A consistent and tempered response was most often exhibited by the best educated. Women showed a more violent response than men, Negroes more than whites, and Kennedy voters more than Nixon voters.[33] Because the assassination provided a successful test of the stability of American political institutions, it produced what a political scientist, Sidney Verba, described as an "integrative effect," reflected in a lowering of partisan feelings and a heightened evaluation of the Kennedy presidency.[34]

A significant or dramatic event makes a subject salient and produces an interest in an area that otherwise might have been forgotten. Thus, immediately after the Kennedy assassination, 37 percent of the people could name the other three assassinated Presidents; Lincoln, Garfield, and McKinley.[35]

A chemical change in the public temper, like that following the Kennedy assassination, may not be fully captured by the particular trend questions through which pollsters seek to measure opinion change over time. In wartime, catastrophic defeats and resounding victories sometimes succeed each other at a rapid pace, with consequences for public morale that are only dimly suggested by survey statistics.

The proportion of Americans who thought England and its allies would win World War II fell from 77 percent at the outbreak of war to 62 percent just before the German invasion of the low countries. It dropped to 32 percent after the fall of France in June 1940. A ten-point increase in those who thought it "more important to help England than to keep out of war," followed the Summer blitz on London in 1940. By March of the following year, after the Battle of Britain and the defeat of the Italian Navy, the proportion predicting Allied victory was back to 78 percent. Such military events as the German conquest of Greece reduced the percentage to 53 percent, while the German invasion of Russia and the growing American commitment to the Allied war effort restored confidence in victory to the 71 percent level by August. When America became involved in December, after the attack on Pearl Harbor, the level of confidence rose to 92 percent.[36] Rising confidence in Britain paralleled rising belief that America would enter the war. These were interdependent judgments, and their generally parallel trend perfectly demonstrates how the publics's assessment of the course of history guides its beliefs on how national policy should be shaped.

It is never the opinion of the moment, but the potential for opinion change which must preoccupy those who seek to exert political influence.[37] It is not necessary for the mood of an entire population to change to create significant shifts in political power. When the overall balance of forces is close, a comparatively minor change of opinion or a shift from neutrality on the part of a small part of the population can swing the political plurality from one party to another and thus bring about a major change in policies and events.

Marked short-run shifts in the mood and morale of a critical subgroup of the population represent significant indicators of social change which may not be reflected in the overall figures of public opinion. We have seen the difficulty of generalizing about the opinions of a large heterogeneous sector of the public like the Negro population, but this does not mean that the typical views of this sector are stable.

Negro opposition to the war in Vietnam grew from 35 percent in 1966 to 56 percent in 1969. In 1966, 74 percent believed the federal government was helpful to Negroes. In 1969 this had dropped two-thirds, to 25 percent.[38] In 1966, 24 percent of the whites and 34 percent of the Negroes were classified by the Harris Poll as "alienated" from the American mainstream.[39] Two years later (and a month before the assassination of Martin Luther King, Jr.) the "alienated" had risen slightly (to 30 percent) among whites but substantially (to 56 percent) among Negroes. [At the same time, even more Negroes (73 percent) than whites (52 percent) believed that there had been more racial progress in recent years than a few years earlier.]

By the start of the 1970s there were visible increases in militancy, and even in revolutionary sentiment among young urban Negroes and a greater tolerance of such views among their elders.[40] The radicalism of many Negro youth must be seen in relation to the fact that nearly one-fourth of *all* people aged 14 to 25 feel that violence is sometimes justified in support of political aims.[41] Younger Negroes were becoming more involved with the *conventional* machinery of politics at the same time that more of them were ready to use other means.

Surveys among residents of central city ghettoes uncovered evidence of a violence-prone minority which, though small as a percentage of the whole Negro population, was still large enough to constitute a potential for considerable trouble.[42]

In the spring of 1970, 31 percent of Negroes (including 40 percent of the teen-agers) agreed that they "will probably have to resort to violence to win rights," compared with 21 percent in 1966.[43] Nine percent classified themselves as revolutionaries and agreed that only "a readiness to use violence will ever get us real equality." (But this must be put into perspective: a 1969 University of Michigan study among a national sample of all American men found that one in five believed that some violence was necessary to produce needed social change.[44])

While moderate Negro leaders like Cleveland's Mayor Carl Stokes, N.A.A.C.P. Executive Director Roy Wilkins, and Supreme Court Justice Thurgood Marshall enjoyed more respect than such militants as Elijah Muhammed, Bobby G. Seale, and Eldridge Cleaver, the gap was not as wide as might be expected. One out of four Negroes said that the Black Panther philosophy is "the same as mine," and the proportion rose to 43 percent among teen-agers. Only 30 percent of Negroes questioned thought the Panthers to blame for the shooting incidents in which they had been involved, and 64 percent said the Panthers had given them a "sense of pride."[45] (By contrast, two out of three whites considered the Panthers a "serious menace," and almost all considered the Panthers themselves responsible for the violence in which they were periodically involved.)

The evidence showed a very large but troubled majority of Negroes resisting appeals to violence, although one in five was sympathetic to rioters and one in ten acknowledged that he was a potential participant. A minority of one in ten with a revolutionary commitment would be a tremendously powerful disruptive force in any society. Responses which would in themselves be indicative of a very serious problem become evidence of crisis when they take the shape of an accelerating trend. Thus, with the opinion of significant minorities as with that of the larger body politic, it is the movement and intensity of beliefs, and not merely their distribution, which demands response from those who hold office.

The distinction between opinion polling and social research is essentially one between a static description of what people say they think at a particular moment in time and a dynamic analysis of why they think as they do and what might lead them to change. We obtain intimations of where such changes may lead when we can compare (either experimentally, or in carefully matched real-life situations) the reactions of similar people faced with different circumstances and different choices.[46]

The importance of opinions is never to be judged by the number of people who purport to hold them. A silent majority is by definition an ineffectual one. It can become a political force only when polls make it self-conscious about its prerogatives, or when political leaders summon its support. Within every majority, silent or otherwise, there is also a latent opposition, and an opposition *within* the opposition ready to find *its* proper expression when the right historical moment arrives. It is precisely at the moment when the popular consensus appears to be jelling that we must hearken to the first faint far-off voices of dissent.

OPINION ON VIETNAM: A CASE HISTORY

Americans have, more than any other people I know, a willingness to change their opinions.

Gunnar Myrdal[47]

Critical incidents that arouse widespread public discussion and emotion have a way of transforming opinions by providing new reference points. Such incidents change the terms of debate; they permit rapid realignments of individual views, buttressed with the rationalization that the objective situation has changed, even though the incidents themselves may have almost no bearing on the objective situation. Episodes of violence are especially likely to have such a catalyzing effect, as we shall see later. The real consequences for public opinion may run far deeper than the surface reactions. The ghetto riots of the late 1960s produced strongly indignant reactions among whites, but they aroused consciences and accelerated the liberalization of racial attitudes and practices. The National Guard's shooting of the four Kent State University students in May 1970 evoked strongly polarized emotions on the subject of campus confrontations, but the more significant effect was to erode popular will to win a war which carried civil disagreement to the point of bloodshed.

No issue in American politics since slavery and the Civil War has aroused as much dissension as Vietnam, nor has any public issue involved greater complexities of judgment in interpreting information, in predicting the consequences of possible actions, and in balancing political pragmatism and idealism, justification of official policies, wishful think-ing, and bandwagon psychology. The surveys of public opinion on Vietnam may have had considerable effect in causing a simple-minded polarization of the population as "Hawks" and "Doves," though they offer, at best, faint reflections of the complex evolution and convolution of thought.

Growing opposition to the war became the focal point for strong, or-ganized political movements that carried their concern over into more fundamental questions about America's social structure, its values, and its economic priorities. Thus the war itself became a critical incident in the evolution of public opinion on a host of other issues. This illustrates how public opinion on any subject of significance is always inseparable from the whole texture of prevailing ideas.

At various times, American involvement in the war became a matter of greater or less salience to the public and alternative strategies seemed either more or less appealing. This had its parallel in an earlier conflict. Early in the Korean War, in the summer of 1950, two-thirds of the American public told the Gallup Poll that American participation was *not* a mistake. After the Chinese sent their troops into battle the balance shifted; by the following March a majority of those with an opinion felt that American involvement *was* a mistake. As the Americans regained lost ground and military positions stabilized once more, opinion pro and con swung back into a more even balance.

Similarly, in the early period of American involvement in Vietnam, a very substantial majority thought it was not a mistake to send in troops. Opinion became evenly balanced in the second half of 1967. It turned decisively the other way in the summer of 1968 at the time of the Democratic convention, and remained at approximately a one and one-half to one ratio for the next two years. The turn of public sentiment against the war was closely linked to events on the domestic scene. After President Johnson announced that he would not seek another term, there were no longer any strong advocates or defenders of the war, either among the incumbent Democrats or among their Republican opponents.

The Communist side made continual references to American and world public opinion as propaganda and negotiating points. United States military and diplomatic policies in Vietnam were formulated with a careful weather eye on American public opinion as mirrored in the polls and the press. A high State Department official commented anony-mously on the decision to negotiate: "Something had to be done to extend the lease on public support for the War. We were focused on what we could do without significant military drawbacks to make clear to people we were serious about peace."[48] General William Westmoreland said on June 30, 1968, "In view of the impact of public opinion on the prosecution of the war, the accuracy and balance of the news coverage has attained an importance almost equal to the combat operations."

If the military planners were constrained by public opinion, the movement of public opinion was also sharply responsive to the course of combat as well as to the shifting prospects for an acceptable political solution.

Only 48 percent of the public in 1967 said they had a "clear idea" of what the Vietnam War is all about." In March 1966, a Stanford University poll found that only 47 percent named Saigon as the capital of the South and 41 percent Hanoi as the capital of the North.[49]

In 1966, half the public favored the administration's current policy, with more Hawks than Doves among the remainder.[50] Opposition to Johnson's handling of the war came from Hawks as well as Doves, and reflected his need to chart a policy between the political extremes.

The Stanford Poll found that those who were best informed about the war were no different from the ill-informed in their willingness to pay the cost of the war, though they were more likely to favor escalation. (Americans were not the only ones who were ill-informed. Of 100 Vietcong defectors interviewed in Vietnam in 1968, 26 could not identify Ho Chi Minh. One former squad leader said, "I don't know. There was nobody in my squad by that name."[51] Two had heard of Lenin. Among a large sample of South Vietnamese interviewed in 1967 for CBS News, only 58 percent identified Ho Chi Minh or Nguyen-ai Quoc as North Vietnamese leaders, and 27 percent were unable to name either Thieu or Ky as leaders of the South). Although men were more hawkish than women in their opinions, and Negroes markedly less hawkish than whites, attitudes (in 1966) with regard to the war failed to show the kind of significant differences by social class that are so often found with respect to great public issues. Even people who had written letters to public officials or newspapers were not different from the rest of the public in their feelings about the overall direction of the war, though they tended to be more extreme in their hawkishness or dovishness.[52] If people were divided, they were divided up and down the line.

The percentage of Americans who thought it was a mistake to send troops to Vietnam rose from 24 in August 1965 to 32 before the February 1968 Tet offensive. In the months that followed it rose, and by September 1969, it had mounted to 58 percent. It was still at about that level (61 percent) in June 1971.

Before the Tet offensive people who classified themselves as Hawks outnumbered Doves five to three. The Tet offensive sharply increased their number, to a six to two ratio, but then a reaction set in. By mid-March 1968, before Johnson's withdrawal from the election race, Doves rose to equal proportions.[53]

In August 1968, 61 percent of the American public opposed a cessation of bombing in North Vietnam; 24 percent favored it;[54] 52 percent opposed a solution of the war in which the Communists would have minimum representation in the South Vietnamese government; 25 percent favored it. Two out of three voters of both parties said they would prefer a candidate who would turn over the fighting to the South Vietnamese and withdraw American troops. In December 1968, Gallup found opinion closely divided on the question of whether the South Vietnamese should take over all the fighting and make all the decisions about peace and dealing with the Vietcong.[55]

Subtle changes in question wording altered the apparent balance of opinion: For instance, in June 1969, Gallup asked whether "troops should be withdrawn at a faster or a slower rate." Forty-two percent said faster, 16 percent said slower, but 29 percent volunteered the response that the present rate of withdrawal was correct. In October, Harris asked a similar question but included the third alternative: "In general, do you feel the pace at which the President is withdrawing troops is too fast, too slow, or about right?" Now the great majority of those responding (49 percent of the total) chose "about right" as an alternative, while 29 percent said "too slowly" and 6 percent said "too fast." Clearly people agreed with the administration policy when it was presented to them as an alternative.

In November 1969, President Nixon appealed to the public for support of his policy of "Vietnamization." This was followed by a modest and short-lived rise in approval of his handling of the war and in agreement that Vietnam was essential to American security.[56] The invasion of Cambodia in May 1970 set off violent reactions on college campuses, including the traumatic episode at Kent State. The polls, however, indicated that the majority of the general public still supported the President.

A Gallup poll in late April 1970, on the eve of Nixon's announcement that he had sent troops to Cambodia, found 58 percent of the public opposed to sending American troops "to help Cambodia" and 28 percent in favor, although a majority approved the sending of military supplies. The President's televised announcement of his action successfully mobilized public support. A CBS poll run immediately *after* the President's speech found the proportions reversed—59 percent approving and 32 percent opposed. A substantial part of the public apparently switched sides on the matter, taking a "my country right or wrong" position. But the underlying anxieties were not altogether dispelled, for opinion was evenly divided on the question of whether the invasion would expand and protract the war or shorten it. Public confidence in President Nixon was as high after the Cambodia announcement as it had been two weeks earlier, though it failed to show the jump in popularity which generally follows any major presidential utterance.

By January 1971 the proportion who favored bringing all troops home from Vietnam before the end of the year had risen to 73 percent, according to a Gallup Poll. A month earlier, nearly nine out of ten were aware of the Laos invasion, and among those with an opinion, twice as many thought the move would lengthen the war as thought it would shorten it. In pursuing its policy of deliberate withdrawal of troops without an announced cut-off date, the administration was following a public opinion that had undergone dramatic changes within a short period of time.

The belated revelations of the Mylai massacre, and the subsequent court martial and conviction of Lt. William Calley, Jr., on murder charges, represented other critical incidents in the evolution of opinion. They gave rise to an overwhelming desire for disengagement, as though the slate of history would be wiped clean as the result of an American withdrawal. In a Harris Poll of May 1971, the public agreed two to one with the statement that it was "morally wrong" for the United States to be fighting in Vietnam, and three out of five wanted United States troops withdrawn even if the South Vietnamese government collapsed.

Mylai and its aftermath produced a tangle of complex feelings, which can be unsnarled only by psychological conjectures rather than by evidence.

After CBS newsman Mike Wallace interviewed former Sgt. Paul Meadlo, who vividly described his participation in the slaughter of women and children, the network received hundreds of messages, of which an overwhelming majority objected to the broadcast.

At his trial, Calley acknowledged both the killing of civilians and the practice of using them to clear minefields ahead of the troops (a practice established by the Nazis on the Eastern Front in World War II), but he insisted that in both respects he was only following orders: "It wasn't any big deal."

While awaiting the outcome, Calley posed for photographers beneath a poster which proclaimed "No More Wars!" and announced that if he was acquitted he would go on a national lecture tour to preach against the evils of war as he had seen them first hand in Vietnam.

Long before the trial, a majority of the public agreed that Calley was a mere scapegoat, and two out of three agreed that incidents like Mylai were to be expected in wartime. Hawks and Doves found common ground to sympathize with the murderer after his conviction. Senate opponents of the war, like William Fulbright and Abraham Ribicoff, charged that Calley was being made a sacrificial victim to assuage guilt shared by the entire military and national leadership (or even, as some critics said, by the entire nation) for conducting an immoral war. When 200,000 demonstrators gathered for an antiwar rally in Washington on April 24, 1971, many of them wore masks in the likeness of Calley, to suggest that they and the whole American people shared the guilt for his crimes.

The pro-military element attacked the verdict as a blow to the morale of the Army and hailed Calley as a hero who had merely done his duty. The Governor of Indiana ordered flags flown at half-staff, the Governor of Georgia proclaimed an "American Fighting Man's Day" in his honor. Two million phonograph records of a song glorifying the convicted killer were quickly marketed.

Heavy publicity was given on television newscasts and in press reports to the protests against the verdict, and to the 100 to one pro-Calley ratio of telegrams and phone calls that swamped Washington. (This ratio changed over the next few weeks. Obviously people who thought Calley deserved punishment for his crimes were not as likely to wire their approval as the critics to voice their indignation). The fast reports on the outpouring of pro-Calley sentiment may have had an effect on many people whose first reaction was that the lieutenant had received his just deserts. A move toward conformity with the mainstream of opinion was then bound to be reflected in polls whose findings in turn could influence the judgments of subsequent courts of appeals in the case— including the President, who hastily reminded the world that he was the last court of appeal. According to Gallup, 79 percent of the public disapproved of the verdict and 83 percent approved of Nixon's intervention. Half of those interviewed said they thought this type of incident was common, and 71 percent said "others" were responsible. Under the mask of discussing war guilt and the inevitable comparisons with Nuremberg, vast numbers of people found it possible to move rapidly from support of the American presence in Vietnam to support of rapid or even immediate withdrawal. The fear of consequences became less vivid than the fear that the war was corroding the American character, as this was revealed not merely by the actions of Calley but even more by the supine compliance of his troops and the eagerness of his associates and superiors to bury the matter when it first came to light.

The publication of the secret Vietnam "Pentagon Papers" in mid-1971 provided new grounds for shifting to an antiwar position. The papers provided a ready rationale for those who were willing to be convinced that the public had been deliberately deceived by its leaders.[57] President Thieu's unopposed reelection made it difficult to sustain any ideological argument in support of the democratic virtues of his regime, and this too had an effect on American opinion.

The surveys on the subject of the Vietnam War were closely followed by government leaders: they were a political force in the conduct of the war itself. Yet they illustrate the perils of interpreting answers to single questions as though they really summarized the state of public opinion.[58] The questions commonly asked gauged public sentiment in terms of support or opposition for the administration's conduct of the war and (in the case of opposition) defined it as being of the Hawk or Dove variety. In early 1966, when the Stanford researchers explored attitudes toward the Vietnam war in much greater depth than had been done in any previously published survey, their data revealed a number of apparent contradictions. For example, well before the American troop commitment reached its peak, a majority of the public supported President Johnson's handling of the Vietnam situation, but at the same time a majority also approved a policy of deescalating the war effort.

The Stanford Poll found that 88 percent were willing to negotiate with the Vietcong, and 52 percent were willing to allow a coalition government that included the Vietcong. Two out of three disapproved an increase in taxes in order to continue the fight, and a majority disapproved any cut in domestic programs. At the same time, however, 61 percent approved raising the number of American troops in Vietnam to 200,000 and 45 percent approved a hike to 500,000.

Among a national sample of young men queried in 1970, a majority agreed that fighting the Vietnam War was important "to protect free countries," "to show other nations that we keep our promises," and "to fight the spread of Communism." But majorities also agreed that the war was "really not in the national interest" and was "damaging to our national honor or pride."[59]

As time went on, the rising antiwar sentiment came from two disparate sources, according to a detailed analysis of Michigan Survey Research Center data. A highly educated, articulate minority opposed the war for moral reasons,[60] and a larger group from the lower end of the economic and social scale opposed the war as a nuisance and for "pragmatic" reasons that came to the fore when the war news was bad. In fact, 63 percent of those who felt the war was a mistake expressed hostile feelings to "Vietnam war protestors"; this was even true of a majority of those favoring immediate withdrawal.[61]

Reexamining the Gallup polls, Irving Crespi concluded that "most people would not be consistently classifiable as either 'doves' or 'hawks,' even though they might hold internally consistent opinion, since such classification does not stem from the positive, underlying basis for opinion on this issue. Instead one would predict that public opinion would endorse *both* aggressive and conciliatory actions."[62]

Press coverage of the Stanford Poll, Nelson Polsby pointed out, tended to dismiss the contradictions among people's opinions as signs of "confusion."[63] The same survey illustrates how people withdraw from the difficult issues with which they are confronted and defer to their leaders the task of making decisions. But polls are themselves news, and the "confusion" of the public is thus itself converted into a public issue, commented upon and debated.

The survey statistics documented changes in the climate of thought which were reflected as well in press and television reports and commentaries, congressional debates, and political demonstrations in the universities and on the streets. Many currents of opinion interacted simultaneously: Views on the importance of the war as a public issue, relative to more immediate domestic concerns; assessment of the military situation and its probable outcome; evaluation of military and political strategy, of the domestic consequences of victory, stalemate, or defeat for the United States; attitudes toward American military and political commitments overseas, feelings about the Vietnamese people and their leaders, South and North, confidence in the American military and in the administration and the President.

Changes of opinion on any one of these dimensions of the situation inevitably carried consequences for all the other dimensions, yet it could not be assumed that such linkages were direct or simultaneous. Passion and discussion were aroused by unexpected episodes like the human dramas of Tet, of Kent State, and of the Mylai affair. Out of such discussion come changes of opinion.

And all of these feverish strains of movement were in some sense mirrored in the responses that the public gave the pollsters, responses that were watched with concern in Washington and Hanoi, and that provided the backdrop against which the tedious drama of negotiations was unfolded. In international politics as on the domestic scene, opinion research was an active force, and no longer a detached and neutral measurement.

Part Four

HOW OPINIONS CHANGE

INFORMATION, OPINION, AND ACTION

Men's value judgments are . . . merely an attempt to bolster up their illusions by argument.

Sigmund Freud

The day after Lt. Calley was sentenced, two conservative Georgia Congressmen who had been consistent Hawks switched to a Dove position and voted against extension of the Selective Service Act, on the grounds that the nation lacked the will to go "all out" and win the war. Their objectives had not changed, but their policy positions had, and these reflected their appraisal of the situation as well as their notions of right and wrong.

The movements of opinion in the mass can be better understood if they are perceived as the movements of many individual minds; however, they can never be reduced to the sum of their individual components. To understand how people change their minds, we must consider how ideas arise in discussion and how they are transformed into acts.

Opinions always start from certain factual premises. But the information we have at hand is usually limited. Our opinions invariably go beyond our real knowledge. The mass media can give us the illusion of knowing the inside story of what in fact we know only selectively and incompletely.

Perhaps the most important and accurate thing that surveys can tell

us is the extent of public ignorance and knowledge. Substantial sectors
of the population are unable to answer correctly such questions as
whether mainland China is Communist or not, or to identify the Vietcong or NATO. Only about one American in three can name his congressman; one in two can name one of his state's senators. In 1966, one in
four thought that Chiang Kai-shek was the head of the Chinese Communist Party.

Such ignorance certainly does not reflect a lack of attention to the
subject by the mass media. Rather, it reflects the selective inattention of
large masses of the population to matters they interpret as having no
direct meaning, relevance, or importance to them. The question of *what*
people think about public issues is really secondary to the question of
whether they think about them at all.

Late in 1969, I asked the editor of a leading Indonesian newspaper
to estimate how many of his country's 60 million adults were aware of
the Vietnam War. He hesitated for a moment and guessed about one
million. How many of these people knew about American involvement?
He guessed one-half million. To the question, "How many have a sense
that the outcome of this war has any meaningful relation to their own
lives in Indonesia?" his estimate was 50,000. Of these he felt 30,000
favored the American-South Vietnamese side.

Assuming that these figures are correct (an unwarranted assumption,
incidentally), how should one have categorized the extent of pro-United
States sentiment in Indonesia: as 60 percent of those who take sides, as
6 percent of the "informed," or as 0.005 percent of the population?
Even if the last figure best helps us to put this knowledge in perspective,
it does not make the informed, politically aware group any less significant or influential.

One need not turn to the underdeveloped world to note that very
few people show strong concern or awareness of the larger arenas of
politics. Alfred O. Hero, a student of American knowledge about foreign policy issues, maintains that less than 5 percent of the population
are really involved in understanding world affairs and follow events
closely in the mass media.[1]

World affairs are not among the topics about which Americans report
they have strong opinions. In a 1964 survey half spontaneously mentioned religion, two in five mentioned bringing up children, and one-third
named each of family life, public education, and the federal government.[2] Topics of conversation do not focus on subjects of public concern,
but revolve more around personal interests. The feeling that an institution needs attention or change is not directly related to the strength of

opinions about it. Comparatively few people at that time were talking about the Vietnam War, civil rights protests—or about the then recent coup and resulting massacres in Indonesia!

Ignorance of the facts, misunderstanding of the issues, inability to visualize consequences—such conditions manifest themselves in the hesitancy which people often display in answer to an interviewer's questions on complicated issues. Uncertainty and irresolution must not be confused with apathy or with a sense of hopelessness about the practical possibility of influencing the course of events.

Political opinion surveys sometimes ask people to indicate on a scale how strongly they hold the opinions they express. Such responses are at least a step in the direction of distinguishing passionate convictions from casual inclinations. But people with certain personality traits (not unrelated to their station in life) are more likely than others to give the extreme responses. This means that measurements of the intensity of opinion sometimes tell more about how temperamental attributes are distributed within a population than about the importance of the issue for the public.

An extreme political position can influence public opinion out of all proportion to the actual size of its support. Unsuccessful minority candidates like Norman Thomas, George Wallace, or even Barry Goldwater, may bring about a greater shift in "middle of the road" opinion than the moderate candidate who is elected. Although voters may reject the extreme position, it becomes part of the context within which they render judgments. "When voters are attracted to middle positions," argues a psychologist, Allen Parducci, "the crusader who wishes to draw the weight of opinion toward his view should take a position that exaggerates his deviation from the center of the political spectrum."[3]

This intriguing theory assumes that the purpose of the crusader is to influence the mass of *opinion,* rather than to seek *power.* Strong advocacy of a cause which the majority rejects for its extremism may pull the center of opinion slightly in the direction of the advocate, but at the same time frustrate his ambition to achieve office by way of popular support.

Public opinion is commonly measured for and against various causes, with the "undecided" as the residue. Often it may be more revealing to measure the degree of apathy, indecision, or conflict on the part of the great majority and consider the opinionated as the residue. The first question a pollster should ask is: "Have you thought about this at all? Do you *have* an opinion?"

Public opinion is a twilight realm between the learning of information and overt behavior. These domains are not wholly interdependent. An increase in information about a subject does not necessarily lead to change in opinions. Similarly, when people talk differently than they used to, this does not mean that they have altered their established ways. There are remarkably few authenticated instances of mass behavioral change that can be directly attributed to changes of opinion induced by persuasive argument.[4]

No attempt at persuasion can be meaningful unless it is channeled to encourage a specific action. It may be tacitly understood that the timing of this action is to be deferred, as in the case of the advertiser who wants potential customers to "file away" the information he gives them about his product, in the hope that it may eventually influence their decision when they are ready to buy. But no amount of advertising can lead to purchase of a product which is not on the shelf of the store when the customer wants it. And no amount of persuasion can move men to act on behalf of abstract causes unless the actions to which they are urged are clearly specified and within their reasonable capacities. A communication urging people to take polio shots produced immediate results among 86 percent of the people in an experimental group, when the shots were available immediately and close by. When people had to wait one day, only 28 percent took the shots.[5]

The overwhelming preponderance of research data gathered by the survey method is in marketing, and much of it deals with reports of purchasing or consumption, which are presumably related closely to the facts of actual behavior. It is difficult to come up with hard evidence on the communications effects induced by product advertising and even more difficult in the case of large-scale information campaigns dealing with abstract concepts.[6] The apparent absence of effect, or a negative or "boomerang" effect opposite to the communicator's intentions, may not be due to any failings of his communication, but rather may reflect its persuasive ability *relative to* what is being said by or for competing causes.

Mass media contributed an estimated $51,500,000 worth of space and time between November 1967 and July 1969 in support of a National Safety Council campaign to increase the use of automobile seat belts. A comparison of two surveys made before and after the campaign found virtually no change in seat belt ownership or use.[7] The connection between the messages and the moment of action was just too remote. Over a period of years, between 12 and 24 million dollars' worth of advertising were contributed annually in fund-raising appeals for Radio Free Europe, a CIA "cover" operation. The funds collected never passed $500,-000 a year. Why? Perhaps there was never any urgency to the appeal, or an effective organizational mechanism to follow up on the advertising itself.

Television spokesmen who testified before the Eisenhower Commission on the Causes and Prevention of Violence argued that no good evidence linked the violent content of programming with overt demonstrations of aggression or anxiety on the part of the viewers. Members of the Commission greeted these statements with skepticism: they pointed out that the television industry sold billions of dollars of advertising time on the premise that the medium could influence action. The apparent anomaly is not so hard to explain. People are more vulnerable to influence by direct appeals on trivial matters (like consumption choices) than by subtle symbolism in the realm of their basic values.

Information can be conveyed more readily than attitudes can be changed, and attitudes are affected more rapidly than actions. (This has been called the "hierarchy of communications effects.") But actions taken for extraneous reasons can also lead to attitude change and to an increase in information. The purchase of a product, on what might appear to be haphazard, accidental, or irrelevant grounds (its chance availability, shelf position, price advantage, or brand familiarity) leads to a formulation of opinions that justify the choice. The product is "good" because it has been tried, and the probabilities of repeat purchase increase precisely because the user has tried it and found it acceptable and must now articulate his satisfaction. Not dissimilarly, a person who for reasons of acquaintanceship, location, or mere accident finds himself swept up in a political demonstration may act with the crowd first, and only later declare himself an adherent on the matter of principle. This is one of the reasons why the collective behavior of a minority may affect history more than majority opinions privately held and never expressed in action.

Human beings use elaborate psychological mechanisms to rationalize their beliefs and unconsciously resolve or reduce the apparent discrepancies among their opinions.[8] Just as an individual reduces psychological tension by "bridging" the inconsistencies in his thinking, so he may minimize any threat to his complacency by exposing himself to information and opinion that reinforce what he already knows or is interested in. Consciously and unconsciously we too often see only what we want to see and confirm what we already believe.

PERSUASION, DEBATE, AND DISCUSSION

In Tel Aviv a widescale public opinion poll was conducted recently. One of the people interviewed was a bright and opinionated housewife who expressed her views in a most convincing manner. When the interviewer finished, he thanked her profusely and walked away. "Please wait, sir," the woman called loudly. "Where can I find you just in case I change my opinion?"

Haaretz, Tel Aviv[9]

What we believe is a composite of what we have sought out and learned for ourselves and of what other people have tried to teach us. We learn things at a different pace and in a different way when we are deliberately trying to learn them and when we are just picking them up "incidentally." We also react differently to persuasion, depending on whether or not we think it is directed at us, and depending further on whether the subject matter has significance for us.

Since human beings generally tend to avoid what is unpleasant, there is a limit to the success of attempts at persuasion which rely on fear. Yet many efforts to persuade people start out by scaring them with the prospects of anything from bad breath to nuclear disaster. We are warned of the ravages of smoking, drinking, drugs, and veneral disease and of the dire political consequences if certain candidates win an election. Such warnings are most persuasive when the anxieties they arouse are acute enough to win attention but not so vivid as to overwhelm the

104

information that follows. People with high self-esteem are more resilient, and hence more receptive to tough messages which evoke fear and resistance from those of frailer spirit. The more vulnerable the individual feels himself to be, and the more he feels the message to be directly focused on himself, the more he will seek to avoid it.[10]

When people are faced with the realization that their actions do not jibe with their expressed opinions, they are most likely to explain the discrepancy by referring to what is *expected* of them by those they consider significant.

From among all the communications to which we are exposed each day, we tend to select, learn, and respond to those we think will turn out to be useful, and useful ideas are not always those that reiterate what we already know or believe. The extent to which a person seeks to buttress his views and reject contradictory ideas or information will vary with the individual's flexibility of character and intellectual quality, but also with the importance he attaches to the subject, the size of the psychological or material stake he has in it, and the amount of information he already has which is at variance with his prior position.[11]

But the process is not always simple. The extent to which people learned "relevant propagandistic information" about the Vietnam War was not related to their own attitudes toward the war, their prior information on the matter, or their awareness of what the experimenter was after. It was, however, related to the novelty of the information; people were most apt to learn information that was different from what they already knew.[12]

Everyone has what Carolyn and Muzafer Sherif and Roger Nebergall call a "latitude of acceptance" for opinions which resemble his own; everyone also has a "latitude of rejection" for those opinions which he regards as objectionable.[13] If a persuasive message falls within the individual's range of acceptability it should produce a shift in attitude. The less the message resembles the individual's original position, the greater the shift of opinion it will effect. But a message that falls outside the range of tolerance may be perceived as even more discrepant than it really is and produce a defensive response which reinforces an established point of view. An attempt at influence is less likely to be successful the more structured and familiar the subject of discussion, the greater the individual's emotional involvement with it, the less prestigious the source, and the more disparate the message from the individual's attitude at the start. To defend deeply held beliefs, a person will overcome his normal impulses to be tolerant or polite.[14]

When we are forewarned that someone is going to try to influence us, our defenses are set in·motion even before we hear what he has to say. However, a forewarning may actually be flattering to us, and thus serve the cause of the persuader if we start with a favorable view of him and his intentions or if he is introduced to us in a favorable light.

In some cases, an advance notice that someone wants to change our opinion represents the first challenge to a position that was previously taken for granted, and therefore it creates an awareness that other alternative views exist. The reflections and doubts that follow this revelation may ease the way for the persuader when he finally appear on the scene.

Forewarning produces different effects depending on whether it is negative or positive in tone.[15] When the warning and the persuasion context are positive, the effect of a communication is enhanced; if they are negative, acceptance is diminished.[16] A neutral warning has no effect on the willingness to accept a communication though it may lead to an effect *before* the communication is received.

When people believe they will have to defend their views, they tend to moderate an opinion which they previously held in private.[17] When we know in advance that someone will challenge our hitherto unexpressed opinions, we tend to tone them down in the subsequent discussion, since there is nothing to lose by being accommodating and since we tend to defer to greater zeal or intensity of conviction on a matter that may strike us as of passing consequence. But if we are already committed by past expression to an opinion that we are told is going to be opposed, we tend to dig in our heels and defend it even more vigorously, and perhaps with a more extreme argument, than we otherwise might. Thus debate polarizes the views of the committed, and at the same time brings the uncommitted from both sides closer to the center, and to consensus.

Our opinions and judgments do not exist in the abstract; we are constantly testing them against those current among people we consider our peers. People measure experience or satisfaction not on an absolute scale of values, but rather in comparison with "significant others" whom they identify with themselves.[18] The influence of a communicator is greatest when he is similar to the audience he addresses; he swings more weight when people can identify with him rather than accept him as an authority figure.[19]

"The reason of man," said James Madison, "like man himself, is timid and cautious when left alone and acquires firmness and confidence in proportion to the number with which it is associated." Most people want to be part of the crowd.[20] Awareness of majority opinion or judgments makes it possible for a person to compare his own ideas and perceptions with those of his group. In the psychological laboratory this leads to rapid reassessments. Experimental subjects have been given simple tests of their judgments of distances, colors, spatial relationships and similar manifestations of what their own eyes and ears tell them. When they are confronted with spurious descriptions of what others report on the same phenomena, they generally "correct" their own judgments to bring them into line with "public opinion."

White people in a New York suburb were found to be relatively less willing to sell their home to a Negro if they thought the climate of opinion in the community was hostile to integration and more willing to sell if they thought the community was not so hostile.[21]

In the political realm, the compulsion to move one's own deviant views into line is expressed in the old slogan, "forty million Frenchmen can't be wrong." The notion that "everybody's crazy but me" is commonly taken as a manifestation of paranoia. Recognition that one is in the minority invariably creates some sense of doubt and uncertainty about the wisdom of one's views, while the adherent of the majority may feel smug and righteous. The fable of the Emperor's new clothes is re-enacted perpetually in the form of a public resistance to any questioning of what the majority takes for granted. (At various times this may be the divine right of kings, slavery, private property rights, or the supremacy of the male sex). There are always isolated voices warning that the Emperor is really naked, but these voices are resented and ignored unless they carry considerable authority or unless they rise sharply in number and volume.

At a certain critical point in outgoing public debates, a minority opinion may gain in strength to the extent that it is perceived as a strong—and therefore legitimate—force. When polls or press accounts suggest that a majority now support this position, a new orthodoxy is enshrined. When power changes hands, opinion shifts in the direction of the victors. A winning candidate always takes office with the goodwill and support of many who opposed him.

Opinion surveys which create the illusion that a "vote" has been taken on a great public issue may tend to produce a bandwagon effect. But as the freshness of a public debate wears off, and as the convinced adherents of a minority viewpoint settle into fixed positions, fully conscious of their minority status, they are likely to manifest greater dedication to their views than is true of the more casual majority. A persuasive message contrary to people's opinions will win proportionately more converts from the ranks of those who hold a majority viewpoint than will a similar (but opposite) message aimed to win converts from the unpopular minority view.[22] The opinions voiced by a group reflect not only the individual convictions which its members bring to it, but their perception of the group itself and of its expectations of them.

For this reason, judgments arrived at in a group situation are less vulnerable to change than those arrived at individually.[23] If we find an ally who agrees with our original opinion before we express it, we stick by our guns even if the rest of the group has another opinion, but if we have already "changed our minds" in public to conform with the group judgment, the belated discovery of an ally has very little effect.

In groups that discuss issues rather than merely vote upon them, the dynamics of debate produce additional changes. Debate produces emotional bonds, as well as an exchange of information and ideas. Into every debate, and the alliances formed within it, there enter overtones of allegiance, affinity, rivalry, envy, loyalty, or hostility which stem from totally irrelevant causes but which produce inevitable and important consequences.

A group is more ready to assume risks after debate than before, since the discussion provides everyone with reassurance that others beside himself are willing to take a gamble. In the course of discussion, the participants come to take on the prevailing attitudes, particularly if the group must arrive at a democratic decision to which all will later be committed. But although discussion leads people to incorporate the majority views as their personal opinion, it may also lead to a sharpening and polarization of differences which do exist and which are merely heightened by the debate. In the words of two psychologists, Serge Moscovici and Marisa Zavalloni, "Society not only moderates ideas, it radicalizes them as well."[24]

We seek reenforcement for our ideas not only in the search for information through the mass media, but in our personal associations, and when our ideas change, we seek the company of others who share our newly acquired views.[25] However, if we are well-informed on a subject we may prefer to engage in discussion with those who disagree with us, if only for the fun of the debate. Discussion invariably heightens our involvement with the subject, but it also summons up our resistances. An attempt to influence people with a message is less persuasive if it is discussed than if the message is merely presented, even though people become more involved with the subject when they participate.

In a bilateral debate positions are polarized on a resolution; one must be either for or against it. But few public issues are so simple; we may support some parts of a proposal and reject other parts of it; we may favor certain modifications; we may have a variety of totally different alternatives to propose in order to cope with the very same problems.

A discussion presupposes a far wider range of choices than a debate, but it also presupposes that the participants are engaged in the search for a solution and are therefore willing to moderate their views, assimilate new information or insights, make concessions and otherwise shift their initial stance. These shifts of position may be more studied or cynical when they are engaged in by people who are actually empowered to make decisions than when the discussants form no functional group and are "only talking." In either case the participants identify their own positions with a range on the spectrum of opinion rather than with only one specific point on that spectrum.

We feel comfortable not only with the views of those who see exactly eye to eye with us, but with others whose opinions we consider to be generally sympathetic or congruent with our own. We tolerate the opinions, the company, and even the authority or leadership of people with whom we may be in profound disagreement, in general because we remain ever conscious of the substratum of more fundamental human values that link us to them, through the nation, Western culture, or common humanity. It takes an extraordinary degree of emotion, as well as a strongly opposed viewpoint, to regard other people's opinions as intolerable, since intolerability implies a commitment to active opposition.

In the era of the New England town meeting, a largely rural America of independent farmers and artisans engaged freely and frequently in discussion, not only as a matter of transacting the public's business, which was everyone's business, but as a common form of passing the time. The tradition of the cracker-barrel philosophers may be little more than a myth preserved by nostalgia for a more intimate scale of life than we know today, but it typifies the free-flowing, widely ranging, continuing discourse that could be carried on in an era when the flow of information was restricted to the relatively small number of events that appeared in the newspapers of that day.

In our own more complex era, the number of news items that are reported daily is almost inexhaustible; the topics of current events cover far too broad an area for most people to be able to comprehend. We have specialized and fragmented interests; whether in city apartments or suburban developments, the twentieth-century metropolitan man maintains a more impersonal, more anonymous life than his rural or small-town antecedents. His opinions are less well known to his neighbors.

The middle-class value system to which most Americans purport to adhere places a damper upon extremism of thought and upon excessive seriousness or emotion in the expression of opinion. Jobs, income, and ethnicity segregate people into neighborhoods, and into patterns of personal association within their neighborhoods, which minimize the likelihood that they will be confronted with discordant ideas. Only the universities are centers of informed and open daily discussion on the full range of problems and issues which confront the society. Thus the steady rise in the proportion of college graduates carries important implications, not only for a higher level of public information, but for a multiplication in the very frequency of debate.

Public opinion can operate on elected officials through polls, plebiscites, and pressures, causing them to support or oppose an administration's policies or a government's course of action. But there is no way in which a nation *en masse* can engage in a reasoned discussion and come up with a detailed solution of problems that are beyond the range of either/or choice.

CHANGING ONE'S MIND

Some ne'er advance a Judgment of their own
    But catch the spreading notion of the Town.
Some judge of authors' names, not works, and then
    Nor praise nor blame the writing, but the men.
Some praise at morning what they blame at night
    But always think the last opinion right.

Alexander Pope

Trend studies of public opinion allow us to trace the progress of a public issue as people shift the responses they give to survey interviewers. On a much smaller scale, the evolution of a collective position by a discussion group can be discerned as its members verbalize their convictions and their hesitations. The processes of opinion change in a single individual are harder to describe precisely since they often take place well below the surface and may not be recognized even by him.

When we speak of people's opinions or beliefs in ordinary conversation, we cover a broad assortment of ideas; we encompass familiarity with a subject and interest in it as well as a predisposition to say certain kinds of things about it and to act in conformity with what is said. "Opinions" include people's perceptions of trivia as well as their most strongly held beliefs about the essentials of life. "Opinions" may express deeply rooted values that give the individual his sense of identity, and that he cannot alter without redefining the whole meaning of his own existence; "opinions" may represent casual judgments which are readily amenable to change.

Theorists of the subject have traditionally distinguished between values, attitudes, and opinions. Values are generally considered to represent the inner core of an individual's beliefs and are reflections of the centrally shared ideas of his culture, or of the subsegment of society with which he identifies himself. Attitudes are usually characterized as predispositions to respond in a certain predictable way to classes of phenomena: people, things, or events. Opinions are ideas about individual cases rather than about broad categories of experience. Attitudes are durable, whereas opinions represent responses to specific questions. To move from values to attitudes and then to opinions is to move both from the general to the specific and from the enduring to the ephemeral; it is also to move from what is deeply engaging to the individual's ego and sense of identity to what is superficial or even accidental.

Scholarly attempts have been made to perfect statistical techniques by which clusters of opinions can be shown to be interrelated and identified in terms of the attitudes which are presumed to underlie them. These efforts are of interest primarily for the methodologist who wants to manipulate data to produce economical descriptions of complex phenomena. But on matters of substance, the threefold classification is arbitrary. The words "values," "attitudes," and "opinions" do not denote separate classes of belief with different degrees of likelihood that they will be translated into action.

We are rarely aware of opinion which is static and universally held. There is little reason to question the general habit of rising in the morning and retiring at night, though there are many alternative ways for people to cycle their time. We take it for granted that things should be this way, yet if we took a poll on the subject we could no doubt find a minority who prefer other arrangements. (By asking a question we would no longer be taking the matter for granted, and we would be bound to find a substantial number of "night people" who might never previously have thought of themselves as such.)

What distinguishes opinions from faith or from mores is their propensity for change. Views which are fixed and held by everyone cannot be called opinions at all; they are simply part of the social fabric. Heterogeneity and dynamism within a society, challenge from nature or human adversaries, contact and conflict with other cultures—all these produce and reflect differences of outlook, judgment, and individual courses of action. Changes in the forms of social organization, in cultural expression, in the balance of political power, in the generation and distribution of wealth, all express themselves in changes of opinion, just as changes of opinion lead to actions which transform human institutions.

People change their opinions because the world changes around them, because their own place in that world changes, because the people around them change; because they are swept up by social movements. All this has always been true, but in relatively recent times something new has been added. That is the deliberate effort to move the minds of people in the mass on matters that have nothing to do with religious faith, but that sometimes arouse an equivalent fervor.

I have suggested earlier that public opinion can be swayed by leaders whose authority of office or personal style commands public confidence. Press and broadcast news shape the public's perception of the world; this fact acquires sinister implications when media are in the hands of those who believe that truth is whatever one chooses to make it. Interpersonal persuasion is the very substance of human intercourse; the prime skill of prophets, orators and political leaders has always lain in their ability to project the intensity of direct personal magnetism to the far reaches of the assembled crowd and to make converts who would carry the message even farther.

The pamphleteer of the eighteenth century was somewhat in this tradition; he used the magic of the printed word to win the attention of the growing number of literate men beyond the sound of his voice. In an era when printed publications were still comparatively few and expensive, such efforts at persuasion could still be direct. Even though the element of interpersonal contact was no longer there, the reader could sustain the feeling that the author was addressing *him*.

In the late twentieth-century world of heavy overcommunication, with its ponderous and highly organized machinery for mass marketing, persuasion is conventionalized and taken for granted; it is not taken personally and therefore can be easily disregarded. The public in mass society is self-consciously aware that many forces want to get it to buy things and do things, to influence what it thinks.

When many competing voices sound at once, the net effect may be to cancel each other. Public opinion often remains static in its overall dimensions, whereas the opinions of individuals who constitute the public are in flux. Studies in which the same people are reinterviewed at intervals often show that while the same proportion at two different points in time say they are on a diet, watched a particular show on television, feel friendly toward the Telephone Company, bought Rice Krispies within the last thirty days, or believe that the foreign aid program should be cut back—they are different individuals at time I than at time II.

As an individual seeks continually to reduce the inconsistencies in his own opinions, to align his views with those of the people with whom he identifies, to check his nonconformist instincts against the prevailing sentiments of his group—so his own expressions are constantly subject to change.

Studies of switches in voting preferences in the course of United States electoral campaigns demonstrate that individuals caught in "cross-pressures," who at first lean toward a candidate other than the one who might be predicted from knowledge of their social background, often tend to revert to the predictable choice when they finally enter the voting booth. Indeed, four out of five vote the way other members of their families do.[26] In an increasingly mobile society, cross-pressures inevitably increase, and it is harder for people to remain totally consistent in their political choices.

A party loyalty formed early in life is likely to persist in its effects on individual belief and voting action even after the party line has changed. The individual may maintain his party affiliation even when he disagrees with the party's policies, with which he may well be unfamiliar. However, in recent years, straight ticket voting for state and local offices and party loyalty in Presidential elections have both declined. (Among whites who voted in both the 1964 and 1968 elections, one-third switched parties; in fact, 40 percent of Nixon's 1968 votes came from people who had voted for Johnson in 1964.) This trend seems certain to continue, since young voters show the greatest independence.

Although common sense might suggest that people with the lowest level of political interest or articulateness might be most likely to switch their candidate preference in the course of an election campaign, this does not at all appear to be the case.[27] Switching betokens a reflective mind and a politically concerned individual. A change of opinion, or a switch of sides on a cause, may represent anything from a mild accommodation under pressure to an agonized conversion.

Sigmund Freud, writing of the process of dream-formation, commented on the manner in which psychological "conflict results in a compromise, so that the communicating force can indeed say what it wants to say, but not in the way it wants to say it; it is toned down, distorted and made unrecognizable."[28] A similar process occurs in the formation of conscious ideas.

At any given moment in time, all of us hold tentative, inchoate, half-formed views on a variety of subjects about which we may have never had a conversation and on which we have never had to take a public position. The extent to which we become publicly committed to the opinions we hold varies not only according to the length, vigor, and frequency with which we have expressed them, but also with the informality or formality of the occasion and the number, familiarity, and importance of those present.

A man who renders an off-the-cuff judgment in response to a casual query by a taxi driver has obviously committed himself far less than if he expressed the same views in a conversation with friends or business associates, and he will show far less inner resistance to taking the opposite tack the next time the subject comes up. On a different plane of intensity, the man who is swept into an angry political discussion in a public meeting is less committed to his position than is someone who comes to the same meeting as an invited speaker with a prepared address. But most people do not go around making speeches, prepared or spontaneous. Outside the realms of religious doctrine, political orientation and social class values, their opinions on many subjects are unpredictable even to their closest friends. (Consumption brand preferences are an excellent example of the "secret" opinions that everyone holds and rarely has an occasion to reveal.)

Opinions expressed in conversation are the ones that carry the most weight, less because of their influence on the listener than because they commit the speaker. Conversational opinion is spontaneous, fluid, and often tentative, and it reflects the emotional response of those communicating to each other, as well as facts and logic. In this kind of interpersonal relationship, people must accommodate to each other. The relationship itself is in ordinary cases and on ordinary matters paramount over the ideas being exchanged. But in accommodating to each other for pragmatic reasons, opinions themselves may be modified if they are voiced in an accommodating manner.

A conversation on matters that do not involve the immediate self-interest of the parties takes on a different aura when the subject shifts to an area of bargaining for a specific outcome. Argument focused on a material goal is apt to entail overstatement, dissembling of one's motives and intentions, and other artifices. Open and closed negotiations differ both in form and in substance, and negotiations carried on by professional plenipoteniaries, like lawyers or diplomats, obey an etiquette of their own: the negotiator is understood by all concerned to be fulfilling a fixed role, and he is not expected to introduce his personal feelings into the debate. *Ad hominem* references are considered bad form. Yet the personal factor in such negotiation *is* vital in determining the outcome, and persuasive skill is sometimes the strongest card in the bargainer's hand.

Once an arrangement has been made, the negotiator must generally justify it to his principals. To rationalize his negotiating skill he must, after the fact, defend this arrangement to his own side as "the best obtainable under the circumstances."

Similarly, public officials defend their policies as the best possible "under the circumstances," and opinion on public issues generally reflects a balance between what is wanted or what is right or what ought to be done and what has a chance of getting done "under the circumstances."

One's change of mind on a topic of discussion may follow simply from a change of perception about an individual who advocates a particular position, or from a change in one's relationship to him. Just as our opinions can be swayed by the authority, prestige, esteem, or affection we feel toward people who have established positions on the matter, so our altered view of a significant person may lead us to alter our own opinions on the subjects with which we identify him. We go through such changes in perception constantly in our associations with other human beings.

Getting to know someone better may lead us to value more or less than before the opinions he holds on particular subjects. Knowing a person in a social context when one formerly knew him at work, or vice versa, changes our assessment of his aptitudes and charms. Knowing a former equal as a superior or as a subordinate brings out new dimensions of character which influence our views of the things we think he stands for.

Such changes also work in reverse; our opinions and feelings about people reflect the congruity of their opinions with our own, as well as the stimulation we get from their opinions and the style with which they are expressed. Studies of interpersonal influence show that people tend to be selective in the way they accept or reject the opinions of others; they recognize areas of special knowledge or competence and distinguish the garage attendant's authority on carburetors from his evaluation of school board candidates. But while they tend to accept leadership in many areas from those above them on the social and educational scale, their peers are the primary source of their principal opinions.

Everyone stands in the midst of cross-pressures from the many people with whom we come into personal contact, toward whom we have varying allegiances and hostilities, for whose views we have different degrees of respect. The formulation, hardening, and shattering of our own opinions is inseparable from the daily joys and strains that accompany our relations to others. But just because people's opinions are often rationalizations of their loyalties and loves, this hardly means that change in opinion is outside the domain of reason. We may change our minds because of a change in the situation, but we may also change our minds on an unchanged situation as we learn more about it.

A group of social scientists on the staff of the Rand Corporation, employed on Vietnam studies by the United States military, issued a public statement in the fall of 1969 calling for American withdrawal. They had arrived at this conclusion, in obvious contradiction to their immediate personal and professional self-interest, by their exposure to mounting evidence of the war's toll in Vietnam and its consequences in the United States. Their underlying political beliefs and premises had not changed; but their changed appraisal of the facts led them to what appeared to be an about-face in policy conclusions. One of these scholars, incidentally, was Daniel Ellsberg, whose transformation from militant Hawk to passionate Dove led him two years later to turn a top-secret Pentagon war history over to the press.

In a television interview, Ellsberg reported that the turning point in his opinions came when he read an account of Army Secretary Stanley Resor's decision to quash the trial of Green Berets involved in the killing of a Vietnamese double agent. This made him vividly aware, he said, that members of the administration had been trapped in a web of rationalizations by their need to justify policy, and he suddenly felt an impelling need to break out of this trap himself.

The Rand scholars' 1969 statement was cited at the time by a friend of mine who had been a strong supporter of the Johnson policy on the war and had similarly undergone a change of heart. Now an advocate of an immediate and unconditional withdrawal, he said that the Rand document "really shook me up, because those fellows were working for the government, they were close to the thing, and they changed their minds." He had recently changed jobs, moving to an organization where he led a youthful staff, many of whom held radical views. Queried further about his conversion, he acknowledged, "I couldn't survive a day in my place if I were known as a Hawk." He went on to argue that the Johnson administration had mishandled the war, and cited its failure to bomb the port of Haiphong. "They could have interdicted the flow of Russian supplies and won the war. They were just afraid of hitting a Russian ship. They should have taken the risk."

There seems to be at least a good probability that my friend's susceptibility to persuasion by the Rand statement was enhanced by the intimate social pressures of his new work environment. Yet his associates in the demand for immediate withdrawal inevitably must have started from totally different premises than his very pragmatic ones: he would hardly have shared the conviction that a Communist regime in South Vietnam would be preferable to the rightist military one in power! One may, in short, arrive at the same position by different paths, and with different supporting arguments. Parents whose sons arrive at draft age are apt to undergo striking transformations as well as crystallizations of opinion. Are their more passionate and articulate views less valid than those they held when personal involvement and self-interest were not at stake?

To "change one's mind" may mean painfully reworking an entire system of belief. More often, it means starting with an emotional judgment from which a ready-made structure of rationalizations follows automatically.

An act of political or religious conversion represents a reorganization of one's perceptions, ideas, and past experiences. Such an act may perhaps be akin to the achievement of insight in psychotherapy, when forgotten, suppressed, or previously ignored relationships suddenly assume coherence and emotional significance. The secret of such insight is very often the recognition of ambivalence of feeling. The patient recognizes the strain of hatred for his objects of love and his love for the objects of his hatred. We know better than to call such events "changes of opinion," for they are indeed much more than that; they are deep changes of heart, and they are beyond the cunning of statistics.

William James describes conversion as an instantaneous process and quotes John Wesley: 652 members of his Methodist Society testified that "the change was wrought in a moment" and not a single one claimed to be "gradually sanctified." "We have a thought, or we perform an act, repeatedly, but on a certain day the real meaning of the thought peals through us for the first time, or the act has suddenly turned into a moral impossibility."[29]

James suggests that a state of apathy or "temporary exhaustion" forms part of the conversion crisis, so that the convert "passes from the everlasting No to the everlasting Yes through a 'Centre of Indifference.' " When emotional sensibility and passive suggestibility combine, at the right psychological moment, the convert attains inner peace and harmony, "the mysteries of life become lucid," and the world seems beautiful and new. In the words of one such "spontaneous" religious convert, "It was as if I had been in a dark dungeon and was lifted into the light of the sun."[30]

People change their outlook as they move into new environments, mingle with new associates, take on different occupations, age into new positions in the life cycle. In the transformation of cadets into officers, of medical students into physicians, ritualized ordeals are employed to give the individual his new identity. Probably one of the outstanding illustrations of a change in outlook and values occurs in the process of immigration and the change of national orientation from the country of origin to the country of adoption. The gradual refashioning of a

European peasant who has emigrated to urban America is a quite distinct process from that of religious conversion, yet no less profound in its effects.[31]

But changes also take place among people whose life position is static and whose personal contacts are restricted to others of similar, or at least predictable, views. These changes of opinion, gradual or sudden, with regard to the events of the day, are set in motion by the larger movements of characters on the political stage, and by the manner in which news media highlight and focus on these movements.

Consider the following case history: Gustav Stresemann had been a loyal supporter of the German Empire and of World War I. As late as 1919 he had written, "I was a monarchist, am a monarchist, and shall remain a monarchist." And yet in January 1923, as Chancellor of the Weimar Republic, he was won over to support a significant symbolic event, official commemoration of the liberal revolution of 1848. Arnold Brecht describes his critical conversation with Stresemann as follows:

"When he hesitated . . . we reminded him that once, as a student, he himself had carried the black-red-gold [Republican] flag at a celebration for the victims of March. We showed him a newspaper clipping about it. He then consented laughingly and heartily, obviously much taken with the plan and especially enthusiastic about the historic support which, he was sure, it would lend his policy of active collaboration with the Weimar coalition. There, and at that moment, Stresemann was won over emotionally to the Weimar Republic. The previous two years, with the fall of Social Democratic predominance on the one hand, and the assassination of ministers and the lust for dictatorship on the other, had made him into a *Vernunftrepublikaner* [a Republican by reason]. But now he was touched at the heart. Now more than tactical opportunism, more than mere reason, came into play. As we sat with him in conversation about the Paulskirche, he suddenly looked once more like that young idealistic student who had carried the black-red-gold flag in honor of those who had fallen in the March days. His secret attachment to the democratic Republic shone from his eyes. The Stresemann of the Wilhelminian policy of expansion—Stresemann the First, one might say, who had still supported the Kapp Putsch—had long been dying. Stresemann the Second was born . . . ."[32]

Persons exposed to extreme situations—battle, prison, disaster—find their attitudes undergoing rapid change. Among American troops in Vietnam, those who had been in intense combat were most negative in their feelings about the war and also about the South Vietnamese.[33] Diplomats, journalists, and other mobile individuals who suddenly find themselves exposed to a new cultural or political environment are particularly vulnerable to a change of outlook.

It is characteristic of the defector that he should feel *he* has not changed, but that *they* have. Janos Radvanyi, the Hungarian chargé d'affaires in Washington, defected to the United States in 1967 after his attempt to institute peace negotiations in Vietnam ran into the pressure of resistance from China. His statement, released by the U.S. State Department, said, "In recent months I came to realize that it was impossible for me to act in good conscience and continue to be the representative of the Hungarian government to the American government." At the same time, in defecting, he denied any disbelief in Communism or disloyalty to his own government.

Such striking instances of conversion are a matter of almost daily occurrence. Calvin Craig, Grand Dragon of the Georgia United Klans of America, announced his resignation from the Klan on April 28, 1967, in order to devote his energies to voter registration work and to help build a nation where "black men and white men can stand shoulder to shoulder in a united America." He announced that his decision to leave the Klan represented "no change in attitudes," but would permit him to "accomplish more of my beliefs."

An act of voluntary conversion may seem sudden to the onlooker, and indeed, on the part of someone with deeply felt and freely expressed convictions, a change of sides in a running debate may be invested with much emotion and drama. But it is the *verbal* expression of opinion which manifests this sudden transformation. An individual with a public commitment to a position, and one who is skilled in marshalling the supporting arguments, may continue to mouth it publicly while he is privately in doubt. Generally there must be a precipitating incident which leads to the first public acknowledgement that he has changed sides. For the political activist the incident may be fraught with excitement, even personal peril, and may come at the moment of decision when action is called for rather than words.

In a democratic society that exercises no sanctions against a changed belief, the first acknowledgment of a shift, in the case of the average private citizen, may come in a discussion with intimates; then as the discussion is repeated the expression of the changed opinion loses its tentative character. As it hardens it may acquire the full set of supporting arguments which are readily available through the media or through the spokesmen for those institutions, political parties, sects or other groupings which have an established point of view, or even a vested interest in the matter. The man who has publicly changed his mind inevitably seeks out the evidence which confirms that he has done so wisely, and the very fact that he has changed must become an example to others.

The forces that impel a man to change his tune in public are not always forces that he can keep under control. Greed, power lust, and other forms of base self-interest may lead an individual to dissemble his real thoughts, and reiteration of the statements eventually leads to acceptance and belief. There is often a thin line between opportunism and the urge to survive, or the altruistic wish to have others survive. The many Jews who "voluntarily" converted to Christianity in Tsarist Russia did so to rid their children, as well as themselves, of the heavy burden of oppression; their predecessors in fifteenth-century Spain converted involuntarily to save their children's lives. Forced conversions produced some of the most fiercely loyal Catholic families in Spain. And many of the frightful Turkish janissaries who cruelly subjugated the peoples of Eastern Europe were themselves abducted Christian boys reared as Moslems.

The testimony of those who have undergone forced conversions is sometimes difficult to distinguish in retrospect from the cases of those who have themselves independently and without excessive persuasion undergone a change of heart. In *Darkness at Noon*, Arthur Koestler has given us the classic portrayal of the false confession which reflects the subtle interplay between a prisoner's fears and his acceptance of the larger ends for which his evidence is being falsified.[34] This kind of pressured "conversion" becomes easier to understand if we acknowledge the multiplicity of opinion which is present in the minds of most people on most political subjects. Pressured conversion is different from traumatic "brainwashing" that is akin to the kind of artificial psychosis experimentally induced in cats placed in an electrified laboratory cage. Brainwashing represents a forcible breakdown of an individual's ego through exquisite forms of psychological torture, so that in a state of apathy and defenselessness he rapidly voices and even accepts ideas contradictory to the values he originally held.

Eugene Loebl was a defendant in the Slansky purge trial who was later "rehabilitated" during the administration of Alexander Dubcek and became head of the Slovak National Bank. He has reported on his interrogations by the secret police in 1949. They lasted sixteen hours a day, followed by marching, sleeplessness, and hunger. Finally drugs were used to force a confession, which he later renounced, only to be forced into another confession:

"This confession was final. I no longer thought of repudiating it. I

felt no shame or compunction about having succumbed and lied. This
state of mind is hard to explain. Before the trial I had to learn my deposi-
tion by heart. A questionnaire was compiled consisting of questions the
judge or the prosecutor would ask me and the exact answers I was to
give. After I had learned these answers by heart, they gave me a test . . .
the terrible thing is that I did not even realize my humiliating role; it
was as if I had lost all sense of human dignity. All one had inherited
from so many generations, all that almost everyone holds dearest and
that becomes part of one's nature, that actually makes one a human
being—all this ceased to exist."[35]

It is time-consuming and very expensive for a state apparatus to
arrange for such individualized conversions. In the larger scheme of
things they have far less importance than the massive but nonetheless
involuntary conversions that take place through the enforcement of an
official dogma, the control of news media, and the suppression of dissent
in both private and public utterance.

A writer in Communist Poland has referred to the anguish of "someone who keeps writing but is always afraid. There are thousands of
things you can't write about. The worst part of it is that these contradictions find their way into you and become a part of you. You find
yourself thinking like a censor; you become as twisted inside as a great
serpent, and you never even know it's happened to you."[36]

But most people are unwilling to expend the enormous psychological
energy and run the risk involved in maintaining the struggle for integrity
and truth. As dissenters are killed, imprisoned, exiled, or muffled, the
official viewpoint inexorably gains control over large areas of thought.
People readjust to changed forms of society, to new leadership, to political reorganization. Obedience paid long enough, with whatever initial
resentment, is eventually rationalized and internalized. It becomes
loyalty—and genuine loyalty at that.

When people are forced to accommodate to a changed social order,
the need for consistency impels them to adopt many of the explanations
by which the new order justifies itself. Direct social pressure and restricted
access to alternative viewpoints may be less important in bringing about
this change than the inner need to feel comfortable with what one out-
wardly accepts.

The fact that there is today apparently an absence of substantial opposition to socialism in Eastern Europe is an indication of the rapidity
with which such basic changes in outlook take place. Even during the
brief period of democratic revival in Czechoslovakia (when honest opinions could be polled) the basic economic-political structure of the country

was not in serious question. A survey conducted by the Institute of Sociology of Prague University found that nine out of ten persons questioned in July 1968 preferred Socialist development and only 5 percent said they wanted a return to capitalism.[37] Yet in 1948 there was no country in Europe more deeply devoted to *petit bourgeois* values. In two short decades of a dictatorial regime imposed by an alien power, the attitudes of centuries had been transformed. There is no reason to assume that more than a small minority of Russians in 1917 were active supporters of the Bolshevik program, or that more than a small minority of Chinese were adherents of Mao in 1948. There is just as little reason to assume that the vast "silent majority" in either country would today favor a sweeping change in the familiar system if they were offered an immediate free choice. (In the absence of survey evidence, such assumptions are only conjectures.)

A compliant majority, in either Communist or Western countries, should not be confused with one that shares strongly felt and clear-cut ideological convictions. A Warsaw University student poll in 1961 found only 2 percent who described themselves as "definitely Marxist," while another 16 percent said they were "on the whole, yes."[38] But for that matter only 2½ percent of the American public are classifiable as "ideologues" with consistent political beliefs.[39]

Even religious beliefs and practices, which people hold more tenaciously than any others, are vulnerable to systematic efforts at extinction. The persistence of religious faith and institutions in the Soviet Union is often cited as an example of extraordinary tenacity, and even exploited as evidence of the regime's "tolerance" in propaganda aimed at the West. It is perhaps more realistic to note that only a tiny minority of believers actively practice their faith in Holy Russia, half a century after the upheaval. In Yugoslavia, where there has never been a comparable antireligious crusade in the past quarter-century of socialism, a recent survey shows that 51 percent do not believe in God, 39 percent do, and 10 percent have "no opinion." People *can* be converted, in spite of their traditions and dispositions, and the dividing line between coercion and other forms of persuasion is sometimes a difficult one to draw.

People rationalize and reduce the inconsistencies in their views and assuage their consciences when they are persuaded or coerced into acting against their normal standards of conduct.[40] Consider, for example, the subjects of psychological experiments who are instructed to administer what they are told are "electric shocks" to a "victim" (actually a confederate of the experimenter) who pretends to wince in pain as they carry out their instructions. The rationale for participation can take a number of forms: the pain is not really all that great; it serves the victim right, since he agreed to participate in the experiment; the subject really was forced to do it, since he needed the money, or the credit for his psychology course. Curiously enough, the higher the "voltage" of the "shock" that he believes he is administering, the less painful the subject avers it to be.[41]

Changes of opinion can be experimentally obtained by getting people to play roles which are in conflict with their own prior beliefs—provided that the subject matter is peripheral to their most cherished values. Experimental subjects who were placed in a "forced compliance" situation in which they had to argue a point of view opposite to their own tended to change their attitudes in the direction that they expressed. Psychologist Irving L. Janis and B. T. King found that the typical individual was "impressed by his own cogent arguments, clarifying illustrations, and convincing appeals which he is stimulated to think of in order to do a good job of 'selling' the idea to others."[42]

In another experiment, John Wallace found that rewarding a person by complimenting him on his success in playing a role produced substantial attitude change in the direction of the debating position he had taken (contrary to his private opinion).[43] As one man put it, "I tend to think of myself as an honest and sincere person. When you told me that the others considered me 'a very good actor,' I was somewhat baffled . . . actually, a little offended. The more I thought about it, the more I became convinced that what I had said in the debate was what I truly believed." By contrast, when experimental subjects were praised for the *content* of what they said, they did not move nearly as strongly in the expected direction. The reason for this, Wallace suggests, was that the subjects knew they were just repeating "hack" arguments that were in the "public domain." "Hence, the subject could verbalize such ideas, receive reward for the reasonableness, logical nature of, and persuasiveness of such arguments but experience little dissonance over and above that expected from simple voluntary compliance." Wallace hypothesizes that "success in role playing increases the subject's involvement in the role. And the greater the involvement of the subject, the more one would expect him to strive for self-consistency."

This kind of artificially induced change is easiest to achieve among those who hold moderate rather than extreme views to begin with. It is easier to see the other fellow's point of view, and to identify with it, if one's own opinions are tentative rather than hardened, relaxed rather than invested with emotion.[44]

Even when a person shifts his attitude to overcome the "dissonance" he feels after expressing commitment to two inconsistent opinions, the process may occur at a low level of emotional involvement when it is studied in the laboratory. In real life the counterpressures of public debate may quickly force attitudes to shift back to the starting point, or to shift again.

On the day in 1939 when Franco's Fascist armies marched into Madrid, the streets were alive with cheering crowds. When these same streets had been full of crowds applauding the troops of the Republic, were the people in the crowds different or were some of them the same? And did either ovation echo the mass sentiments of the moment? Throughout this century this phenomenon has been seen over and over again.

At the end of World War II, I participated in the project of recruiting high officers of the Luftwaffe to assist the American Air Force in the continuing war against Japan. When these officers were asked if they would turn against their former allies, there was not the slightest glimmer of hesitation, doubt, or ambiguity in their response. Nor, indeed, does there appear to have been any in the case of the Italians, Rumanians, and other military forces whose rulers switched sides in the course of the war.

Does this kind of sharp reversal of sides reflect a change of opinion? Does not the phenomenon of sudden political change rather reflect the coexistence of antagonistic systems of thought, alignment, loyalty, and opinion in the minds of the same people? These coexisting systems can reverse their dominance when this seems to be called for by the objective realities of the situation or by immediate short-run personal self-interest.

For the highly political man who recognizes the inconsistencies, weaknesses, gaps, and fallacies in his own intellectual value system, there already exists in embryo the contradictory argument, the antithesis to his thesis. It was not necessary for Bukharin, Radek, and the other defendants in the great Moscow trials to be coached on the details of their imaginary crimes any more than it was necessary for Galileo to receive indoctrination in Ptolemaic astronomy in order to present a "disproof" of what he had demonstrated.

Part Five

AMBIGUOUS OPINIONS

THE CAUSES OF INCONSISTENCY

Do I contradict myself? Very well, then, I contradict myself.

Walt Whitman, "Song of Myself," *Leaves of Grass*

"And still it moves!" Galileo muttered. His inquisitors no doubt sensed the insincerity of his public recantation, but his verbal obeisance kept the facade of religious conformity intact. If there is often an incongruity between what people think and what they say, there are also often inconsistencies in what they think and never say. These inconsistencies reflect the pulls and pressures of our conflicting affiliations and loyalties, the distortions and inadequacies of our different sources of information. Complex personal motives sometimes cause our emotions to rule our judgments and then force our reasoning to follow suit.

Contradictory opinions can be traced to the multiple roles which individuals assume in different situations. They can also be detected in the collective movements of political temper. Public issues are created by a clash of views reported in or initiated by the mass media. It is through this interplay of reportage and argument that people come to formulate opinions on the many subjects that lie beyond the scope of their personal experience.

"In the United States," wrote de Tocqueville, "the majority undertakes to supply a multitude of ready-made opinions for the use of individuals, who are thus relieved from the necessity of forming opinions of their own."[1]

129

In fact, an individual's ideas on any public matter are likely to follow a *system* of opinion which may or may not be shared by the majority, but which has already been expressed in the media by specialists and pundits. Such systems of opinions, in which all the ambiguities are straightened and all the loose ends are tied up, surround the great controversies of our time. They need not extend to the comprehensive scope of a doctrinaire ideology, "revealed" in the works of self-anointed leaders, but they carry with them a full panoply of arguments and rationalizations.

Public issues tend to align themselves in terms of established groups or personalities toward which people have varying degrees of identification or opposition, empathy or revulsion. Our opinions on specific matters of discussion generally reflect our predispositions to side with or against the various forces who have already been heard from on the matter.

People often accept political labels without accepting the ideology which is generally associated with them. Lloyd Free and Hadley Cantril estimate that two-thirds of the public can be described as "liberal" in their views on the operational activities of government, but that "Americans at the ideological level continue to pay lip service to an amazing degree of stereotypes and shibboleths inherited from the past."[2] In fact, only a minority of those who call themselves Democrats also describe themselves as liberals.[3]

Many people who have opposing political allegiances resemble each other in their answers to specific questions, though not necessarily in the reasons which led to those answers. For example, at an early stage of the 1968 election campaign (in April), supporters of Nixon, Wallace, Humphrey, and McCarthy were far less sharply differentiated than might be supposed in their racial views, and not very different in their answers to questions about the war and the state of the nation. Each candidate evidently drew initial support from a broad spectrum of opinion.[4]

The response to a candidate's personality or style allows his supporters to project their own views upon him. Yet the political consequence of one candidate's victory rather than another's could represent a polar opposite in government policy.

In the 1968 New Hampshire primary race, a plurality of McCarthy's supporters objected to the administration's conduct of the Vietnam War on hawkish grounds rather than for McCarthy's own dovish reasons; they voted for him as an opponent of administration policy without understanding or agreeing with his stand.

But by the time the national election campaign had come to its close, the issues that divided the candidates had sharpened. The people who actually voted for a candidate in November were more homogeneous in their opinions than those who had favored him in April. There were substantial differences in outlook between whites who voted for Wallace and those who voted for one of the other candidates: favoring segregation, 40 percent versus 10 percent; favoring a tougher police line with demonstrators, 87 percent versus 55 percent; taking a stronger stand on Vietnam, 67 percent versus 36 percent.[5] None of these issues found all the proponents on the side of one candidate and all the opponents on the other. But the closer the point of real decision and action, the less inconsistent opinions will be.

Public opinion surveys often reveal a contradiction between people's opinions about what is right and good and proper and their personal willingness to do something to support their beliefs. In the course of the 1968 election, only one person in five agreed, and over half *disagreed* with the proposition that "taking part in protest meetings or marches that are permitted by the local authorities" was one of the proper "ways for people to show their disapproval or disagreement with government policies and actions."[6] It is unlikely that a majority would cheerfully renounce the right of protest for *themselves.*

A California Poll in January 1968 found 52 percent who agreed that "professors in state supported institutions should have freedom to speak and teach the truth as they see it," but at the same time, 52 percent (obviously including at least some of the same people) agreed that "professors who advocate controversial ideas or speak out against official policy have no place in a state supported college or university."

In the area of racial attitudes we find similar inconsistencies. Thus the trend of white opinion shows an unmistakable and striking liberalization of outlook in recent years, but this coexists with a heightened awareness of even sharper changes in Negro expectations and a consequent sense on the part of many whites that they are being "crowded."

Among the most anti-Semitic third of the population a majority agree that "Jews are warm and friendly people," and that "the more contact a person has with Jews the more he likes them." Among those classified as "extreme" anti-Semites (15 percent of a nationwide sample), three out of four thought big companies should "hire the best people whether they are Jewish or not" and 75 percent said it would make no difference if they had Jewish neighbors. (Another 5 percent say they would *like* to have some).[7]

A captured Luftwaffe pilot who had fought through the Russian campaign and had, for a period of time, been based at airfields deep in conquered Russia, commented about the approaching end of World War II: "I would like to travel when the war is over and peace is restored. I would like to see how people live in their own countries. I would like to go back to Russia and find out how they *really* live—how it is there in peacetime." There was still in some realm of his imagination another Russia, a real but mysterious Russia, perhaps one he had first encountered in the writings of Gogol, Turgenev, and Chekhov, which existed outside of what he had personally seen and observed and experienced.

Do we not all encompass in our memories diverse and incongruent impressions of the same people and places as we knew them in different contexts and at different moments of time? Our responses to family, friends, and acquaintances are invariably colored by our recollections of past shared experiences, encounters, and conflicts. These recollections are themselves evoked by our disposition to love, admire, and revere or to disparage, resent, or hate, in relation to the contacts and the demands of the moment.

Total consistency of belief, expression, and action is as rare within a society as it is within an individual. For an infinite variety of reasons, we think, speak, and act differently on different occasions. Our individual outlooks change not only with time, but with the need to adapt to circumstances. We respond to specific situations in terms of predispositions which may lead us to totally disparate courses of behavior. Every conflict of motives, judgments, values, and allegiances leads to its own characteristic synthesis or resolution which, once arrived at, serves as a precedent to be justified.

A frequently cited experiment showed that an Oriental traveling with a white companion was often accepted as a guest in hotels that in response to an earlier mail inquiry had said they would not accept Orientals.[8] How could this be? Very simply, the energy expended in being inconsistent was far less than the energy which might have been generated as the result of a (consistent) refusal encountered by objection and bitterness.

Our words and our actions are likely to show the least inconsistency when we are unobserved and anonymous, unrestrained by the bonds of the groups with whose values and habits we identify ourselves. The more deviant our opinions are from those of the group, and the more openly we have to disclose them, the more likely we are to manifest inconsistency.[9] During the school integration crisis in Little Rock, Arkansas, which was resolved by federal military intervention, ministers who were in favor of desegregation did not express their positions in front of segregationist congregations.[10] At such a time, silence is dissembling.

It is not unusual to encounter the residual traces of childhood beliefs rejected in adolescence or adulthood. *Young Communist,* a Soviet magazine, did a poll in Gorky which showed that 60 percent of the babies were baptized, although most of the parents had listed themselves as atheists. The writer Kornei Chukovsky reports a conversation overheard between two small children in a Moscow park. One boy of seven asks another, "Is there a God?" The slightly older one replies, "We Communists don't believe so, but of course maybe he does exist anyway."

James Joyce once told Harold Nicolson that a man had taken a copy of *Ulysses* (which was on the papal *Index*) to the Vatican, hidden in a prayer book, and that the Pope had blessed it. Nicolson commented later, "He was half-amused by this and half-impressed. He saw that I would think it funny, and at the same time he did not think it wholly funny himself."[11]

When an employee asks his supervisor, "How well am *I* doing my job?" the answer he gets is apt to be different from the one that might be given to a third party who wants to know, "How well is *he* doing his job?" That answer will, in turn, be different if the third party is the supervisor's boss, his competitor, or another subordinate on the same level as the employee.

This variation in the replies does not mean that the person expressing the opinion is honest in one answer and dishonest in the others. It means rather that he has defined his verbal response in terms of the uses which he infers will be made of it and the latent meanings which he assumes will be read into it.

The traditionally good interpersonal relations of whites and Negroes in a small Mississippi town was delimited by the mutual acceptance of the boss and worker roles. Once either party perceives his relationship to the other as capable of taking on different forms and having greater complexity, the established structure of expectation changes. The new perception of status relations creates a whole new framework of attitudes and feelings and of behavior as well.

Inconsistency in our opinions often reflects our awareness that self-interest is at variance with loyalty to others, or to our higher ideals. It is not always easy to predict whether a man will behave in terms of the norms expected of him or in terms of what he privately thinks is right. An individual who at home may be highly critical of his country's foreign policy will often defend that same policy when he travels abroad. This isn't necessarily dishonesty or phoney patriotism. When he argues the issues with a compatriot, he takes for granted a certain fund of common information. It is hard to make these same assumptions when the same subject is discussed with someone (however intelligent) who starts from hostile or inaccurate premises. Both sets of opinions, along with the supporting arguments, exist simultaneously, though only one at a time is in charge.

The views we hold are always comparative, always expressed with a wary eye on the "significant others" by whose standards we choose to be identified. We consider ourselves frustrated or advantaged by comparing ourselves not with the reigning monarchs of the world but with those we consider our peers. And we are capable of making such comparative judgments on different levels, as Muzafer Sherif and his associates point out:

"The self-identity of the person consists of more than just one commitment or one stand; it is multi-faceted . . . a person takes all these stands, but not to the same degree. He is tied more strongly to some groups than to others; he commits himself on some issues more intensely than on others. His ties with other people can also be ranked by their importance to him. His stands on various social issues can be differentiated, . . . by the importance he gives them. If the hierarchy of a person's ties and commitments is ascertained, a great deal may be learned about his behavior in different situations. Many apparent contradictions in his actions may be explicable, especially in cases where he makes a verbal statement on a specific issue and then acts in a contradictory fashion."[12]

Opinions can never be isolated from their context. A psychologist, Milton Rokeach, has suggested that attitudes have both generic and specific components. He differentiates between the attitude toward an "object" and attitude toward a "situation"; the object placed in one situation arouses a different response than it does in another.[13]

Because of union regulations, the publisher of a very large newspaper had to get permission to visit the floor of his own plant from the pressroom shop steward. In granting him this permission, the shop steward observed to him, " I wouldn't go through this if *I* were running this paper!" What, in this case, is the "real" opinion of the shop steward? Is it his private opinion, expressed on a man-to-man basis when he puts himself in the executive's place and thinks in terms of abstract justice, or is it the opinion to which he would give voice as a union functionary if the rule were violated?

We all express judgments, prejudices, and emotions in the bosom of our families that would be outrageous if we heard them on the lips of strangers. Are these any less the expression of our "real selves" than the more reflective statements we make when we are on our best behavior?

After the military takeover of the Greek government, in the spring of 1967, a reporter interviewed an old man in a small Greek village. He asked (a typical unbiased reporter's question): "Are people unhappy with the new regime?" " 'They like it,' he said firmly. Then with a smile, 'They have to like it.' And finally with a shrug, 'Most don't like it.' "[14]

On any given subject an individual does not necessarily have just one public opinion and one private opinion, which may or may not be the same. Rather he may at the same time hold a *variety* of opinions, articulated or vague, public shading into private. These multiple opinions correspond to different roles he plays in life or to different reference groups to whom he relates. They may be contradictory or incongruent. They may be actively at war with each other and arouse in him an uncomfortable sense of conflict, or they may be no more than low-charge reflections of the opposing viewpoints to which we are all subjected through mass media and in conversation. Just as the same object may arouse alternating emotions of love and hate, depending on circumstances, so we are capable of simultaneously incorporating a belief and its opposite or seeing the best and worst in two alternative courses of action.

An ordinary citizen often expresses views on public policy—even expresses them strongly—while acknowledging that they would be wholly untenable if held by people in power. Sometimes such deviant opinions are held or expressed in the context of an implicit assumption that they are unrealistic.

A person may feel that by holding nonconformist views—advocating elimination of the income tax, unilateral disarmament, free access to narcotics, or whatever—he is exercising pressures which can help to dislodge the authorities from an entrenched but obtuse position. An individual holding opinions on this basis might freely acknowledge, when challenged, that they exist "for talking purposes" only, and that he would be forced to modify them if he had the responsibility for taking action. Conversely, someone who supports the responsible authorities is often quite willing to admit that his views would be quite different if his own life role changed: opinions on student unrest or the laws governing marijuana might change if one had a child in college who had gotten into trouble; opinions on military adventures might change if one had a son in the Army; and opinions about the Middle East crisis might change if one had relatives in Israel or Lebanon.

The political scientist John H. Bunzel recalls a conversation during the Cuban missile crisis in 1962 with a woman who had just wired President Kennedy in protest against his quarantine policy. Asked what she would do if she were President, she acknowledged after a relentless step-by-step interrogation of the logical consequences of her reasoning, that surrender would be better than war.

"But in terms of deciding what is the best policy, which is what the President must deal with—"

"My position, I admit, is completely emotional. It has nothing to do with policy. I don't know what the President's policy should be. My telegram to the President just expressed my own personal feelings. I just don't want a war."[15]

As Bunzel wisely comments, such a reduction of choices to the emotional dichotomy of peace or surrender "has nothing to do with political alternatives or the processes by which difficult decisions are made."

Public opinion is more likely to exhibit an appearance of inconsistency, the greater the intricacy of a subject, the more ambiguous the facts, the greater the number of alternative solutions, the larger the number of parties involved. An issue thrust upon the public without prior warning, which persists as an issue without a desire on anyone's part to keep it alive, is bound to entail disparities between what people ideally want and what they think can be done about it, between short-run gains and long-run goals, between instinct and reason, between the desire to be wise and the need to appear consistent.

Public opinion encompasses that part of the domain of ideas which is the subject of free and open discussion. The "public opinion" of an individual, says sociologist Jean Stoetzel, is precisely that which he is willing to express overtly and to which he is willing in effect to sign his name.[16] The thoughts, impulses, fantasies, and schemes which are never revealed to others are at the heart of any person's identity. Our mental processes pursue a different form and sequence in private and in public.[17] Thoughts expressed to others invariably must strain to assume a semblance of logic and orderliness. Apparent inconsistency may reflect nothing much more than fuzziness of expression or ambiguities of language. Thoughts voiced on serious subjects, like those which deal with trivia, invariably reflect the interpersonal relationship, real or putative, among those engaged in communication, their respective evaluations of each other's social rank and personal utility, the social tissue out of which the discussion grows, the purpose to which it might be put. One's words on any subject are bound to depend on whether or not one speaks with authority *vis à vis* one's interlocutor, on how well one knows him, and on the importance one attaches to the issue.

But private thoughts on the same subject are plagued by none of these considerations. They may weave back and forth through fantasy and

digression, double back on their tracks, and acknowledge themselves
to be in contradiction or bewilderment. Original and creative ideas
stem from such search and trial. But private thoughts must always be
tested in the forum, and once articulated they must inevitably break
forth, be repeated, and find their way into the arsenal of firm assertions,
clichés, and prejudices with which every individual defends the fortress
of his inner self.

When freedom of expression is suppressed, individual opinions continue to exist, though they are not openly exchanged. Baron Jacques
Necker, Louis XVI's Minister of Finance, referred to the aggregate of
privately held opinions as *"l' opinion du peuple,"* in contrast with public opinion proper, which he identified with the free flow of discussion
among courtiers in the royal antechambers and salons. In this dichotomy,
"public opinion" represents a truly collective force which embodies the
highest motives and the best capacities of society, whereas "the opinion
of the people" represents the low grumblings of the uninformed masses.

Translated into contemporary terms, the "popular opinion" of individual Soviet citizens with respect to an event like the invasion of Czechoslovakia contrasts with the Soviet "public opinion" manifested by the
official apparatus of *Izvestia* articles, trade union meetings, and television
newsreels.

When political power changes hands and people feel free to openly
express thoughts that were formerly restrained, private opinions burst
forth in tumultuous public discussion, as happened in Prague during
the Spring and early Summer of 1968.[18]

In a police state, serious political conversations are carried on in a
whisper between persons who have already established some basis for
mutual trust, and in places outside the range of eavesdropping or hidden
microphones. The most delicate probing, testing, and tentative conversational gambits are used by people of deviant political views to establish
contact and a sense of mutual confidence in a world of conventional
thinkers, rigid ideologists, and informers.[19]

Even in the freest of societies, harsh criticisms of authority or of
generally accepted dogma are rarely uttered by sober people. This self-
imposed limitation is a necessary form of accommodation to the demands
of civilized social intercourse; it is an instinctive way of reducing the
tensions of daily life in a heterogeneous country peopled by individuals
of varying backgrounds, life-styles, and interests.

It is precisely the itinerant stranger to whom people are always able
to unburden themselves without worry. The individual who reveals all
his private beliefs to a friend or acquaintance may be risking gossip, a

wound to his reputation, the appearance of hypocrisy. At worst he may even be opening himself to blackmail, revenge, reprisal, and sanction. The sharing of a painful or shameful secret is an act suffused with emotion and often followed with anxiety; it is only in the sacramental privacy of the confessional or on the psychoanalyst's couch that the catharsis of self-revelation is uncontaminated by resentment toward the confessor. Secrets always in some way involve the individual's relations with others. The branching web of these relations sets restraints on the free expression of what one knows or thinks.

"The more unpopular an opinion is," warns Samuel Butler, "the more necessary is it that the holder should be somewhat punctilious in his observance of conventionalities generally."[20] It is wise for the advocate of an unpopular opinion to moderate his voice so long as he seeks adherents for his cause from among the conventional-minded majority. But the revolutionary who rejects the possibility of working within the framework of the established order may choose deliberately to speak with indignation and a sense of outrage, to defy the conventions and to show his contempt for established institutions and their spokesmen.

Open statements of political opinion are generally inhibited if the ideas expressed are likely to arouse irritation, outrage, annoyance, or disgust from those within earshot and thereby carry consequences for the social acceptability of the person expressing them. The process of setting words down on paper for dissemination in public forces a writer or speaker to reexamine his stance and to reduce the inconsistencies in his position.

Most people who speak or write for an audience do not do so anonymously. If they speak or write on serious subjects, their views as stated must often be modified versions of their unexpurgated opinions—if only because the time or space is limited, because certain literary conventions must be observed, or because incomplete communication is better than getting a load off one's chest with nobody listening.

The rare individual who criticizes sacred institutions runs a severe risk of being regarded not merely as a bigot, zealot, or heretic, but as an eccentric whose opinions cannot be taken seriously on any matter. He must, therefore, always weigh his purposes against both the substance and the manner of his criticism.

If his commentary is voiced merely for the purpose of self-expression, then he can be as bold as he likes—provided that he is willing to accept the disadvantages and reprisals which even the most liberal society imposes upon those of deviant views. On the other hand, if his primary objective is to achieve changes in the institutions he criticizes, he must inevitably temper his manner and censor his content, in order to exert the maximum amount of social pressure compatible with the maintenance of his own respectability, credibility, and authority. At this point he takes on a new role, that of the public man.

PRIVATE OPINIONS AND PUBLIC ROLES

When one runs with wolves, one must howl.

Wladyslaw Gomulka

Self-consciousness of role has always linked politics and the theater. An editorial cartoon in the *London Times*[21] shows two men driving on a California highway adorned with a billboard advertising (at the time of his first campaign), "Ronald Reagan for Governor." One driver asks, "Why shouldn't a film star make a good Governor—after all Henry Fonda made an impressive President in 'Fail Safe,' and Peter Sellers made an excellent President in 'Dr. Strangelove.'"

The entry of movie stars into public life is not unique to the United States. In India, N. G. Ramachandran, the "Tamil Errol Flynn," was shot in the neck and critically wounded by another film actor, M. R. Radha, who has generally played villain roles. Both men were prominent in political life and Ramachandran was sure of election in spite of the fact that he had to campaign from a hospital bed and was unable to talk. At the same time, his latest movie was "a stupendous success. What makes it irresistible is the casting of the real-life assailant in the villain's role."[22] Cambodia's former chief of state, Prince Norodom Sihanouk, produced and starred in at least five feature films.

A practicing politician must forever be on stage, even when there is no audience present to enjoy his posturing.[23] During a minor "invasion" attempt to overthrow the dictatorship in Haiti, the lifetime president, the late "Papa Doc" Duvalier, adorned himself in military uniform and directed the counterattack from his well-guarded palace. His official mouthpiece, *Le Nouveau Monde,* referred to him as "this intellectual dressed in the uniform of a soldier." (Curiously enough, the pitiful handful of "invaders" were themselves play-acting. They arrived wearing camouflage uniforms with labels marked "Big Game Styled by Broadway.")

In the royal palace in Madrid, the bedroom of Alfonso XIII, the last King of Spain, is kept as he left it when he abdicated in 1934. The visitor may note that among the monarch's bedtime reading was a pre-World War I book, in English, entitled, *Behind the Scenes at the Russian Court.* Alfonso was learning from books "how to do it." ("The King dreams he is King," Calderón de la Barca wrote centuries ago.) But from here it is only a step to the case of the actor who plays the role of a statesman, imagines that he actually is one, and is eventually elected to the office by voters who live in the same world of fantasy.

The politician whose words are chosen to suit the occasion and to soothe or cajole the particular group he is addressing always presents himself in the guise of a man speaking his own mind. His play-acting may be utterly cynical and self-consciously dishonest, yet the etiquette of politics demands that he present this guise as a genuine expression of his own nature.

This is an expectation totally different from that of the professional actor, whose words are taken *not* to be his own. The masks of primitive shamans and of ancient Greek actors similarly reflect this disengagement of words from speaker. The tradition has been preserved through the centuries by the classic conventions of the theater; the patent artifice of stage, scenery, and curtain; the unnatural poetic cadences of dramatic speech, the brevity and structured tension of the play as an art form.

The relation between actor and role has been profoundly altered in the theater of the twentieth century, shaped as it has been by naturalism in the novel, verisimilitude in film, and commercialism in production. The actor as star, as real or putative idol of the masses, must role-play offstage as well as on; his wealth, glamor, and important worldly connections create for him a *persona* he must live up to with as much skill and consciousness of effort as he must apply to his other roles. The actor who played the part of the head of the Rothschild clan in a successful Broadway musical was deluged with requests for money—as though he had taken on the wealth as well as the fictional identity appropriate to his role.

In the new "guerrilla theater," actors appear to forsake their stage roles for verbal and physical assaults on the middle-class audience, breaking down the conventional barriers between the theater and the real world. The purpose of the theater of participation is just the opposite of classical drama, for the audience must depart not with its emotions exalted and purged, but in a state of profound irresolution, malaise, and discomfort.

"Guerrilla" actors posed as student editors at a meeting of the College Newpaper Association; they infiltrated the program and made fiery speeches. Listening to one, radical leader Jerry Rubin asked, "Is this guy real? Or part of the Washington Theater Group? I don't know. But did it make any difference? Everything was real and unreal."[24]

Many of today's professional revolutionaries see themselves as political actors, on stage for the benefit of the larger public to whom their antics will be reported and projected through the mass media. Abbie Hoffman, arriving before the House Un-American Activities Committee in a Santa Claus suit, thereby demeaned the dignity of his inquisitors and charmed the press.

In the buildup to the 1968 Chicago demonstration, the Yippies threatened to introduce LSD into the city's water supply and claimed that 230 "hyperpotent Yippie males" were being formed into a special battalion to seduce the female retinue of the Democratic convention. Jerry Rubin urged his supporters to bring "pot, fake delegates' cards, smoke bombs, costumes, blood to throw, and all kinds of interesting props; also football helmets."

The defense of Rubin, Hoffman, and the others who were tried for their part in the Chicago disturbances was precisely that their activities had been a "put-on"—the "Yippie myth," in the words of their attorney. "The secret to the Yippie myth," writes Rubin, "is that it's nonsense."[25] A film intended to rebut the city of Chicago's own documentary interposed photo sequences of the confrontations with scenes from old movies showing Keystone Kops and medieval battles.

Conventional politicians, no less than revolutionaries, must use the devices of the theater to win attention and support, and they often do so without a saving touch of innocence. (Consider Richard Nixon's tear-jerking "Checkers" speech of 1952, and the candidate's own comment on it in an address to a group of broadcasting executives: "An efficient 'off-the-cuff' appearance on television, creating the illusion of intimacy so desirable to win the viewers, according to Mr. Nixon, entails many hours of preparatory work."[26])

The exigencies of public office require a rapid adaptation of personal views to meet diplomatic necessity. John Freeman, former British Ambassador to the United States, was editor of the *New Statesman* during the early 1960s. In one article he described Richard Nixon as "a man of no principle." When he was appointed British Ambassador in February 1969, Freeman observed, "My feelings about him have changed completely."

Governor Paul B. Johnson, Jr., who unsuccessfully sought to defy federal power in the desegregation of the University of Mississippi, traveled to Caracas shortly afterward as part of a group of Mississippi businessmen. Facing an audience ill-disposed toward North American racist doctrine, Johnson told the Venezuelans who questioned him on the subject, "As you know, integration is the law of the land, and we have integrated all our schools. Prejudice exists, as in other parts of the world, but the problem will be solved through education."

Judge G. Harrold Carswell, named by Nixon to the Supreme Court in January 1970 (and rejected by the Senate), repudiated a political speech he had made in 1948 in which he said, "I yield to no man . . . in the firm, vigorous belief in the principles of white supremacy, and I shall always be so governed." After his nomination, Judge Carswell said these sentiments were now "abhorrent" to him, and his supporters dismissed the remarks as a "youthful indiscretion" (made at the tender age of 28). "A wise man changes his mind often and a fool never," said Senate Republican leader Hugh Scott. Review of Carswell's background produced evidence that at an even more tender age (26) in 1946, he had written a newspaper editorial attacking Eugene Talmadge's racist campaign tactics. One of Carswell's home-town political cronies dismissed his vacillations with the remark, "Ol' Harrold was just playing the game."[27] (Such a defense assumes that the game-playing has stopped at whatever moment the inconsistencies of outlook stand revealed.)

Playing the game, too, was Heinrich Himmler, who in the final days of World War II harbored the fantasy that he would be accepted by the West as the leader of postwar Germany. Himmler made no effort to argue in favor of the policy (of which he was in charge) of exterminating Jews; he simply denied that it was taking place. Receiving a representative of the World Jewish Congress, Himmler complained of "distorted" reports about the concentration camps: "The bad connotation of these camps is due to their inappropriate name. They should have been called 're-formatories'. . . . The treatment in the camps was hard but just." Himmler conceded that crimes occasionally happened in the camps but added, "I also punish the persons responsible."[28] Was this "acting"? Or was Himmler, *while* he lied, expressing genuine opinions that he had held all along *at the same time* he was engineering the "final solution"? He undoubtedly made his statement with the same honesty as an SS general I interrogated in May 1945, who expressed utterly convincing disbelief and shock at the photographs of naked bodies piled up in concentration camps. It was another self that spoke.

This is a rare and outrageous example, but any man who appears in a public role must adapt his instinctive personal style to the requirements of his position. The controlled consistency of role which is expected of political figures in a dictatorship contrasts with the agonized inconsistency which may beset even the most hardened politicians in a parliamentary democracy.

Robert McNamara, as Secretary of Defense, was rumored to be in private disagreement with the Vietnam War policy which he implemented in practice, but this could never be confirmed by any public utterance. When he was nominated to head the International Bank for Reconstruction and Development, a newspaper report commented, "What the private Robert S. McNamara believes and feels remains obscure. Even the reason he conveys these differing impressions is unclear."[29] He was described as "an intensely complicated man who conveys one impression of his beliefs and emotional attitudes to friends who share these convictions and feelings, and who conveys a significantly different impression to friends who do not."

In frank and private discussion among equals, or between a leader and his intimates, the complexities of a situation may be fully revealed, doubts and indecisions may be voiced, and the contradictions that beset any policy-maker can be made explicit.

Alan Westin has compared the individual's need for privacy and reflection to the organization's need for executive sessions as a prelude to the presentation of its public face:

"Much of the behavior of both private and public organizations involves irrational decision-making procedures, harsh and/or comic discussions of 'outside' people and causes, personal motivations for decisions, and highly disorderly procedures to cope with problems seen by the organizations as intractable or insoluble. . . . It is useful to recall that the Constitution of the United States was itself written in a closed meeting in Philadelphia; press and outsiders were excluded, and the participants were sworn to secrecy. Historians are agreed that if the convention's work had been made public contemporaneously, it is unlikely that the compromises forged in private sessions could have been achieved, or even that their state governments would have allowed the delegates to write a good constitution. Once the Constitution had been drafted, of course, it was made public and its merits were freely debated and discussed as part of the ratification process."[30]

Organizations, even the most authoritarian and rigidly hierarchical, may tolerate internal discussion and debate and still require their adherents or members to present a united front to the outer world. It is not uncommon to use dissenters as the spokesmen for an official position with which they have privately disagreed in order to bind them to the new policy and to reaffirm the primacy of organizational loyalty over personal belief. Monsignor Ferdinando Lambruschini, a moral theologian at the Lateran University, was a member of a commission of 55 clerics and laymen named by Pope Paul VI to study the question of birth control. He was among the signers of the majority report, which approved modification of the Church's ban on birth control, and which was overruled by a secret high commission that advised the Pope on theology. Subsequent to this, he was selected to present to the press on July 24, 1968, the Papal Encyclical, "Of Human Life," which reaffirmed the total ban on contraception. According to *The New York Times*, "Monsignor Lambruschini carried out his mission loyally, giving no hint either in his initial exposition of the Encyclical or his answers to many challenging questions on it of his own dissent." He was appointed Archbishop of Perugia on October 15, 1968.

It is easy to scorn the man whose changes of stance open him to charges of opportunism. But public men must be judged by the consequences of their acts, rather than by what we take to be their motivations. Individuals in history, from Alexander to Hitler, may have hated their fathers and siblings and loved their mothers to excess; knowledge of such biographical facts helps us understand why they did what they did, but is not especially relevant to the judgments we pass on them. As Alexander Hamilton wrote, "We are not always sure that those who advocate the truth are influenced by purer principles than their antagonists. Ambition, avarice, personal animosity, party opposition, and many other motives not more laudable than these, are apt to operate as well upon those who support as those who oppose the right side of a question."[31]

A candidate for high public office borrows dignity and decency from the demands of the position he seeks for himself. George Wallace, by running in 1968 as a national rather than a regional candidate, was forced to eschew an overt display of bigotry and thereby moved his bigoted constituents in the direction of the national mainstream. Role-playing which disguises the politician's motives and true nature is not to be condemned if it makes him behave as a statesman.

A lawyer may express posttrial opinions critical of a client he has represented in court; such incongruities between formal role and personal belief are taken for granted. But there are some roles that demand total agreement between official and personal opinions when these are voiced in public. The well-known head of a large industrial corporation, at a press conference, reads a statement forecasting a rosy outlook for the general economy and for his own industry and firm. A few hours later, at an off-the-record meeting with a group of fellow-businessmen, he distinguishes between the views he expressed in his capacity as a corporate spokesman and his personal opinion, which he stresses is highly pessimistic. The effect of the second statement is to wipe out the first one.

Vice President Spiro Agnew, in a speech which attacked antiwar demonstrators as "an effete corps of impudent snobs who characterize themselves as intellectuals" was, according to the White House press secretary, expressing "his personal feelings." Similarly, President Nixon "was expressing his personal feelings" in a letter voicing similar skepticism of protest, though not in the same rich rhetoric.

Is it really possible for presidents and vice presidents to express "personal feelings" which are not embodiments of an official position? Certainly this is true in domains of taste which a democratic society excludes from considerations of politics. President Truman's threat to punch a music critic in the nose because of an unfavorable review of his daughter's singing was indeed a statement of personal opinion, as was President Eisenhower's expressed (but harmless) dislike of abstract painting. (The same views expressed by Soviet leaders would have consequences of considerable public concern.) But when a head of state or his second-in-command speaks of political matters how can his words fail to be taken as authoritative?

This accounts for the extraordinary interpretative exercises that follow every presidential press conference. Even the most banal and casual utterances are invested with deep undertones of meaning. Clues as to the meaning and future shape of government policy are sought even in the most simple, brief, and half-articulated replies to questions on which it is obvious that the President has devoted little thought.

Can we assume that the public statements of public men reflect less of their personal convictions than their private statements do? The man who is in the public eye necessarily speaks in accordance with a role, but it is a role that he has chosen, and one that carries with it the responsibility of withholding his doubts and indecisions from view.

The rest of us are no more immune to ambivalence and self-contradiction merely because our thoughts go unrecorded. Our increasingly segmented lives demand that we play a diversity of roles, each with its appropriate set of attitudes. A very old Orangeman, who on his deathbed converted to Catholicism, explained to his shocked family, "better one of them should go than one of us." Honesty may have little relevance to the task of weeding rationalizations and role-play from "true" opinions. Men believe their own lies when they repeat them often enough, and in the absence of free discussion they will voice the repeated lies of others. Yesterday's rationalization becomes today's conviction. What opinion analyst can tell when a lie becomes a truth in the mind of the person who voices it?

Part Six

UNHEARD OPINIONS

ACQUIESCENCE AND FEEDBACK

Power is based on opinion. What is a government not supported by opinion? Nothing.

Napoleon Bonaparte

Beliefs are subject to coercion because men's minds often harbor contradictory impulses. Beliefs are always creatures of circumstances; they alter with new conditions and with shifts of power. To trace such change is the continual task of public opinion research, but this task can be undertaken only under political conditions of freedom and order—freedom for opinions to be expressed openly, and order so that they can be gauged without interference.

Most of what I have said so far about public opinion relates to its formation and expression in a democratic society, in which divergent views can be freely held and freely measured. Only a fraction of mankind lives under political systems in which opinions can be formed through open debate, and in which published polls offer instant feedback on the state of the changing mood. But in no part of the world, and under no form of government, are people's opinions without interest for those who rule and lead them.

All regimes, no matter how repressive, brutal, and violent, no matter how illegitimate or unorthodox their assumption of power, proclaim themselves as the protectors of the people, and as the spokesmen for its true needs and will. Josef Goebbels claimed that the Nazi Party always "advocated as the best course of government that the problems uppermost in everybody's mind should be explained with utter frankness . . . to put every case before the people and discuss it openly is a sign not of weakness but of supreme assurance. We Germans are living in a true democracy, however autocratic the methods of its leadership may sometimes be."[1]

The trappings of representative government may be retained or adopted to provide the semblance of popular support. Even colonial governors purported to rule in the best interests of the natives rather than of the exploiting power. Native chiefs, tribal elders, councils of dignitaries, voting colleges of *"évolués"* have all been used to provide the illusion of a genuine responsiveness to the grass roots. The rituals of the fake plebiscite and the rigged election are part of the paraphernalia which any tinhorn autocrat now regards as essential to the dignity of his office. He must rule with the help of "public opinion."

If our understanding of public opinion is inseparable today, as suggested earlier, from the findings of public opinion surveys, this is only the case in those countries where surveys are permitted. By definition, an authoritarian regime bans open polls, a free press, and other indications of the popular will. It therefore can claim majority support in the absence of contradictory evidence.

Every modern dictator uses his propaganda apparatus to create a popular portrait of himself as folksy and responsive to the mass. Mussolini is a simple hearty fellow surrounded by old wartime cronies; Stalin is a pal to Young Pioneers and collective farm tractor drivers; Lenin absentmindedly tends an old lady's cooking pot. Even Hitler beams upon little pigtailed girls in Tyrolean costumes, bestowing bouquets. Hitler's solicitude for the daily habits of the German people was brought home by Robert Ley, his labor leader: "He says 'take a shower instead of a bath. Why? Because I am worried that a mother might bathe her children one after the other in the same water. I don't want that.' "[2]

The purpose of such imagery is not merely to glorify the Leader by contrasting his residual streak of humanity with what is known to be his absolute power; the purpose is also to proclaim his oneness with the people. He is not merely the ruler; he is the executor of the people's will. He listens to simple men; he communes with them; they understand each other, and this is an understanding that transcends more formal expressions of opinion, such as we take for granted through representative government, a free press, and free political institutions, or for that matter through opinion polls.

A report from Cuba describes Fidel Castro talking in a crowd: "A white-haired lady appears, and for twenty minutes Castro listens. Lips purse, eyes squint. Then from the breast pocket of his olive green uniform he produces a notebook and pen, scribbles a hasty note. This scene is played all over Cuba. Where Castro appears the government of Cuba is at work. That is the Cuban dictatorship?"[3]

A German newspaperman reports on a trip with the Communist leader of Rumania, *after* the liberalization of his regime: "As soon as Ceausescu appears, standing up in the back of a Cadillac convertible (which is preceded by a Jaguar limousine filled with bodyguards and followed by a Mercedes SEL in which Ceausescu rides when it rains), people break through the police barriers. With gestures of supplication, they hand their 'beloved leader' letters. I am told that, formerly, anyone who attempted to do this was gunned down on the spot. Ceausescu, however, accepts the letters, which are petitions requesting redress for their grievances. No one tries to hold the petitioners back, no one starts taking down their names. But these people who walk back into the cheering crowd, their faces showing joy and relief, do not see what happens to their petitions. Nicolae Ceausescu throws them away a few moments later like soiled paper towels, tosses them to the ground—and there they will lie, unread, among the crushed flowers along the side of this road where he passed in triumph."[4]

Although there may be nothing but pretense in the public display of his willingness to hold court and hear grievances, no dictator can fail to be concerned about the popular mood. His power depends upon public acquiescence or toleration, if not upon love or active support.

The significant constituency for a ruler need by no means be identical with the total population he rules. Slaves, serfs, colonials, or other lower orders may be kept by terror or custom in a state of total subjection, and without any particular concern about their feelings on matters of state. Since they are nonpersons, it is easy for the dominant group to delude themselves into thinking that the others are intellectually incapable of formulating serious opinions; when evidence of seditious sentiment arises it is handled by military rather than political means.

We noted earlier that the essence of public opinion is the clash of opposing thoughts and of differing interpretations of the same political phenomena. It is therefore difficult to visualize political "public opinion" in any country where people cannot freely speak their minds or consult more than a single source of news. But this is a matter of degree, for dictatorships may be all-encompassing in their demands for conformity in the domains of taste as well as of politics, or they may be restrictive in only a narrow part of the spectrum of political thought. Consider a Central American dictatorship where the press censors itself in its references to the regime, foreign media rarely have occasion to comment and are banned only when they do, and people feel generally free to talk as they will about the state of the world, except that they know better than to talk too loudly about El Presidente and his family. In such a country there would certainly be, at least among the literate sectors of the urban public, a genuine and open public opinion about world affairs, and even about many domestic issues. Even in the most totalitarian country public opinion may exist with respect to that restricted list of subjects on which people talk to strangers without self-consciousness.

But our concern with public opinion goes beyond conversation about the weather or tastes in food. Public opinion is of significance only to the extent that it deals with the most urgent and poignant questions of public life, and it is precisely these questions on which discussion is generally inhibited by a dictatorship. People in Batista's Cuba felt perfectly free to say anything they wanted to about the United States, or Russia, or the price of rum, but when they talked about the rebels in the Sierra Maestra they lowered their voices.

An isolated dissenter in a totalitarian state does not necessarily see himself as part of a universe of the like-minded. As long as he thinks of his own opinions as those of a solitary deviate he is unlikely to express them, or to take himself seriously as a potential member of the opposition.

In her memoirs, Nadezhda Mandelstam, widow of a poet who died in one of Stalin's prison camps before World War II, writes as follows:

"In his letter to Stalin, Bukharin added a postscript saying he had been visited by Pasternak, who was upset by the arrest of Mandelstam. The purpose of this postscript was clear: it was Bukharin's way of indicating to Stalin what the effect of M.'s arrest had been on public opinion. It was always necessary to personify 'public opinion' in this way. You were allowed to talk of one particular individual being upset, but it was unthinkable to mention the existence of dissatisfaction among a whole section of the community—say, the intelligentsia or 'literary circles.' No group has the right to its own opinion about some event or other."[5]

When free institutions are suppressed, the stifling of unwanted information is always only one aspect of the stifling of dissent. Goebbels stated the objective clearly: "The people shall begin to think as a unit, to react as a unit and to place itself at the disposal of the government with complete sympathy." A contemporary of his, Elizabeth Noelle (now known as the female "Pope" of German public opinion research[6]) observed in 1940: "The role that public opinion plays in America and Germany is very different. In the great 'democracy' on the other side of the ocean it has the function of a corporation whose millions of stockholders dictate the policy of the enterprise. In National Socialist Germany, it seems to us rather as the body of the people (*Volkskörper*) which receives its orders from the head and guarantees their accomplishment, so that through the working together of head and limbs transcendent political and cultural values can be achieved. In one case public opinion rules; in the other it is led."[7]

The authoritarian myth of the People which thinks but one thought and thinks with but one voice (that of the Leader or the Party) is the counterpart of a belligerent stance. The proclaimed national uniformity of outlook is transformed from a psychological advantage into a military asset: national unity and dedication.

Goebbels wrote smugly, "By simplifying the thoughts of the masses and reducing them to primitive patterns, propaganda was able to present the complex process of political and economic life in the simplest terms. . . . We have taken matters previously available only to experts and a small number of specialists, and have carried them into the street and hammered them into the brain of the little man."[8]

Mussolini and Hitler adapted from the Russians the technique of the massive rally, with its theatrical aura of bunting, banners, and spotlights, and the self-reenforcing excitation of the mob under the control of the Leader and his Party apparatus. The Fascists also adopted the technique of the Party Line in the mass media, the ruthless exaction of conformity with regard to every bit of information and every expression of opinion.

Sources of information which are at variance with the official line are automatically labeled as enemy sources; they are either the false propaganda launched by foreign adversaries or the false rumors and defeatist gossip of domestic traitors. Thus the flow of information in a totalitarian society theoretically follows a perfectly closed system; information which enters the system from unauthorized sources must have been introduced for treacherous motives and hence should be rejected with as much vehement incredulity as though it came from the enemy himself.

Misinformation, like information, is a prime source of public opinion, and no doctrinaire ideology can manage without it. A closed-off system of thought must manage facts so that they conform to its design. It is a curious testimony to the vitality of democratic ideals that the enemies of democracy feel impelled to use distortions and lies in their efforts to win and retain adherents. The most satanic autocrats of modern times have a delicate reluctance to flaunt their crimes; the need to deny or disguise them shows a recognition of public opinion as a force to be taken seriously. As we shall see, the term "public opinion" is brandished as a verbal weapon in the world propaganda war even by those who would never tolerate its free expression.

Lies have been and always must be the cornerstone of any totalitarian state, for the only reason to suppress dissenters is that the truth is intolerable; access to conflicting versions of the truth will topple confidence in the state and in its leadership and institutions. Falsification of evidence can muddy the waters, raise doubts, confuse issues, or provide sudden alternative views of events already accurately reported—provided that sufficiently opaque barriers can be interposed between independent newsmen and the evidence.

The landing of men on the moon was kept out of the news media in China, but it cannot be kept from the Chinese. Every propaganda apparatus must reckon that such momentous news will sooner or later filter back into the system through clandestine channels. Propaganda must always be conducted on the assumption that the existence of really significant events will eventually come to light.

Georges Clemenceau was asked by a German diplomat to guess how future historians would assign the guilt for the outbreak of World War I. His reply was, "This I don't know. But I know for certain that they will not say Belgium invaded Germany."[9]

Early in 1945, President Roosevelt was shown evidence of Stalin's massacre of the Polish officer corps at Katyn, but he dismissed it as "German propaganda and a German plot." When George Earle, an intelligence officer, insisted that he would publish the story, Roosevelt ordered him not to do so and transferred him to Samoa.[10] To this day the Soviet government, Soviet media, and Soviet scholarship fail to acknowledge what happened at Katyn, yet those in the Soviet Union who are concerned with Soviet-Polish relations cannot ignore the reality of what took place. There can hardly be a politically conscious person in Russia who is unaware of Khrushchev's denunciation of Stalin at the Twentieth Party Congress, although this speech has not yet been reported in the Soviet press.

Hitler's decision to exterminate the Jews was reached with the sneering question, "Who today remembers the Armenians?" Over half a century later there is, indeed, little awareness in the West of the Turkish massacres. But apart from the Turks, and from the surviving Armenians, *history* knows it. Every propagandist knows in his bones that he cannot wipe the record clean forever. But he can try to wipe it out for long enough to accomplish what he seeks in the short run. He can win breathing time, time for his masters to win the advantage and make their point, time for memories to fade, not only of the event itself, but of his attempt to suppress its traces.

It is one thing to try to consign the landing of man on the moon into the memory hole; it is another and easier matter to obliterate minutiae, the deeds of individual men, the records of particular institutions. The Nazis ascribed Heine's *Lorelei* to anonymous authorship; the works of Trotsky are not listed in the card catalogue of the Great Lenin Library.

The propagandist must be wary of losing credibility with his target audience, by denying the existence of what will sooner or later turn out to have occurred—a city securely occupied by the enemy must eventually be acknowledged as lost. But for each city lost, ten are contested.

The easiest way to change the public's impression of events (and history's) is not to try to turn them into nonevents, but to bury them with invented events. The propagandist confronted with an unwelcome fact may seek to obliterate it by denial or avoidance. He may try to reduce its importance by surrounding and muffling it with other, often irrelevant facts, or by creating a new and fictitious version of the same events, and thereby transforming it from the domain of established truth into the realm of conjecture, debate, and opinion. As Hannah Arendt observes, it is "relatively easy to discredit factual truth as just another opinion."

Television newsman Reuven Frank has described a now familiar figure, "the Soviet UN delegate who keeps saying, 'as is well known' about things which are not well known at all." By the familiar device of incessant repetition the official version of history can be imposed upon the public awareness and the ambiguous records of what really happened can be cropped into more memorable form.

At every historical moment there are always numerous things happening which may or may not be considered relevant to the mainstream of politics. Perceptions of the same occurrences vary with the observer. Therefore it is sometimes hard to tell the boundary line between a genuine interpretation and a misleading one and between a misleading interpretation and a fabrication.

The propagandist's best opportunity to alter the record is by inventing new events after the fact (Stalin's role as Lenin's principal aide in the October Revolution, the American use of germ warfare in Korea, the American military participation in the Six-Day War, and so on) or by rearranging real events into a different sequence or pattern of meaning which gives them new interpretations and turns winners into losers and villains into victims.

A former Vietcong propaganda cadreman notes, "The Vietcong tactic is to exaggerate all the bad news and bad public opinion as far as the government is concerned. For example, the students demonstrate against the government. The Vietcong will exploit this and exaggerate this incident. They will say that the demonstrators have been ruthlessly suppressed. They were killed and arrested because they opposed the government. However, the Vietcong don't make up stories from nowhere. They always base their rumors on real fact or on general public opinion. What they do is simply to exaggerate that piece of news or that public opinion."[11]

Documentary photography has been around for a hundred years and has given us a fulsome record of major historical happenings, including the Russian Revolution. Unfortunately, the real photographs of the major events of the time inevitably portray a great many old Bolsheviks who later fell into disgrace, so they were destroyed during the Stalin period, or replaced by prints so heavily retouched that the original faces are unrecognizable or simply obliterated. Soviet historical museums are full of such photographs, so painted over that they readily merge into the world of illusion from which come the heroic paintings of Lenin addressing the workers, Lenin leading the assault on the Winter Palace, Lenin addressing the Congress of the Soviets, Lenin alone in the garden, pondering. The use of the official court painting is perhaps as typical of the Soviet regime as it was of the Napoleonic period in France. The paintings of Socialist Realism glorify and make permanent events that might otherwise appear to be trivial and transitory. They also serve to place in the realm of fantasy and of historical remoteness happenings which actually remain in the memories of men still living.

Fabrications can provide the appearance of consistency, justice, and reason, even when any or all of these may be absent. The thirst for power, plunder, or advantage must be masked from those who fight the battle, from victims and from onlookers alike. If black and white opposites can be reduced to varying shades of gray, indignation against the aggressor gives way to a sense of confusion over the complexities of the issue, and confusion about the rights and wrongs always provides grounds for apathy and disengagement. Hitler justified the invasion of Poland on the grounds of intolerable Polish provocations. "The South Koreans claim the North Koreans invaded them, and the North Koreans claim it was the South," Communist sympathizers said at the time, objecting to the American intervention and giving both parties equal benefit of the doubt.

There is under every totalitarian regime a subterranean stream of forbidden ideas and information, but it surfaces only when the ground is weakened through other causes. Foreign propaganda in itself cannot convert the trickle of buried whispered private opinions in a tightly controlled society into a free-flowing surge of public opinion which sweeps an unpopular regime out of power. There must be other compelling reasons which lead to disillusionment and make men turn against the state they have been raised to honor.

Every modern dictatorship exacts uniformity of thought on the grounds that the nation is a beleaguered bastion in which deviant ideas are treasonable. Party Secretary Leonid Brezhnev warned Soviet intellectuals, in March 1968, that "Western ideologists had succeeded in winning influence over some groups in Soviet Society. . . . Our enemies in the camp of imperialism clutch with great tenacity at any manifestations of ideological immaturity and hesitations among individual representatives of the intellectuals."[12] Hesitations there are indeed!

The concept of "the public" implies a single body politic, whether or not this is considered to be composed of uniform and homogeneous individual components—as implied in the philosophy of one man-one vote. There is no place for public opinion in the political theory of Marxism-Leninism, which puts emphasis on the separate publics represented by social classes, to each of which an appropriate political ideology corresponds.[13] The significant clash is accordingly that of the publics themselves, of their powers and essential interests, which opinions serve only to rationalize. Opinions that deviate from those appropriate to one's class are irrational; those unrelated to class interest are irrelevant.

Authoritarian societies taboo political polls because they reject the principle of feedback through channels other than those which the authorities can control and manipulate. The existence of dissent or opposition might not, beyond a point, be kept a secret, whether in today's era of fine-meshed communications, or in the cruder, more slowly moving police states of the past. But the nature and extent of opposition are comparatively easy to disguise when no independent measurements are being made. Demonstrations, clandestine publications, and terrorist acts can all equally well be dismissed as the work of a handful of troublemakers. The wider influence of the dissenters, their personal dedication, talent, or influence, can carry no weight amenable to exact measurement or description, and the state's control of the communications media arrests the public's awareness of what is really going on. This control is, however, a two-edged sword, for in the absence of a genuine feedback system, rumors flourish, and small groups of opponents to the regime can cast an extremely long shadow in the eyes of the masses and even of the persecutors.

In a dictatorship, there can be no dividing line between the assessment of the public temper, political intelligence, and police espionage. From Frederick II to Nicholas II, the agents of the King or Emperor were at one and the same time eavesdroppers on the conversations of the mass and detectives ferreting out individual subversives who threatened the established powers. A neat combination of the two was a project of Louis Philippe. A British observer reported as follows on the use of "revolutionary" newspaper vendors as a way of checking revolutionary sentiment in the Paris of 1834: "The town has been infested for the last six weeks with wretched itinerant venders of the most disgusting trash, and abuse against the royal family,—the lowest species of caricatures. I have watched them in the streets; no one noticed them, none purchased their wares; it seemed indeed a most unprofitable trade; but still it was continued, without check on the one side, or encouragement on the other. I at last expressed my surprise to a friend at their impunity. 'Oh,' said he, 'it is an *attrape;* they are agents paid by the police, to sound the feelings of the multitude.' "[14]

Similarly, the block warden system employed by the Nazis used a large network of grass-roots "trusties" to collect information on what their neighbors were talking about.[15] These intelligence data, funneled back, sifted and interpreted at successively higher levels, provided a remarkably objective picture of what Germans felt and worried about as the war progressed, and gave Goebbels invaluable guidance in manipulating the release of good and bad news through the press. At the same time that the system of surveillance uncovered subversives, the universal awareness of its existence discouraged not merely subversion but the expression of defeatist sentiment, antiregime jokes, and other dissident remarks which, if left unchecked, might have become forces in the development of public opinion itself.

There are limits to the systematized collection of data from observation and eavesdropping rather than from direct questioning, since the instruments by which the evidence is gathered can not be standardized, like survey questionnaires. Mass Observation, which started in Britain during World War II, followed the same practice of "tuning in" to what people were talking about, and quoting their remarks verbatim. The underlying supposition is, of course, that what people spontaneously bring up in conversation in public places is a far better index of their real concerns than what they reply to an interviewer on questions they may not previously have thought about.

The survey technique is a worthless instrument in the hands of a dictatorship, since direct political questions are bound to produce answers that accord with the official line. Yet as survey research becomes more widely taken for granted, particularly as an essential tool of marketing and advertising, the mechanics of public opinion polling are maintained today even when dictators rule.

OPINION UNDER "PROLETARIAN DICTATORSHIP"

> *We appeal to world public opinion, and in the first place to Soviet public opinion.*
>
> Moscow petition, 1968

Opinion polling, like other forms of empirical social research, was proscribed in the Soviet Union as "bourgeois social science" until several years after the death of Stalin. (The actual technology of survey research has of course been familiar to Soviet specialists and was used for intelligence purposes in occupied Austria as early as 1946.) In the past decade and a half a new generation of young Soviet sociologists has come to the fore with a strong interest in Western scholarship, theory, and research methods.

At the Spring, 1966 Communist Party Congress, Brezhnev gave the green light: "The development of the social sciences and the implementation of their recommendations are of no less importance than the utilization of the achievements of the natural sciences in the sphere of material production and development of the people's spiritual life. . . . Sociological research, based on a materialist understanding of history and generalizing the concrete facts of life in Socialist society, is day by day playing a bigger role in the solution of practical questions of politics, production, and education."[16]

Although the Party bureaucracy has maintained firm control over publications and Western contacts, there have been increasing participations in international social science meetings, apprenticeships with the French branch of the Gallup organization, and a growing volume of research in the Soviet Union itself, on subjects without overt political content. Soviet industrial sociologists have done highly sophisticated studies of work motivation and youthful job aspirations that document the persistence of strong social class differences in the classless society.[17] Preferences for films and television programs are studied by another research institute at the University of Leningrad, and questionnaires in the press have solicited opinions of consumer goods and services. *Pravda* was itself revamped as the result of a readership survey. Moscow now has an Institute of Public Opinion which has done extensive surveys on how urban Russians spend their time; the results have been published in the Soviet press just like any Gallup Poll in the West, and they have similarly begun to enter the realm of general discussion: Grigory Z. Anashkin, a Justice of the Soviet Supreme Court, called for judicial reforms in an article in *Literary Gazette*. To support his suggestion for strengthening the role of defense attorneys in criminal cases, he cited an opinion poll of 159 policemen, of whom half did not think defense lawyers were necessary.[18]

A poll of 900 Moscow scientific workers under the age of 30 found that 97 percent followed international affairs attentively. A Party savant, Ivan I. Artobolodovsky, cited the detailed findings of this survey as evidence of "skepticism, apolitical attitudes, non-class interpretations of such concepts as democracy, personal freedom and humanism, and a misunderstanding of the roles of the press and other means of mass information."[19]

In East Germany, all local authorities were commanded in March 1968 to cooperate with researchers conducting a public opinion poll on behavior at work, school, and leisure, to determine how young East Germans are "motivated to become useful Socialist personalities." In Rumania, consumer surveys have been hailed as a vital tool of centralized economic planning. In Poland, a strong pre-Communist tradition of social research has been vigorously revived.

Thus, in spite of all ideological resistance, polling has inevitably come into use in the Communist countries as a necessary information resource for an advanced industrial society. The need for consumer surveys and other research on what appear to be safe apolitical subjects produces a corps of practitioners whose expertness depends not merely on their statistical knowledge but on their skills as questioners and analysts. These skills run into areas of greater depth and seriousness than appear on the surface of the subject matter. Once the survey mechanism is set in motion, it cannot be confined to the trivia of consumer preference or job satisfactions, because these can only be understood in the light of a deeper understanding of the values that men cherish. There are no safe subjects for independent investigation in societies where freedom is constrained.

The brief flowering of liberalism in Czechoslovakia during 1968 was accompanied by a considerable amount of press and public attention to political polls and their findings. Under the Dubcek regime the Action Program of the Czech Communist Party called for systematic use of opinion research. In March, a poll conducted by the Research Institute of the Academy of Science showed only 23 percent of the public were in favor of General Svoboda as president. (Svoboda subsequently became a hero of the resistance to the Russians.) The interesting point is that such survey results were prominently published in spite of their damaging implications for the regime. After the Soviet invasion, polling in Czechoslovakia was redirected into safer channels, but it did not disappear.

Outside the Soviet bloc, in Yugoslavia, a variety of research institutes conduct mass media audience studies, market research, and a surprising amount of polling on politically charged subjects. The report of one such survey, which delved into public interest and opinions on issues confronting the Congress of the League of Communists, was distributed to all delegates to the Congress as essential background material for their deliberations. In Cuba too, polls are run to guide officialdom.

In spite of the long-standing Communist suspicion of public opinion *research,* the phrase "public opinion" has been heard more frequently on the lips of Communist spokesmen, always, to be sure, in contexts where no objective verification is possible.

The broader the public whose opinion is described, the more vague and ambiguous that description must be. It is therefore not surprising that in the Communist lexicon, "world public opinion"—which is of course unmeasurable—occupies a more prominent place than Soviet public opinion, which could be measured and published but isn't, on any subject that really matters.

Comparatively early in the Vietnam war, spokesmen for the Communist side began to use references to American and world opinion in their public statements.[20] As early as August 5, 1964, Radio Hanoi denounced the American imperialists "before world public opinion." The next day the North Vietnamese press wrote, "We call on world public opinion, particularly United States public opinion, to sternly condemn the United States ruling circles."

Later, as negotiations proceeded, such references were continually advanced by the Communists to support their bargaining positions on any point under discussion: American proposals for private talks were merely an attempt "aimed at deceiving and calming public opinion. . . . The progress or the deadlock of the Conference depends on the United States public opinion at large which demands that the United States adopt a more serious attitude." There was an "irreversible tide of public opinion against the war in the United States, including popular refusal to accept further casualties." The purpose of American troop withdrawals was only to "placate American public opinion and bide time."

Such references were never accompanied by any actual citations of American poll results. Although these did show an unmistakable trend toward antiwar sentiment, they also showed majority support for the war policy of both the Johnson and Nixon administrations at the time of the Communist statements.

The North Vietnamese did not stand alone among the socialist democracies in calling upon the heavenly forces of public opinion to condemn the American imperialists: The premier of Outer Mongolia, Yumzhagiin Tsedenbal, added his mite: "Public opinion in Mongolia resolutely demands that the United States of America should stop the dangerous provocations aggravating tensions in this area."[21]

In an interview with *Life*,[22] Premier Alexei Kosygin referred scoffingly to the South Vietnamese government as one which "has no support either of the people of South Vietnam or of world public opinion."[23] The Americans were not the only target of Soviet criticism in which public opinion was used as a weapon. In a speech to world Communist leaders in Moscow on June 7, 1969, Brezhnev warned that "A section of progressive world opinion still believes that the present Chinese leadership has revolutionary aspirations, believes its assertions that it is fighting Imperialism." Note that the significant constituency in this case was restricted from "world opinion" to "progressive world opinion"—a universe definable at the option of the speaker. (The Chinese Communists were, for that matter, also fascinated by the same magic phrase. On one occasion the Red Guard tabloid accused the former Mayor of Peking of confusing his words with Mao's "so as to pass fish eyes for pearls and mislead public opinion.")

The periodic resurfacing of libertarian sentiments after years of dictatorial subjugation—in Spain, Hungary, East Germany, Poland, Czechoslovakia, and the Soviet Union—shows how hardy are the seeds of human curiosity and critical intelligence. The new generations which come of age under a dictatorial regime rediscover for themselves the forgotten truths of history and the continuing values of Western civilization. In spite of the most stringent controls over what children learn in the schools and what everyone learns from the media, it is simply not possible to stanch completely the flow of fresh information and rebellious thoughts.

With the rulers of Russia making easy references to the power of public opinion, it is not surprising to find similar references cropping up from the Soviet underground. After the crushing of Czech freedom, Anatoly T. Marchenko addressed these words to Czechoslovak and Western Communist newspapers and to the British Broadcasting Corporation: "Our newspapers have been trying to misinform public opinion in our country and at the same time to misinform world public opinion on our people's attitude 'toward the events in Czechoslovakia'. . . . The newspapers present the position of the Party leadership as the position— even the unanimous position—of all the people."[24]

A young scientist, Yuri Morozov, in a letter addressed to pupils in his hometown school, wrote, "A huge part of my generation has developed a persistent immunity against ideological demagogy." The newspaper *Soviet Russia* published his letter with a rebuttal that referred to a survey showing that 96 percent of the young people in Moscow and Leningrad read the official press (as though they had any option!). The paper acknowledged defensively that "there are people who, like Morozov, seem to shut their ears to repetitions of official ideas. But does the interest and value of an idea depend on whether it is official or not?"[25]

To address letters to the foreign press would have been unthinkable in the days of Stalin. In today's less brutally monolithic era, appeals to foreign opinion have been followed by imprisonment rather than by execution, and the inevitable punishment has been an acceptable price for those brave enough to puncture the official myth of unified public support. A Soviet poet, Natalia Gorbanevskaya, arrested and beaten on Red Square for protesting the invasion of Czechoslovakia, later sent a letter to foreign newspapers addressed to "world public opinion." She says: "My comrades and I are happy that we were able to take part in this demonstration and that we were able even briefly to break through the sludge of unbridled lies and cowardly silence and thereby demonstrate that not all the citizens of our country are in agreement with the violence carried out in the name of the Soviet people."[26]

Larissa Bogoraz-Daniel, also condemned to prison for protesting the invasion, said just before she was sentenced, "The prosecutor ended his summation by suggesting that the verdict will be supported by public opinion. I, too, have something to say about public opinion. I do not doubt that public opinion will support this verdict, as it would approve of any other verdict. The defendants will be depicted as social parasites and outcasts and people of different ideologies. Those who will not approve of the verdicts, if they were to state their disapproval, will follow me here to this dock."

The injustice meted out to Soviet dissenters is beside the point of this chapter. What is important here is that both victims and persecutors feel impelled to appeal to the higher force of world public opinion as the arbiter of ultimate justice.

The very notion that *vox populi* should be heeded is, I have said, a sharp departure from the dogma of class conflict. The dictatorship of the proletariat has always been justified as a temporary device necessitated by the political immaturity of backward sectors of the working class, as well as by the need to crush counterrevolutionary opposition. But the public transcends class boundaries and the world public reaches out even farther. At some point, Party ideologists will have to reconcile Marxist theory with their own continuing reliance on public opinion as a political super-ego. The problem will be all the more challenging for them because survey research is now too well established and too useful to their country to be abandoned or ignored. Even unpublished studies of public opinion must give the Soviet leaders a greater sensitivity to the wishes and needs of their people, and thus be a force for change.

IS THERE A WORLD PUBLIC OPINION?

Opinion ultimately governs the world.

Woodrow Wilson

It is not only in the Communist countries that the phrase, "world public opinion," has become a commonplace. In recent years world opinion has been cited by statesmen around the globe to support their positions on such matters as the Greek constitutional crisis, the Arab-Israeli conflict, the Pakistani-Indian war, an unsuccessful leftist coup in Indonesia, the hijacking of airplanes, and, as already noted, the Vietnam war.

In the gamesmanship of disarmament negotiation, world opinion may be a powerful force—or it may be used cynically as a ploy. Harold Agnew, Director of the Weapons Division of Los Alamos Laboratories, complains (presumably on behalf of the last word in nuclear weapons), "Nothing is more stifling to innovation than seeing one's product not used or ruled out of consideration on flimsy premises involving public world opinion."

Is world opinion a reality to study and contend with? Or is it no more than a rhetorical artifact, a latter-day version of the particularistic and protective Deity who served every national cause in the wars of the past?

Nearly a century and a half ago Alexis de Tocqueville predicted that "By whatever political laws men are governed in the ages of equality, it may be foreseen that faith in public opinion will become for them a species of religion, and the majority its ministering prophet."[27] It is undoubtedly a sign of the times that selfish national political causes are today defended with the cry that they are supported by world public opinion rather than by celestial powers. Since the preferences of world opinion are no less difficult to establish than those of divine partisanship, such claims to higher patronage are hard to dispute.

To speak of "the opinions of mankind" (as the American Declaration of Independence did in 1776) implies that there are subjects of broad consensus throughout the ranks of humanity. Are there indeed such subjects? Perhaps on the rules of interpersonal conduct: hospitality to guests, deference to the aged, courtesy to strangers. The collective opinions of mankind on major issues (peace, economic growth, scientific progress) resolve into a series of platitudes. Lack of agreement about means rather than ends represents the chief obstacle to a world-wide public opinion.

In the eleventh edition of the *Encyclopedia Brittanica* (1911), an article on Balkan history refers to the shocked reactions of world public opinion to atrocities committed in the course of the Greek war for independence. If one can speak of an articulate international public opinion in the 1820s, can one speak of an incensed public opinion at the time of the Crusades, of the Hun invasions, or of the Goths and Vandals centuries earlier?

When rapid and fundamental transformations of opinion lead to drastic political upheavals, they generally do so within the geographical limits fixed by history. Social revolution, with rare exceptions, has taken place within the framework of national states. Even when revolution has been international, it has not been world-wide. The political ideal of a world order remains remote.[28] There is no "responsible" political mechanism involved in world public opinion analogous to that in the national state. International organizations like the United Nations have as their constituents individual nations rather than the population of the world at large.

The mechanics of survey research may help to create the illusion that opinions are international, because they can be traced from one country to the next. In every major Western country, opinion research is now routine. Several commercial research networks make it possible to run parallel surveys with the same questions in many different parts of the world. Even where public opinion research in the Western sense is not regularly carried on, there is apt to be some occasional practice of the survey method. United Nations teams research the incidence of medical symptoms in remote villages of the African bush; market researchers check the consumption of soap in Latin American shantytowns.

The State Department has for years conducted opinion surveys in a number of countries to check the comparative popularity rating of the

United States and the Soviet Union, like any manufacturer checking his brand of soap against a competitor. Most of this research has been conducted without any attempt to disguise its sponsorship.

The Central Intelligence Agency tested the political mood in Greece in the spring of 1967 with a "secret opinion poll," according to the German magazine *Stern,* which charged that this brought about the military *coup d'état* and forestalled elections.[29] The poll allegedly predicted that the opposition Liberal Center Union and Left would win 63 percent of the straw votes, which would mean the end of the conservative regime and possibly of the royal dynasty, "the two pillars of American policy." Whether or not this report is accurate, it reflects a widespread impression abroad of international surveys as a tool of American intelligence. Since the debacle of Project Camelot in Latin America, United States government-sponsored research abroad has been done circumspectly, if at all.[30]

Sociologists Irving Louis Horowitz and Lee Rainwater regard one aspect of the Camelot affair as particularly tragic: "not that the C.I.A. supported research in sensitive areas, but that nearly all 'respectable' agencies lacked either the wisdom or the funds to support such research."[31] In fact, the C.I.A. and the Pentagon planned the Bay of Pigs invasion without consulting a thoroughgoing analysis of Cuban public opinion that had already been prepared and that would have warned them not to expect any popular rally to support the invaders.[32]

The emergence of polling on an international scale suggests that public opinion is itself now a worldwide phenomenon. But does multinational polling prove any more than that parallel research exercises may be carried out in many places at once, like the spring maneuvers of armies not allied? When the findings of cross-country surveys are published, the implication is that similar answers to the same questions reflect similar salience or significance for these questions in different countries. Yet identical responses may emerge by coincidence from entirely different causes, or in entirely separate historical or cultural contexts.[33] Similar percentages responding "yes" in Italy and England, say, may actually reflect deep-seated convictions in one case and in the other no more than a conventional playback of the prevailing views expressed by the institutions of mass persuasion. For understandable pragmatic reasons, reports of multinational surveys customarily ignore this type of qualitative distinction.[34]

In every country, the national system of mass media is prominent among the institutions that raise invisible barriers to circumscribe the outlook of the citizenry.

The psychoanalyst Harry Stack Sullivan refers to "parataxic distortions" that arise in interpersonal conduct.[35] These distortions represent one individual's self-centered and narrow views of events that involve other people. Sullivan is not concerned with paranoid delusions, but with the common misperceptions that arise in the stress and strain of ordinary interpersonal conduct. Private motivations and needs shape perception so that the same objective reality takes on completely different meaning in the eyes of two participants.

There is an obvious parallel between this type of neurotic behavior at the level of lovers, parents and child, husband and wife, superior and subordinate, rivals or competitors, and the behavior of nations engaged in a conflict of vital interest.

In the classical Chinese opera, the faces of the actors are painted in a masklike manner to designate symbolically the character of the personages they portray: virtue, duplicity, vengefulness, and so on. What the characters actually say and do is almost irrelevant because their true nature has already been revealed by the color of their face paint.

In today's mass media, particularly in wartime, not only cartoons and caricatures but verbal clichés and stereotypes are used to represent the character of the national adversary. What the adversary says or does may be irrelevant if his inherently evil nature is already known to us by the color of his mask. His motives are predictable; his actions can no longer be explained by ordinary human standards. This kind of distortion is more or less generally true of the way in which media in most countries depict the outer world, and particularly those sectors they define as hostile.

The mass media are essentially parochial in character.[36] In every country they look at the world from a national perspective. They focus strongly on local interests and personalities. Not only in the press but in audiovisual media, the "news" tends to be what is happening close to home. Things happening nearby are perceived as familiar and amenable to control. Disproportionately little attention is typically paid to distant events of far greater ultimate consequence. This parochialism exists in socialist and capitalist, in industrialized and underdeveloped countries. It is true in spite of the existence of worldwide news services, in spite of the widespread dissemination of films, recordings, and television programs. Those common threads of information that filter though all the many different selective nets of national media systems become worldwide knowledge in spite of those national systems and not because of them.

The mass media reflect the power structures of national states. This is clearly and unmistakably a matter of intention in those countries where the media express the official position of the government or the Party and where they are assigned a definite mission in mobilizing public support for national policies. It is no less true in Western countries in which operational control of the mass media is in private hands, but where their financial foundation is inseparable from the prevailing economic institutions. Whether under private or official control, mass media tend to be voices of conformity. This inherent conservatism reinforces their tendency to be parochial in outlook.

In recent years there has been a rapid acceleration of the forces making for global unity of information and culture. But this tendency has taken place largely within the framework of national mass media systems rather than through international mass media, communicating directly with a worldwide audience. Whereas specialized or technical publications have international audiences, as is true for the living arts—literature, painting, music, and theater—this kind of international public does not exist for the mass media as we usually define them. Here tremendous barriers still exist.

First and foremost is the barrier of language. Most people in most countries are unable to communicate except in their native tongue. And even among those who know other languages, few indeed have either the intellectual stamina or the incentive to eavesdrop, as it were, on broadcasts or publications addressed to the audience of another nationality.[37]

Media distribution across national boundaries is inhibited by a variety of nonpolitical factors; the expense or physical difficulty of transporting publications, records or films, the absence of needed equipment or trained technicians, the slowness of transport.

There are differences in the popular tastes and interests of different cultures, as in the case of national games, dances, and musical forms. This is often carried over into areas of intellectual content. In any case, the effect is to discourage voluntary exposure to media of nonlocal origins.

Another barrier arises from differences in the mores of different societies. Even when they are clearly communicated, symbols do not necessarily signify the same meanings, nor do they have the same importance to people of different cultures. This is all the more serious because people tend to insulate themselves from experience or information which is in any way not in conformity with what is customary and comfortable. In an institutionalized form, this kind of barrier is defined as political or ideological in nature. Countries in many parts of the world and of varying political persuasions censor or restrict access to incoming foreign mass media in order to protect their citizens from communications which are deemed to be hostile, tendentious, or false. Sometimes what appears to be a political barrier may actually have a very simple economic basis, as when countries limit the importation of films because they lack foreign exchange. All these factors together have inhibited the emergence of international mass media, with only a few exceptions, of which the *Reader's Digest* is perhaps the most remarkable, since its editorial origins are predominantly American.

In impoverished preindustrial countries the messages of the mass media are carried by word-of-mouth far beyond the primary audience to reach many people who themselves have no direct contact with radio, television, or the press. Today every folk society must contend with an increased flow of new information and with the repercussions of events in the world at large. The common symbol of this is the Bedouin on his camel looking up at the jet airplane in the sky. Even in the most primitive areas of the world there is at least a dim awareness that the price of salt or kerosene is in some way influenced by the decisions of powerful men a long way off. The names of these men and the slogans that identify them are known even in the depths of the bush. Lord Ritchie-Calder reports that he has "mushed" with Eskimos "who had Geiger counters on their dogsleds to seek uranium and battery radio receivers to pick up the quotations of the Montreal metal market to see whether it was worth looking for uranium."[38]

Mass media establish commonly understood reference points. These may have technological or even political connotations, as do Sputnik and Apollo, but more often they are in the domain of popular culture such as the Beatles and Mickey Mouse. One of the curious by-products of the newer mass media is that they have placed political figures, imaginary cartoon characters, and movie actresses in the same fantasy world of stardom.

Broadcasting changes the requirement that public opinion be dependent on mass literacy. Broadcasting makes significant personalities and events familiar to more people; perhaps even more important, it creates an illusion of familiarity where it may not be justified. Power over broadcasting is generally more concentrated than control of the press; moreover, nationwide broadcasting systems tend to create a centralized common experience, whereas the reading of a newspaper or magazine is selective both in the reader's choice among periodicals and in his choice of items to read.

A truly closed information system is inconceivable in a world of radios, a world in which literate people live in large metropolitan aggregations that strain the capacities of police surveillance and in which even the most isolated and poverty-stricken state sends diplomats and cargoes overseas and accepts others in exchange.

The adoption of the German song "Lili Marlene" by the British Army in World War II and the growth of the Soviet black market in Western music both demonstrate how readily popular culture leapfrogs boundaries. The fashions and tastes that predominate where culture is totally free from official controls emerge from underfoot wherever an oppressive state apparatus keeps the media under its heel.

In spite of radio jamming or restrictions on the importation of foreign publications, no nation can be totally isolated from the world's cultural and intellectual mainstream. Even in the United States, a 1966 survey found 2 percent of the public claiming to listen to foreign short-wave broadcasts at least once a month; the percentage may be small, and is probably overstated, but it projects to an audience of millions.[39] The 27,000,000 short-wave radios in the Soviet Union are a significant link with Western ideas and with alternate sources of news. As much as two-thirds of the Soviet public is estimated to listen regularly to Western broadcasts.

It would, however, be a mistake to assume that where listening to (or viewing of) foreign broadcasts takes place, whether clandestine and punishable (as in China today) or tacitly tolerated (as in Yugoslavia or even as in Hungary), it manages to attract any substantial part of the population on a regular basis.[40] It is mainly in times of crisis that people in a dictatorship listen to the "enemy" radio in the hope of gleaning information or insights that they would not have otherwise. At such times, rumors circulate quickly.

After five decades of Soviet censorship a young university student in Moscow could ask a foreign visitor about one of his intellectual idols, "Is Sigmund Freud known in the United States?" But in Alma-Ata, a few miles from the Chinese border, in a play written by a local Russian playwright and performed by an amateur cast, the hero's fantasies were of Brigitte Bardot (whose films were known in the Soviet Union only by second-hand reportage).

Since the earliest years of this century, the motion picture has been a tremendous force for the creation of universal symbols and values and for the sharing of common human experiences. Seen in the dark, under conditions which arouse the most intense dramatic identification on the part of the audience, motion pictures can create empathy with protagonists who stem from a different culture, speak a strange language, and live in an unfamiliar geographic environment.

When this quality of audiovisual communication is translated through documentary television into the worldwide reporting of great events at the moment they happen, new possibilities are opened to the sharing of collective experience. Thus far, international television has been largely limited to sports, entertainment, and ceremony, like the funeral of Churchill. But the intensity with which strong mass sentiments can be mobilized, as at the times of the Kennedy assassination or the moon landings, suggests the beginnings of a new dimension in the creation of history.

Communication satellites have revolutionized international communication, with great implications for the eventual creation of a worldwide public opinion. Within a few years it will become technically possible, with only minor adaptations, for both radio and television signals to be sent (or jammed) from any transmitter to any receiver in the world. But until this is a reality, the universal flow of ideas and information must depend on the national mass media systems which mediate, edit, and interpret for their own audiences.[41]

What is the meaning of "public opinion" in societies where literacy is universal and where the media are highly developed, compared to its meaning in those societies whose mass media are within access of only a small literate elite? Can the same phrase, "public opinion," be applied to countries that enjoy a high degree of political freedom and those in which deviant utterance is repressed or discouraged? Can one regard public opinion as comparable in countries where polls are a familiar part of the life of politics and marketing and countries in which the state of public opinion is itself a matter of diverse opinion among experts? Such questions raise their own doubts about the meaningfulness of a world opinion which takes so many different shapes.

The absence of a common political constituency makes the "opinions of mankind" unmeasurable. When opinions are unmeasurable, either by surveys or at the ballot box, they often go unheard and usually go unheeded.

Part Seven

OPINIONS IN REVOLUTION

FORCING SOCIAL CHANGE

The transition of an oppressed nation to democracy is like the effort by which nature arose from nothingness to existence. You must entirely refashion a people whom you wish to make free, destroy its prejudices, alter its habits, limit its necessities, root up its vices, purify its desires.

Committee of Public Safety[1]

Political opinions must exert their pressures within the constraints of political systems, responsive or indifferent as these may be to what people think, and reluctant or eager as they may be to direct people's thinking. The essence of a democratic polity is its sensitivity to the emerging views of significant minorities as well as to the mood of the majority. Since opinion research reflects the diversity of goals and priorities in contemporary society, it is incompatible with the totalitarian illusion of monolithic national unity; it is also an obstacle to those who seek to hasten the processes of social change by tactics that bypass the normal machinery of persuasion.

Such extralegal methods must interest us insofar as they are intended to jolt established beliefs; the rationale for their use returns us again to the question of whether and why public opinion should be obeyed by those who hold power, and thus to the question of whether the polls are a meaningful measurement of public opinion.

What is the justification for the use of revolutionary tactics under a

177

political system which freely permits deviant opinions to be heard and their advocates to seek office? The answer first given by Marx and Engels, and repeated with embellishments and local variations over the years, is that bourgeois democracy merely provides the illusion of freedom for the masses, whose leaders are placed over them by monopoly capital, and whose access to information and opinion is limited to what their rulers impose upon them. The workings of democratic institutions represent no more than the mythological facade by which entrenched economic power perpetuates itself. The public opinion of the moment is therefore little more than what the oligarchy wants people to believe, in order to suit its own selfish and sinister purposes. Herbert Marcuse writes, "The majority of the people is the majority of their masters; deviations are easily 'contained'; and concentrated power can afford to tolerate (perhaps even defend) radical dissent as long as the latter complies with the established rules and manners (and even a little beyond it). The opposition is thus sucked into the very world which it opposes—and by the very mechanisms which allow its development and organization."[2]

The social philosopher Norman Birnbaum, like Marcuse, writes of a "manipulated" consensus: "The control of access to information, the control of the mass media of communication, the command of the system of education allow those who dominate the political order to impose their ideological will upon an intellectually inert population. How often, in industrial society, does one hear ordinary persons repeating as if they were their own the most insipid, the crudest of clichés derived from the channels of mass communication."[3]

Is American public opinion no more than the reflection of biased reportage and interpretations of events, imposed upon the population by mass media operated in the political interest of the ruling "power elite" as well as for their profit? This is not the place to defend the democratic virtues of American institutions, nor to analyze the complex processes which govern the output of news and opinion in the American press. We have already observed that under *any* system the media are centers of power and inevitably linked to the other centers of economic and political power. Can the truth and the public interest ever be served when these powers are linked in a monolithic structure? The free movement and clash of ideas on public issues can take place only as long as control of the media is diversified and their management operates under professional constraints. Revolutionaries may regard the press and the broadcasters as the principal force by which their enemies poison opinion against them. But whatever support they muster derives from their ability to generate news and thereby make their position known to the public, through the very media whose integrity they scornfully reject.

At a time of revolution, wrote de Tocqueville, opinions are "reduced to a sort of intellectual dust, scattered on every side, unable to collect, unable to cohere."[4] When opinions are volatile, they are also resistant to accurate measurement. Political instability must inevitably prevail when authority is under attack and no one really knows for sure where popular sympathies lie. How can there be civic order when inferences about what people find acceptable or consider important must be made from rumor, from the official utterances of the state, or from the terrorist actions that threaten its stability?

Needless to say, the prevalence of violence—or the distrust which surrounds the threat of violence—inhibits even the most innocuous forms of polling. The simplest consumer surveys presented difficulties in the last months of Batista's reign in Cuba, when bombs went off regularly in public places. The difficulties become greater under conditions of open civil war, as in Vietnam, where polling was introduced by American tacticians of counterinsurgency.[5] Great errors and uncertainties are apparent to the professional as he examines the results of polls conducted in times of trouble; moreover, the findings are generally held suspect by the public itself. No one knows what public opinion really is under these conditions. Thus not merely the regime but its militant opposition may *claim* the support of the majority, and acts of terror and counterterror may equally be justified as manifestations of broad public opinion.

A stable and orderly society depends on the sense of cohesion between its members and its ruling institutions. It is not necessary for the merits of these institutions to be respected, or for their leaders to be loved, but it is necessary for their legitimacy to be accepted. The destruction of public order, whether it takes the form of littering the streets, looting the supermarket, or burning the university, represents a rejection of the social bond between the individual and the state's apparatus and traditions. In a revolutionary period, this type of alienation may become so widespread that the prevailing authorities find no supporters when their power is violently assaulted.

Violence has always been an appropriate form of political action under a police rule where normal channels of expression are unavailable to dissenters and where the way to peaceful change is barred by an oppressive state power. Acts of terror against the hated oppressor are then regarded as the *true* outcries of public opinion, and independent observers may report them as such in the press of the world outside. In the nineteenth century, assassination and arson were common weapons of revolutionaries faced with autocratic imperial regimes such as those of the Tsars or the Hapsburgs. In the twentieth century the use of violence has been an effective weapon of nationalist revolutionary movements confronting an established colonial rule.[6]

The struggles of African peoples for independence have successfully (in Kenya and Algeria) or unsuccessfully (in Angola) employed terrorist tactics that seem grisly and barbaric to anyone who feels the slightest empathy with the victims (who characteristically are innocents selected at hazard). The most vicious and oppressive colonial governments have appealed to "law and order" to justify their brutal countermeasures (which, also characteristically, claim far more innocent victims than the original terror).

Any occupying force, even when its proclaimed objectives are exploitation, enslavement, and genocide (for example, the Nazis in Russia), imposes a facade of legitimate authority, complete with its ceremonies, office holders, uniforms, and orderly systems and procedures of administration. These are necessary for effective control and to maintain at least some semblance of an economy.

Those who challenge this forcibly imposed authority (vicious or benign as it may turn out to be) are invariably in the position of disrupting the routine of civilian life which demands that banks be open, railroads run, and the streets be safe. Just as the average citizen's desire to avoid trouble can lead to the toleration of guerrilla activities ("Maybe if they get what they want it will stop; I don't want to get involved!"), so the desire to avoid trouble inhibits mass opposition even to the most intolerable of regimes.

In such a situation the task of dedicated rebels must be to raise the level of disorder and violence to the point where authorities lose their illusory aura of legitimacy; where they break their own rules through random reprisals against innocent victims; where, in short, they represent the same kind of menace to personal security that is represented by the revolutionaries, and with less moral reason to support them.

A disciplined revolutionary party apparatus does not have to use guerrilla violence to achieve direct military objectives. It uses violence for its psychological effect on public opinion, for its ability to give the world at large the impression of a *threat* to power.[7]

In Cuba and in Algeria, isolated acts of terror were used by the revolutionaries to demoralize the forces of the state. These incidents aroused anxieties directly among the defenders of established authority and thus served an indirect military purpose. More important, they raised questions about the regime's ability to maintain that order which is the fundamental criterion of a viable government. These questions were raised in the minds of the population, of the world at large, and of the regime's own functionaries. If they equate guerrilla actions with public opinion (which may or may not be the case), officials must become privately convinced that they are sitting on a powderkeg of popular hostility.

Algerian terrorism was directed at the disenchantment of metropolitan France, not at the destruction of the French Army, and it succeeded brilliantly, just as the Vietcong's militarily futile Tet offensive succeeded in disillusioning the American public about the imminence of victory in Vietnam. On the other hand, the terrorist tactics of the Algerian *colon* O.A.S., both in Algeria and in France, were unsuccessful, as were the comparable but less bloody outrages of the Weathermen who smashed windows and bombed buildings in the United States at the start of the 1970s. In both instances, the guerrillas had no significant popular support, and there was no confusion as to where authority firmly lay.

The philosophers of freedom have always defended the use of force to undermine the "law and order" imposed by tyranny. The problem is that any regime can be termed a tyranny by those who seek to destroy it. "There is a violence that liberates and there is a violence that enslaves," said Mussolini. "There is moral violence and stupid, immoral violence." One's own violence is, of course, always the moral kind. Lenin likened the disagreeable aspects of revolution to the breaking of eggs in making an omelette.

From the vantage point of subsequent history, the anti-Nazi partisans of World War II (who have served as a model for the Communist guerrillas of Latin America and Southeast Asia, as well as for the Arab *fedayeen* and the Angolan rebels) appear to be the genuine exponents of their national aspirations, and the legitimate spokesmen and representatives of their people in the struggle against the foreign oppressor and his puppet government. Only a tiny number of Frenchmen were in the Maquis, and a numerically far larger number served as loyal functionaries of the Vichy government, just as they had earlier served the Third Republic and then went on to serve the Fourth and Fifth. Yet history acknowledges that the few brave men who put their lives on the line against the enemy expressed the national conscience to a degree not manifested in their numbers.

There is abundant evidence that the partisans of World War II had the tacit support of a large part of the silent population. But the same tactics can be used effectively even when the population at large has no particular interest in the rebels or sympathy for them, *provided* that the established authorities similarly enjoy no strong measure of popular support.

Even a comparatively popular uprising ordinarily involves only a fraction of the population. After the 1956 rebellion against the Soviet-imposed Kadar regime in Hungary, a refugee survey conducted by Radio Free Europe estimated that 11 percent of the population had fought with gun in hand, 16 percent had actively participated without fighting, and 8 percent had provided other support. The same survey estimated that while 2 percent of the public opposed the revolution, 63 percent were inactive, though not against it.[8]

Social revolution may emerge from the force of a public opinion whose expression finds no legitimate channels. But it may also result from the effectively organized actions of a minority which seizes control of state institutions and thereby acquires legitimacy, authority, and leadership over public opinion itself.[9] Newspaper plants and broadcasting transmitters are always among the first targets of a revolt.

Every mass political movement has always begun with a handful of dedicated people who have the will to persist in their organizing efforts through periods of adversity and indifference. Prince Kropotkin describes the revival of the Socialist movement in France after the bloody suppression of the Commune:

"Our beginnings were ridiculously small. Half a dozen of us used to meet in cafés, and when we had an audience of a hundred persons at a meeting we felt happy. No one would have guessed then that two years later the movement would be in full swing. But France has its own ways of development. When a reaction has gained the upper hand, all visible traces of a movement disappear. Those who fight against the current are few. But in some mysterious way, by a sort of invisible infiltration of ideas, the reaction is undermined; a new current sets in, and then it appears all of a sudden, that the idea which was thought to be dead was there alive, spreading and growing all the time; and as soon as public agitation becomes possible, thousands of adherents, whose existence nobody suspected, come to the front. 'There are at Paris,' old Blanqui used to say, 'fifty thousand men who never come to a meeting or to a demonstration; but the moment they feel that the people can appear in the streets to manifest their opinion, they are there to storm the position.' "[10]

In Kropotkin's day, the objective of revolutionary conspirators was still primarily to establish a mass following rather than to seize power with the disregard for public opinion that characterizes an élitist *coup d'état*.[11] The storming of the Winter Palace was a deliberate military action; the storming of the Bastille was the spontaneous outburst of an angry mob. Though only a few hundred men were involved in the actual attack on the Bastille, there were a quarter-million Parisians under arms during those days of July 1789.

In George Rudé's description, "A more or less peacefully disposed Sunday crowd of strollers in the Palais Royal was galvanized into revolutionary vigor by the news of Necker's dismissal and the call to arms issued by orators of the entourage of the Duke of Orleans. From this followed a sequence of events that could not have possibly been planned or foreseen in detail by even the most astute and determined of the court's opponents."[12]

Compare this accidental scenario with the skillful maneuvering of Lenin and his associates, directing the minority of Bolshevik activists from the stronghold of the Smolny Institute! Today we are apt to visualize the Russian Revolution in terms of the romantic myth concocted in Sergei Eisenstein's cutting room. Actors costumed as "The People" rush across the vast open plazas on the banks of the Neva. Red banners flutter; the guns of the Aurora sound.

In truth, riots, confrontations, and urban guerrilla warfare are pinpricks to the daily routine of a great metropolis. Life went on pretty much as usual in Petrograd in October 1917. The stores were open, the trolley cars ran.[13] People assumed that if they simply ignored the trouble, it might just go away.

"Ten men acting together," wrote Count Mirabeau, "can make 100,000 tremble apart." In guerrilla operations, tremendous military leverage can be exerted by a small number of armed men—regardless of whether they have a civilian following (as in Cuba and Algeria) or do not (as in Bolivia, Malaya, and the Philippines). The same principle—exacting an enormous retributive price for very little expenditure of effort—is easily translated to the urban scene.

Today's society, dependent upon complex technology, is highly vulnerable to sabotage, hijacking, kidnaping, and disruption. Contemporary revolutionary theory starts with this fact. On the one hundred and seventh anniversary of the Emancipation Proclamation, the Black Panthers issued a message which read, "The United States of America is a barbaric organization controlled and operated by avaricious, sadistic, bloodthirsty thieves. . . . The power we rely upon ultimately as our only guarantee against genocide at the hands of the Fascist Majority is our strategic ability to lay this country in ruins, from the bottom to the top."

This is bluster, to be sure, but not every such threat can be laughed away. A handful of determined zealots *can* throw a great city into a panic, and small-scale nuclear weaponry will in the near future provide opportunities for a few individuals to terrorize vast populations.[14] When public order is vulnerable to blackmail and public morale can be cowed, then public opinion can also be at the mercy of those who relentlessly seek power.

SHOCKING OPINIONS

Those who profess to favor freedom yet deprecate agitation, are men who want crops without plowing up the ground; they want rain without thunder and lightning. They want the ocean without the awful roar of its many waters. . . . Power concedes nothing without demand. It never did and it never will. Find out just what any people will quietly submit to and you have found out the exact measure of injustice and wrong which will be imposed upon them, and these will continue till they are resisted with either words or blow, or with both. The limits of tyrants are prescribed by the endurance of those whom they oppress.

Frederick Douglass[15]

Demonstrations, strikes, lobbying, and publicity in the hands of impassioned minorities have long represented an accepted part of the process by which opinions are formed and public policies fashioned in a democracy. The civil rights movement of the late 1950s and early 1960s was an extraordinarily effective illustration of organized peaceful protest that led to massive social change. But what is to be done when institutions are rigid and unresponsive, when the procedures that permit peaceful change fail to work, when the channels for communicating grievances are clogged?

In contemporary America, "revolutionary" acts of disruption and terrorism represent a deliberate effort to move new items onto the agenda of government, to accelerate decisions that might otherwise come slowly, to create a sense of urgency and crisis with regard to matters that might otherwise appear insignificant.

While quiet protests through legitimate channels often produce shrugs of unconcern from an entrenched bureaucracy, broken windows and shouted threats bring out the television cameras and rouse the indifferent authorities. "With one match I can bring about more change tonight than with all the talking you can ever do," a ghetto rioter told an Urban League official who wanted to "cool it."[16] Arson and looting spurred the nation's business elite into an awareness of the urban crisis social scientists had warned of for years.

Violent acts and words produce political awareness where there was none before. Today their impact is multiplied through the power of the mass media, which produce feelings of shock or outrage far beyond the immediate scene of events. Conventional clichés are challenged, and the previously disinterested party, now sucked into the drama as a kind of participant, acquires a sense of involvement and responsibility for a solution. He must ask himself, "What drives these people to such mad and desperate actions? Why do they feel so strongly? Could they perhaps have a point?"

Violence fills the political air with excitement. It makes opinions more volatile, more subject to rapid persuasion, more polarized. New heroes arise suddenly and old authorities topple. The changes of opinion that occur in an emotional atmosphere reflect an allegiance to the words and style of leaders rather than a response to the clash of ideas. They gravitate from the realm of reason to the realm of faith, and in the realm of faith is the triumph of the reactionary demagogue as well as of the radical.

Revolutionaries seek power, knowing that opinion will be molded by it. Reformers seek to sway opinion, and so to bend power to their purposes. Violent tactics may be intended to forcibly change the distribution of power and thus the prevailing system of government, but they may also be intended to shock public opinion into awareness of grievances and thus to accelerate reform within the system itself. No fine line can be drawn between the kinds of pressure tactics that apply in one instance or the other. Confrontations can lead to violence that turns reformers into revolutionaries.

In the excited atmosphere of confrontation, unpredictable occurrences can have awesome consequences, actually changing the course of history with a force out of all proportion to the precipitating incident. The Boston Massacre was committed by eight men with unloaded muskets, faced with a violent mob of four hundred; its five victims became the symbolic martyrs of the American Revolution.

Acts of violence (or the threat of violence) to persons and property are often regarded by their politically motivated practitioners as a direct extension of the traditional forms of dissent. Terror and "trashings"[17] represent a means for a minority to express strongly felt emotions with maximum attention value, when it cannot win majority opinion to its side through the ordinary machinery of persuasion and politics.[18]

The revolutionaries of the past thought in terms of the *coup d'état*, in which the objective was to shift power at the center of the government by eliminating those who stood in the way. Assassination, arson, and the other weapons of individual terrorism were used against specific targets, real or symbolic, that represented obstacles to the reassignment of state authority and the restructuring of political forms.

In the present day, revolutionary terror (as practiced, for instance, by the Tupamaros in Uruguay) has been put to a new purpose: to traumatize the population at large by introducing a large element of uncertainty into daily life, and thereby forcing the reconsideration of all traditional values, loyalties, and dogmas. The shock of having one's customary routine destroyed, of feeling oneself vulnerable to attack from unexpected enemies, of seeing the landmarks of authority crumble all around—all those destructive and deeply disturbing events produce a toleration of ideas that would formerly have been ruled out of bounds, and above all a yearning for peace, order, and stability reestablished at any price.

Social revolution has always entailed a full measure of emotional excess and wanton brutality, as normal restraints are unleashed. What is new in the twentieth-century pattern is the use of brutality as a calculated tactic, on the part of coolly dedicated professional revolutionaries, to hasten the reorientation of the masses of people.

Innocent bystanders become committed to "the cause" to the extent that they are sucked into complicity in revolutionary acts. Peasants who are ordered to kill their former landlords become participants in revolutionary reeducation; show trials of counterrevolutionaries become dramatic spectacles and the onlookers become accomplices. Terrorist blows met by mass reprisals turn a previously noncommital public against the forces of order (and repression). Once the battle lines are drawn, a matter that has been of transient or trivial interest is redefined in the vital terms of "us" versus "them."

In the United States, most of the public has declared itself strongly unsympathetic to forceful tactics.[19] A "counterrevolutionary" response is welcomed by those Left ideologists who proclaim that it serves the valuable function of "radicalizing" the formerly apolitical masses. David Dellinger, who helped plan the 1968 Chicago demonstrations, said their objective was to "strip the facade of liberal policies from the Establishment and expose the raw machinery of force and repression beneath it."

The purpose of inciting hate or violence is not so much to destroy or discomfit its object; (that is a side-benefit); the real purpose is to transform the thinking of those who experience the emotions or actions as perpetrators or as spectators. The bourgeois revolutionists of an earlier day spoke of freedom, brotherhood, love, and national fulfilment. Today's bourgeois romantic revolutionist *par excellence,* Ché Guevara, writes, "People without hate cannot triumph over a brutal enemy." Hate, once generated, can be turned, as a diffuse emotion, into channels different from those in which it was first directed. Anger against those who initiate terror is easily turned against those who come to prevent it.

A 19-year-old Negro militant at San Francisco State College was blinded and maimed by a bomb which exploded prematurely in his hands while he was preparing to plant it in the Creative Arts building. The chairman of the Black Students Union described him as "the innocent victim of the racist oppressive society that is perpetuated at San Francisco State College." Aggressors commonly define themselves as victims.

In the confusion of charges and countercharges which surround any critical incident, it becomes irrelevant to ask who was responsible; the important thing is that there is crisis, that hitherto unmentionable issues are raised for discussion and resolution.

In contemporary America, revolutionary sentiments have been accompanied by a bloodthirsty imagery which has not been seen in political life since the glorification of death by the Black Shirts and the wilder moments of *Der Stürmer.* A militant feminist wrote in the Berkeley *Barb:* "[Eldridge Cleaver] asked me once if I would kill for women's liberation, and I replied that I thought there were more important fronts in the struggle where killing would be necessary. His response . . . 'when you are fighting for your own liberation you fight to the death on all fronts.' "[20]

The slogan of the Mothers, the "Acid-Rock" faction of S.D.S., was "The future of our struggle is the future of crime in the streets." Their *New Left Notes* proclaimed, "There are no limits to our lawlessness." One splinter group of the S.D.S. at the University of Michigan termed itself the "Jesse James Gang." In New York, the S.D.S. sponsored a "Pretty Boy Floyd Memorial Lecture" at the New School for Social

Research in commemoration of the gangster who was the principal perpetrator of the "Kansas City Massacre," in which two detectives, the chief of police, and an FBI agent were killed, and two federal agents were wounded.[21]

To some of the revolutionaries, Sirhan Sirhan, Robert Kennedy's assassin, was a hero, as was Charles Manson, the commune leader convicted as mastermind of a mass murder in Beverly Hills. One comment by Bernardine Dohrn, a leader of the revolutionary Weathermen: "Dig it, first they killed those pigs (Sharon Tate and her friends), then they ate dinner in the same room with them, then they even shoved a fork into a victim's stomach! Wild!"[22] A Los Angeles underground paper, *Tuesday's Child,* named Charles Manson "Man of the Year" while the Weathermen, according to the Liberation News Service, said "Manson Power" made 1970 "The Year of the Fork."

Obscenity was also used as a studied device to deprive adversaries (like policemen or professors) of their dignity, and to reduce their response to an animal level of emotion. "Alienating people is a necessary process in getting them to move," writes Jerry Rubin, the Yippie leader. Speaking at Kent State University in May 1970, a few days before the turmoil that ended in the infamous killings, Rubin said, "The first part of the Yippie program, you know, is to kill your parents. And I mean that quite seriously, because until you're prepared to kill your parents, you're not really prepared to change the country, because our parents are our first oppressors."[23]

In an atmosphere supercharged with anger, outrageous and valid ideas or slogans appear equally plausible. At Chicago, the Yippie manifesto included certain *plausible* demands as objectives of the "Second American Revolution" (immediate end of the war in Vietnam, withdrawal of American troops from foreign bases, end of the draft, cable TV, elimination of air and water pollution, legalization of marijuana and psychedelic drugs, abortions when desired, and so on) along with *implausible* demands (abolition of money, full unemployment, with people "free from the drudgery of work . . . let the machines do it," decentralization of political authority into "tribal groups," television time reserved to show love-making, and free love in general: "We believe that people should—all the time, anytime, whomever they wish").

Mad slogans are not incapable of winning mass support, as the history of the twentieth century makes quite clear. Revolutions have been made by handfuls of "fanatics" and "madmen" spouting what appear to be absurdities. Most people are unable to recognize the signs of mental illness. When they encounter the symptoms they tend to dismiss them as eccentricities or temporary aberrations.[24] It is small wonder, then, that insane words and actions often encounter toleration and apathy.

It is of some passing interest to note how many phrases of the new revolutionary movement are borrowed from other places, and other times. The slogan, "Power to the People" follows the cry of "All Power to the Soviets"—a demand raised in 1917 in opposition not to Tsarist autocracy but to the bourgeois democracy of the Provisional Government.

There are echoes of John Reed in Staughton Lynd's description of an antiwar demonstration in Washington: "It was unbearably moving to watch the sea of banners move out . . . toward the Capitol. . . . Still more poignant was the perception that as the crowd moved toward the seat of government . . . our forward movement was irresistibly strong. . . . Nothing could have stopped that crowd from taking possession of its government. Perhaps next time we should keep going, occupying for a time the rooms from which orders issue."[25]

When demonstrators at the University of California in 1968 occupied a University-owned lot in Berkeley to make a "people's park," a leaflet distributed by students to the National Guardsmen who eventually took over the lot began, "To our brothers!"—a nostalgic echo of the October days. Buildings occupied by the students at Columbia and other universities were described as "liberated zones" in the vocabulary of the Eighth Route Army—as was the area where the demonstrators were permitted to remain in Grant Park, Chicago, during the 1968 convention week. A sign read. "Today the Park, tomorrow the country."

Mark Rudd, the S.D.S. leader, proudly revealed that he had never seen the site of Columbia's proposed gymnasium, although he made it the major issue in the student revolt and succeeded in blocking its construction. Similar cynicism has been voiced by other radical leaders: "First we'll make the revolution, and then we will find out what for," said Tom Hayden.[26] "If there had been no Vietnam war, we would have invented one," Rubin wrote in another context.[27]

The use of confrontation tactics to radicalize a campus stems from the well-taken premise that substantial numbers of nonrevolutionary students are motivated by social idealism and a passionate desire for peace, and that they share with the rebels a distrust of administration, trustees, and outside civic authorities, including the police; they are also generally sympathetic to the underdogs on whose behalf the citadels of power can be assaulted: instructors not recommended for tenure appointments, janitors employed at "starvation wages," dwellers in rent-controlled buildings about to be demolished by the heartless university to make room for dormitories to house the growing number of students.

A mail survey of Columbia students after the spring disturbances of 1968 found 11 percent who felt it was justified to hold a dean captive, and even more who approved the copying of documents from President Grayson Kirk's files. In the words of Allen Barton, who directed the study, "In a referendum or an election, 19 percent of the vote does not amount to much. On the other hand, 19 percent of 17,000 students amounts to 3250 people—a formidable picket line, sit-in group or crowd."[28]

Surveys like Barton's allow us to gauge the extent of the passions that make headlines, but it is easier to describe or televise the behavior of a mob than to sample the thoughts of a scattered multitude. Mobs act, and enact their own dramas, while scattered individuals find no common voice. In discussing the notion of the constituency, we noted that the high visibility of any militant group makes it easy to perceive their actions as reflections of mass sentiment in the absence of evidence to the contrary.[29]

Troubled conditions do not often lend themselves to systematic research of any kind. A study at Cornell University after the disturbances and racial incidents of 1969 found that 35 percent of the students described the unrest as a "groundswell," whereas 39 percent said it reflected the feelings of a "small minority." But among the faculty 46 percent said it was a groundswell (28 percent a small minority) and among university administrators 54 percent called it a groundswell (25 percent a small minority). In short, the administration was far more impressed with the breadth of the student movement than were the students themselves.

The strength of student revolutionaries must be appraised in relation to two facts mentioned in an earlier chapter:

1. Right-wing sentiment (as reflected in pro-Wallace feeling in 1968) far outweighs left-wing opinion among *all* American youth.

2. Young people are *on the whole* far less likely than their elders to be voters or active participants in the political process.

But these facts emerge from empirical research and, like many not so obvious truths, are invisible to the naked eye of the casual observer.

Revolutionary critics dismiss the findings of opinion surveys as "irrelevant." They *know* the answers, they say, and research wastes time and money and is beside the point. ("What they paying you all that money for to go around and ask them damn fool questions," a Negro interviewer was challenged, "when for 50 cents and a pint of wine I can tell you what's what?")

As a result of this attitude, research may be most distrusted precisely where it is most needed. For example, the causes of student unrest were the subject of a 1971 study sponsored by the National Institute of Mental Health, with backing from the American Council on Education and the Carnegie Commission on Higher Education. The Commission's distinguished chairman, Clark Kerr, explained that the study's aim was to learn students' views "so that the qualities and relevance of our colleges and universities may be assessed and hopefully, improved." The project met massive opposition and calls for noncooperation in sectors of the student press. Although the data were set up for processing in a manner that safeguarded anonymity for the respondents, the real objective of the study was alleged to be a form of espionage: "To what extent can the student's subsequent participation in protests be predicted from information available at the time of matriculation?"

It has always been hard to persuade interviewers to go into the slum neighborhoods of American cities, and when they do go there the task of getting willing respondents is extremely difficult. A Columbia University study on the relation between poverty and adolescent health ran into problems in Harlem after three uncooperative Negro interviewers were discharged.[30] They formed an "Ad Hoc Citizens Committee Against Columbia University," to protest the study, charging that it was "just one more method used by the ruling class to determine how best to suppress the black people with the least amount of trouble."[31]

A Negro psychologist, Charles W. Thomas II, says, "White psychologists have raped black communities all over the country. Yes, raped. They have used black people as the human equivalent of rats to run through Ph.D. experiments and as helpless clients for programs that serve white middle-class administrators better than they do the poor. They have used research on black people as green stamps to trade for research grants."[32]

In recent years, graduate students and young instructors organized as the "Sociology Liberation Movement" have demanded the disengagement of the "sociological Establishment" from its "dependence" on the "military-industrial complex." At the September 1969 meetings of the American Sociological Association, a resolution approved by the "nonvoting" persons present, though defeated by the minority of voting members, began, "Whereas, the prostitution of academic sociology to the institutions of corporate imperialism is clear to all who care to see. . . ."

At the same time, the same faction also insisted that sociologists devote more attention to the study of "socially relevant" issues instead of to the comparatively dry descriptive problems on which so many members of the profession have been engaged. There is a poignant dilemma in the espousal of these two positions; it is the essential dilemma of today's social science, rather than the particular problem of survey analysts. The difference between serious study of serious problems and mere speculation about them is the difference between well-funded, large-scale empirical research (well-funded from tainted Establishment sources) and the individual exercise of free inquiry unhampered by a need to muster evidence in support of one's theories.

In whose interest shall research be conducted, and to what ends? These are fair questions, but however they are answered, wisdom can come only by adding to the sources of information, and never by cutting off any that now exist. Social research emerged from a tradition of social reform. Social scientists first left their armchairs to observe and to interview people systematically because they assumed that a better understanding of social problems was the first step to their solution. By contrast, revolutions are led by men of conviction, whose faith often makes them impatient with a studious sifting of the facts.

It would be as inane to equate opinion polling with social research as to equate the shock tactics I have described in this chapter with the predominantly peaceful and politically heterogeneous radical movement to change American society. Shock tactics have often proven to be counterproductive; their use is on the wane in the United States though not in the world at large. In their efforts to shock, revolutionaries are preoccupied with the business of changing public opinion. However, their rejection of survey research carries with it an implied disdain for the public opinion they wish to change.

Part Eight

OPINIONS AND RESPONSIBILITIES

OPINIONS AND RESPONSIBILITIES

Public opinion is a permeating influence. It requires us to think other men's thoughts, to speak other men's words, to follow other men's habits.

Walter Bagehot

Opinion polls can be troublesome and even dangerous, I noted at the outset of this book, not only when they are done badly or dishonestly but when they are done well and taken too literally. Political decision-making might be even more troublesome if there were no systematic surveys to lift awareness of public opinion beyond the realm of conjecture.

Most survey research is devoted to the study of trivia; it is the study or minor preferences in the marketplace and in the media. To a very large extent it is not a study of opinion at all but of purchasing and product usage. Of the remainder, which is really devoted to the study of public issues, much deals with subjects of transitory interest that are unfamiliar to most people or incapable of arousing strong feelings pro or con.

Except at election time, most of us do not expect our casual conversations about politics to eventuate in direct action. The real decisions we make in daily life are in large measure decisions on consumption (either of goods or of time) and these do not commonly involve discussion (except for such unusual major purchases as a house or a car, on which everyone seeks counsel).

Political questions are clearly more important than the questions of consumer choice which most commonly confront survey respondents. Yet the average individual has no control over political decisions, or over the problems that they represent, except within the framework of collective social action. The questions asked in opinion surveys often seem irrelevant to a world of barricades, guerrilla warriors, and lumbering armies.

When an interviewer confronts me with questions about my brand choice in beer or automobiles, he is dealing with preferences that relate to past and possible future actions over which I exercise the primary control regardless of what influences may be brought to bear upon me. When the same interviewer asks my opinions about China, Rhodesia, or the European Common Market, he is asking about matters on which my opinions can be translated into action only through the appropriate institutions of society or through expressive behavior that bypasses the institutions. As consumers we may act as individuals; as political beings we act in the context of collective movements whose chemistry transforms the beliefs of the participants.

Opinions become meaningful only when they are linked to a consciousness of responsibility. The translation of opinion into action requires a combination of strong motivation and the sense that action can have meaningful consequences. It is only through action that opinion influences history. On the great issues of the time opinion may move in fits and starts, by jumps and leaps, rather than by a slow process of change or attrition.

When are people impelled to do something about their beliefs, apart from the ritualized timetable of the electoral system? Under what circumstances are opinions translated into direct social action, whether this be signing a petition or starting one, giving money or calling a meeting (the traditional forms of expression in our society) or disrupting a City Council meeting, ripping up the paving stones, or burning a supermarket?

Powerful private, personal motivations may underlie a political act—friendship, family or ethnic ties, ambition, revenge, hunger. But there are also motivations which are *truly* political, whether they exist in pure form or represent a veneer of rationalization for the private motives. Political opinion which is carried through from conversation to action almost always carries with it a sense of outrage or injustice.

At this point it is no longer opinion at all in an intellectual sense, but rather a state of emotional shock, a visceral response of readiness for action. There is a feeling of deprivation, a direct threat to the ego. Such a reaction is what people normally feel when they learn of a particularly vicious crime. To the extent that the crime itself is important or interesting enough to come to the attention of the entire community, there is a common instinctive feeling that something must be done. This kind of clear-cut emotional response cries for expression. When opinion is divorced from feeling, its nuances are infinitely more difficult to trace and test; it is harder to find a consistent point of view. A sense of outrage may be widespread, as it has been after mass killings of civilians in Biafra and Bengal, but there may be no universal agreement on what to do next. A vague or confused state of public opinion crystallizes into sharp divisions when specific alternative choices are in the balance.

A generalized sense of outrage is hard to translate into concrete measures. People usually prefer to assume that the legitimate established forces of order and justice have matters under control. Events like a municipal graft scandal or a wartime massacre of civilians can be accepted and assimilated by the public as long as it feels the authorities are investigating, prosecuting, and taking care of things.

In assessing public opinion we are always faced with the question of how likely individual views are to be transformed into effective forces in the political process. It is not necessary to elaborate on the point that some individuals, and some levels of society, carry more influence in the political process than others do, even under a system of one man-one vote. Among the public at large, 28 percent claim to have made a campaign contribution within the past five years; 18 percent to have worked in an election campaign; and 24 percent say they have written to an elected official about some matter of public interest.[1] Four percent claim to have addressed a political meeting; 18 percent to have written to the editor of a newspaper or magazine; a full 6 percent say they have published an article in a trade or professional journal within the same time period. (Unquestionably all these claims are substantially exaggerated, but they serve at least to indicate the comparative orders of magnitude of these different types of activity.)

Political participation is by no means evenly distributed throughout all social ranks. The United States has a long tradition of *grass-roots* political activism by agrarian populists, labor unionists, and more recently by unskilled and indigent urban minority groups. This type of lower-class political action has sometimes been vigorous and effective, particularly when oriented to short-run, immediate local goals rather than to broad, comprehensive programs of social reform.

But Welfare Mothers and Knights of Labor notwithstanding, greater participation in the political process has generally been linked to higher social position. (It must not be forgotten that many student radicals are the children of upper-middle-class suburbia.) Higher social status has always meant greater financial means and greater leisure to devote to political causes. It also carries a broader range of access to ideas and information, a bigger vocabulary, greater self-confidence, and greater familiarity with the means of manipulating public institutions.

Alexander Hamilton presented a rationale for his aristocratic political outlook when he suggested that representative government did not require that legislators be drawn from the ranks of the particular social strata they represented.

"The idea of an actual representation of all classes of the people by persons of each class is altogether visionary. . . . Mechanics and manufacturers will always be inclined, with few exceptions, to give their votes to merchants in preference to persons of their own professions or trades. . . . They are sensible that their habits in life have not been such as to give them those acquired endowments without which, in a deliberative assembly, the greatest natural abilities are for the most parts useless."[2]

A not dissimilar argument was still being advanced two centuries later in South Africa to justify the requirement that colored voters be represented in Parliament by whites. Curiously enough, an echo of the Hamiltonian philosophy may also be detected in a suggestion offered by Yugoslavia's leading pollster, who is disturbed that a representative sampling of opinions turns up too many of the wrong kind: "In countries with a high percentage of peasants in the composition of population this social group, usually conservative and old-fashioned in its manifested attitudes and opinions, can actually control dominant opinion by sheer majority. The part played by industrial workers and the intelligentsia in the economic and political life of a country is more important, but this is not sufficiently expressed in the dominant opinion. We would have an ideal solution if it were possible to find a method of weighting the opinions of selected social groups and thus to establish a basis for obtaining an adequate final picture."[3]

Political influence reflects the flow of ideas from one individual to another, as well as the willingness to work directly within politically oriented organizations. The direct interpersonal influence that an individual brings to bear upon others is circumscribed by the range and character of his daily contacts. Most people deal as whole persons primarily with others akin to themselves in social class, interest, and outlook, whereas their socially more varied contacts are made in terms of narrowly defined roles which sharply limit the subject of conversation. (There are of course subtle influences in such contacts between members of different social orders, as when servants, shop clerks, or head waiters adopt the upper-class mannerisms of those they serve.)

Most of us tend to defer to the specialized information of those whose authority we respect, but our casual exchange of opinions and facts on important matters is most likely to take place with our peers, with whom we feel comfortable and whose vested interests we identify with our own.

Relatively little direct communication about world affairs takes place between members of different social groups.[4] People of higher status talk more about politics because they simply talk more. Their conversations are longer and more frequent—about anything. The same influential individuals tend to volunteer their own opinions and ask other people about theirs.[5] Those who influence others make particularly active use of the media to provide evidence and arguments to back their views.[6]

To talk about a subject, even to have an opinion on it, signifies that one has accepted its reality; by implication one accepts a certain sense of responsibility for coping with this reality. Saul Bellow's hero Herzog is afflicted with a disease he calls "humanitis." He is sick with worry about the state of mankind; he makes all its anonymous troubles his own personal ones. This affliction, however, is far less prevalent than its opposite, which Jacob Chwast, a psychologist, has named "spectatoritis," the ability to stand apart from the afflictions and troubles of others.

On an inside page of the newspaper, a brief United Press International dispatch reports that in Miami "a wounded driver of a bakery truck bled to death tonight while 20 witnesses to the shooting stood by without notifying the authorities."

A seventeen-year-old boy bled to death after an assault by a juvenile gang in a New York subway train while eleven other riders sat by. They did not summon assistance or help him, even after the attackers had left the car.[7]

An eighteen-year-old switchboard operator was raped and beaten while alone in her office in the Bronx, New York. She escaped momentarily and ran out naked and bleeding to the street screaming for help. Forty passers-by gathered and watched while the rapist tried to drag her back upstairs. No one interfered until two policemen chanced to come by.[8]

Such incidents seem commonplace, barely meriting attention; from them a direct line can be traced to the world's complacent acceptance of starvation and mass murder. What an individual defines as important cannot be separated from what he feels he has within his control. The mass media have familiarized us with what was formerly mysterious and exotic, but this very sense of familiarity arouses a greater frustration over our inability to cope with the powerful and distant forces that affect our welfare.

Paul Goodman says pessimistically, "People believe that the great background conditions of modern life are beyond our power to influence. . . . History is out of control, it is no longer something that we make but something that happens to us. . . . We read—with excitement, spite, or fatalism, depending on our characters—the headlines of crises for which we are unprepared."[9]

In our bureaucratized world it is easy for individuals to abjure responsibility not only for their acts but also for the consequences of the opinions they hold. Adolf Eichmann, as we know, "only followed orders." It is now conventional to ascribe to one's superiors the motivation and blame for one's own socially unacceptable acts. It is no less common for those superiors to pass the blame to their subordinates or (again) to the "System."

In *War and Peace*, Tolstoy describes Napoleon on the battlefield at Borodino as a hostage to history, powerless to control the destinies of the armies he had set in motion: "Even before he gave that order the thing he did not desire, and for which he gave the order only because he thought it was expected of him, was being done. And he fell back into that artificial realm of imaginary greatness, and again—as a horse walking a treadmill thinks it is doing something for itself—he submissively fulfilled the cruel, sad, gloomy and inhuman role predestined for him."[10]

The symptoms of "spectatoritis" are evident in physicist Ralph Lapp's description: "The Long Island housewife who assembles tiny electronic components for a bomb mechanism does not associate herself with a weapon that may bring death to some victim. She lives in her own microcosm and, if queried about her occupation, may shrug off the questioner with a reply, 'a job is a job.' The scholarly professor who probes the chemical secrets of certain compounds may fail to associate his research with destructive defoliants. The industrialist who mass-produces napalm may brush aside any qualms he may have with the contention that he simply fulfills orders given to him by his government."[11] As a matter of fact, Lewis Frederick Fieser, who led a Harvard team in developing napalm during World War II, *did* tell a reporter that he was free of any guilt. "Just because I played a role in the technological development of napalm doesn't mean I'm any more qualified to comment on the moral aspects of it. . . . I was working on a technical problem that was considered pressing. I distinguish between developing ammunition of some kind and using it. You can't blame the outfit that put out the rifle that killed the President."

Occasional reports in the press reveal the presence on American soil (and even as American citizens) of former concentration camp guards and other war criminals. Brief hubbubs of concern over their presence quiet down very quickly. Who has the energy or the will to exorcise these ghosts of the recent and unpleasant past? The reluctance to engage in acts of retribution is no more than a mild symptom of the same moral disengagement that permitted the crimes in the first place. Someone else, someone higher up, was assuming responsibility.

When we go to the theater or movies, we go braced for a shock; we go in the anticipation of the dramatic, the extraordinary. In ordinary life, it is hard for us to adapt to the dangers that confront us at every waking moment. In an era in which paranoid demogogues have controlled great nations and in which the means of mass destruction are easy to come by, how can one plan ahead except by assuming that all will work out for the best?

Four out of five large-city residents queried on the very weekend of racial riots in Newark, in 1967, felt that trouble in *their* city was unlikely.[12] We want the accustomed things in their customary places. It takes time to adjust to the realization that the world is full of uncertainties, and that the things we take for granted, physical safety, personal dignity, the tolerance of our fellow men, may no longer exist.

By maintaining the semblance of routine, people strive to negate the intrusion of danger, like the storekeeper who continues to wait calmly on a customer in the face of a hold-up man carrying a gun. We may fool ourselves by defining a dangerous situation as nonthreatening or by denying it altogether.

When President Guido was forced out of the Argentine presidency by a military coup, tanks marched into the square in front of the Casa Rosada in Buenos Aires, but they were ignored by a huge crowd on the way to a football match. A typical scene of this period was that of a man sitting in front of his store reading his newspaper, while behind him, glowering, a soldier manned a machine gun. (We could hardly expect the same definition of the situation in the event of a parallel *coup d'état* in Spain or Cuba, with theirs histories of bloody civil war. Tanks and machine guns would be seen by the average citizen as a real personal threat, not just for show.)

During World War II, concentration camp inmates living just a few hundred yards away from the gas chambers and crematoria denied knowledge of them. Bruno Bettelheim reports the case of a prisoner who broke away from a group destined to be killed. "Some of the fellow prisoners selected with her for the gas chambers called the supervisors, telling them she was trying to get away. . . . The separation of behavior patterns and values inside and outside of camp was so radical, and the feelings about it so strong, that most prisoners avoided talking about it; it was one of many subjects that were 'taboo'. . . . This attitude of denying 'reality' to events so extreme as to threaten the prisoner's integration was a first step toward developing new mechanisms for surviving in the camp. By denying reality to overwhelming situations, they were somehow made bearable; but at the same time it constituted a major change in experiencing the world."[13]

The more atrocious an event, the more remote it is from normal experience, the easier it is to shut it out: "Prisoners hated guards who kicked, slapped or swore at them much more than guards who had wounded them seriously." Bettelheim reports that on the same day there was "news of an anti-Nazi speech by President Roosevelt and a rumor that one of the SS officers was to be replaced. New prisoners discussed the President's speech excitedly and paid scant attention to the rumors. Old prisoners were indifferent to the speech but devoted their conversation to the rumored change in camp officers."[14]

Chaim Aron Kaplan's remarkable journal of the Warsaw ghetto has the following entry for June 7, 1942: "When the news doesn't tell us what we want to hear, we twist and turn it until it seems full of hints, clues, and secrets that support our views . . . and the news from Reuters always contains a certain intonation or expression to satisfy and comfort a spirit thirsting for a speedy and quick redemption."[15]

If, under such conditions, people can deny the imminence of their own doom, how much easier it is to deny reality to the unpleasant events which we know about only at second or third hand, which happen to faceless statistics rather than to individual human beings with whom we can empathize! Why should be have opinions about such matters? If we "think about the unthinkable," must this not become an obsession that makes all normal activity impossible?

In November 1944, one-fourth of the American public said they did not believe reports of the Nazi concentration camps, or had no opinion.[16] Of the remainder, one-fourth had a realistic notion of the number of victims, one-fourth had no opinion, and another fourth estimated the number to be 100,000 or less. Over two decades later, only one-third picked from a roster of possibilities the figure of 6 million victims, and a quarter insisted that the figure was too high after they were told it was correct.[17]

Soviet history still makes no acknowledgment of the fact that the Nazis singled out Jews as special victims. Neo-Nazis in Germany insist that "only" 1, 2, 3, 4, or 5 million Jews were killed, as though the seriousness of the crime would be diminished in proportion to the number of victims.

In an earlier chapter I commented on the shock effect of Mylai upon American opinion about the Vietnam war. The facts about Mylai emerged only because a few dedicated individuals (Ronald Ridenhour and Seymour Hersh) insisted on tracking them down and making them public. If the press was slow to investigate the first reports of the massacre, and if the military authorities in Vietnam were satisfied with the first investigatory report, which whitewashed the episode, this merely manifested the deadening of nerve endings that occurs among generals, newsmen, and public alike when reports of civilian casualties become a matter of daily routine.

Truth slips easily through the meshes of public forgetfulness. When people can ignore what they don't want to know they can also believe what they want to believe, and find excuses for the most outrageous actions. The difference between right and wrong is easily obscured when powerful voices insist over and over again that wrong is right.

In the laboratory under controlled conditions we can verify what recent history illustrates in gruesome detail—that human beings can be readily induced to behave in contradiction to their deeply felt opinions and moral standards, provided that they have some kind of socially acceptable rationale (such as "obedience to authority") to sustain them. The police of Paris who rounded up the Jewish children in the Vel d'Hiver for transport to slaughter were the same men who took to arms against the Nazis only a few months later when the hour of resistance came.

The intensity of aggressive behavior diminishes the closer an aggressor is to his victim and the greater the victim's opportunity to talk back.[18] But modern technology makes it easy for aggression to be depersonalized to the point where neither aggressor nor victim perceives their mutual connection. Hence it becomes easier to behave in contradiction to one's principles when the contradiction is not glaringly evident. The soldier who kills in battle as part of a ritualized and socially sanctioned assignment is no more likely than anyone else to become a murderer when he returns to civilian life. His battlefield activity is a specialized and temporary role which he in no way connects with his normal civilian personality.

Our tolerance for injustice, and even our participation in it, may arise, paradoxically, from our very need to believe that the world is really a reasonable and just place. This at least is the conclusion drawn by a social psychologist, Melvin Lerner, from a series of experiments: "Most people cannot for the sake of their own sanity believe in a world governed by a schedule of random reinforcements. . . . If this is true, then the person who sees suffering or misfortune will be motivated to believe that the unfortunate sufferer in some sense merited his fate."[19] Thus an accident victim who is reported *not* to be responsible for his accident is considered a less attractive person than a victim whose own responsibility for his accident is in doubt.

Lerner notes that "at the verbal cultural level we find that martyrs are loved and admired, innocent victims are reacted to with affection and concern; and people who get themselves into trouble are condemned and considered to be naughty."[20] His experiments showed just the opposite. There is obviously a deep contradiction between the values that people profess in the abstract and the way in which they translate their attitudes into actual behavior.

We define a situation as an emergency by observing the reactions of others before we react ourselves. The more people who watch a victim in distress, the less likely he is to get help. Psychologists John Darley and Bibb Latané found that experimental subjects responded more slowly to an "emergency" affecting another individual when a third person was present as a bystander. When there were four other bystanders present, nearly half the experimental subjects did not report the emergency at all; the reaction time of those who did respond was exactly half as fast as when there was no other bystander and the subject had to take on all the responsibility. In the last case, the subject had to perceive the situation as one in which he *alone* could summon help.

"We are taught to have a decent respect for the privacy of others, and when surrounded by strangers, express this respect by closing our ears to their conversation and by not staring at them—we are embarrassed if caught doing otherwise. The fact that everybody in a crowd is on his best public behavior—staring off into space or down at the ground—however, may prevent anybody from noticing the first subtle signs of an emergency."[21]

The sense of responsibility is connected with those altruistic sentiments that lead an individual to commitments and actions. At the point when individuals resolve to act they must eliminate the inconsistencies and ambiguities in what they think. Reality inevitably comes in many shades of gray, and our ideas may be similarly fuzzy and self-contradictory as long as they are merely personal opinions, and not strategy or policy to which others must be bound.

The exercise of responsibility toward others is often an act of self-interest. Indeed, the recognition, awareness, and expression of self-interest is a necessary force in the political process, and often even an honorable one. Self-interest may demand a recognition of the self-interest and grievances of others which, if unpropitiated, ultimately pose a threat to one's self. Social progress requires the resolution of incongruities between real self-interest and the perception of self-interest based on superstition, habit, prejudice, and other forms of distorted thinking.

When the electorate of a town or country votes down a proposed school bond issue, it is deferring future need to present interest. Such a decision often works to the disadvantage of good sense and equity if the choice is between an immediate personal sacrifice or disadvantage and a long-term advantage which is collective, abstract, and destined for generations to come.

Society can mobilize the resources required to manage its larger collective needs only by sacrificing the fulfillment of at least some of the personal, visible, tangible needs of which citizens as consumers are incessantly reminded by our elaborate system of marketing communications.

Everyone wants pollutants eliminated from automobile exhausts, but almost no one wants to pay extra for the devices required to eliminate them; a few years ago there would have been a loud outcry against laws making such devices mandatory, and thus raising the price of an automobile. Shortly such laws will inevitably become universal, or the Detroit manufacturers will themselves make them standard equipment, raising the price. The outcry will be minimal; the public is ready, because the media have helped make air pollution an issue, with the public alerted to its social cost.

People can be persuaded to accept the need for traffic controls and regulations when these represent inconveniences and restrictions on their freedom. Can they be persuaded to accept the long-term benefit of opening residential housing to Negroes in general when it means that tomorrow a Negro will move in next door?

A sense of involvement and responsibility can move men to acquiesce in, or even to support policies that must mean sacrifice of their prejudices or higher taxes and higher prices. President Nixon's 1970 State of the Union message urged that "to the extent possible the price of goods should be made to include the costs of producing and disposing of them without damage to the environment."

Inevitably the price the consumer pays for a can of peaches, a bottle of beer, or a newspaper will have to reflect the cost of hauling these goods away and recycling them into future productive use. But public opinion polls will always show a majority opposed to such measures— until they are established by legislation and accepted as common practice.

Collective needs, and the perception of their urgency, will continue to grow. Thus the public and its elected representatives will increasingly face the necessity of deferring direct present material satisfactions for the sake of enjoying indirect advantages in the very remote and uncertain future.

The changes required in social and economic policy to accomplish this can be enacted only with the concurrence of a public opinion which sees the elimination of social problems as a personal benefit comparable in value to the acquisition of new consumer goods. And public opinion cannot concur in such radical solutions (for radical they must be in order to be solutions) unless the problems themselves seem personal and urgent.

To deal with such problems as discrimination, poverty, pollution, waste, and ugliness requires that people define them as matters within their sphere of personal control and responsibility. This means that they must first define themselves as victims with a stake in the solutions rather than as disinterested observers. Compulsory free education, emancipation of slaves, elimination of child labor, shortening of the work week, minimum wage laws, establishment of Social Security and Medicare—all such measures for social improvement disturbed the *status quo,* not only challenging the vested interests of the minority, but in many instances upsetting the majority's notion of what was right and proper. In every case the citizens and taxpayers of the day were willing to accept a burden for themselves in order to make life better for succeeding generations. Is there any other means of progress?

In a segmented society social problems arise from the inability of the public at large, or of significant sectors of the public, to perceive where their true interests lie and to accept the short-run disagreeable consequences of that recognition. The "opinions" of the apathetic and the disengaged are not to be equated with those of a public that recognizes its stake in the issues under discussion and its accountability for the consequences of the policies it favors. Opinion research forces this kind of awareness by illuminating the differences in values and goals among different sections of society. This makes polls a factor in the political process rather than merely an account of it.

NOTES

Part I

1. Len Giovanitti and Fred Freed, *The Decision to Drop the Bomb*, Coward-Mc-Cann, New York, 1965, pp. 166–168.

2. *Harper's*, December 1961, p. 20.

3. *The New York Times*, February 1, 1970.

4. In the summer of 1971 a series of polls were conducted by John Kraft on behalf of the American Business Committee on Public Priorities, an anti-war group, among samplings of 240 voters in each of ten Congressional districts, including those of the Speaker, the minority leader, and other key floor leaders and committee chairmen. Few of the voters questioned knew how their representatives had voted on major issues, and most of them favored policies opposed to their representatives' positions on Vietnam, the draft and the supersonic transport plane. Cf. Warren E. Miller and Donald E. Stokes, "Representation in Congress," quoted by Bernard C. Cohen, *The Press and Foreign Policy*, Princeton University Press, Princeton, N.J., 1963, p. 240.

5. Personal communication.

6. Larry L. King, "Inside Capitol Hill: How the House Really Works," *Harper's*, October 1968, p. 70.

7. In the formation of the federal government, William Carpenter observes, "No member of the [Constitutional] convention could say what the opinions of his constituents were at this time; much less could he say what they would think if possessed of the information and rights possessed by the members here." William S. Carpenter, *The Development of American Political Thought*, Princeton University Press, Princeton, N.J., 1930, pp. 93–94. Quoted by Hannah Arendt, *On Revolution*, Viking, New York, 1963, p. 239.

8. *The Public Pulse*, January 1969.

9. Harold Mendelsohn and Irving Crespi, *Polls, Television and The New Politics*, Chandler, San Francisco, 1970, p. 17.

209

10. *Ibid.,* p. 62.

11. *The Real Majority,* Coward-McCann, New York, 1970.

12. Every's formula for success is to look for a catchy campaign slogan and to keep the candidate from making personal appearances, since the candidate who talks is a bad risk. "He makes a speech and then exposes himself to foolish questions from some nut who makes him look bad." Every points out that 80 percent of the people do not even know the name of their Congressman; "99 percent don't know whether an incumbent running for reelection has kept his earlier campaign promises." *The New York Times,* January 9, 1966.

13. "Communications in Government," in Nigel Calder, ed., *The World in 1984,* Vol. 2, Penguin Books, New York, 1965, pp. 51–57.

14. Lewis Chester, Godfrey Hodgson, and Bruce Page, *An American Melodrama: The Presidential Campaign of 1968,* Viking, New York, 1969, p. 447.

15. The same anti-ABM ad was later placed in three Vermont newspapers in an attempt to influence Senator George Aiken, whose vote was uncertain.

16. The question was, "Taking everything into consideration, do you think President Nixon was right in ordering the military operation into Cambodia, or do you have serious doubts about his having done this?" (*The New York Times,* May 26, 1970.)

17. *The New York Times,* March 13, 1970.

18. *The New York Times,* May 5, 1969.

19. Walter Lippmann, *Public Opinion,* MacMillan, New York, 1922.

20. Clinton Rossiter, ed., *The Federalist Papers,* Number 50, New American Library, New York, 1961, p. 319.

21. From an unpublished paper by John Wahlke and Milton G. Lodge, summarized in *Science News,* December 5, 1970.

22. E. J. Kahn, Jr., *The New York Times,* April 12, 1971.

23. Charles Y. Glock and Rodney Stark, *Christian Beliefs and Anti-Semitism,* Harper and Row, New York, 1966, p. 199

24. Leon Festinger, *A Theory of Cognitive Dissonance,* Row Peterson, Evanston, Ill., 1957.

25. E. M. Forster, *Aspects of the Novel,* Harcourt, Brace & World, New York, 1947.

26. News media naturally give prominence to polls they conduct or commission themselves, and few of them differentiate between surveys made by professionals and those run on an amateur basis. Elmo Roper, criticizing the press' "inability or unwillingness to discriminate between the available polls," cited as an instance the Gallup Poll's 1966 prediction that the Republicans would gain between 35 and 55 seats in the House, while the press, in its own surveys, tended to predict a much smaller gain. Ignoring the Gallup estimates, a headline in *The New York Times* on the day after the election read, "Republicans Stronger Than Expected in Off-Year Vote."

27. *Editor and Publisher,* January 2, 1971.

28. The preceding three paragraphs are derived from the author's essay, "Social Sciences in the Mass Media," in Frederick T. C. Yu, ed., *Behavioral Sciences and the Mass Media,* Russell Sage Foundation, New York, 1968.

29. Gerhart D. Wiebe, dean of the Boston University School of Communication, concluded that in *The New York Times'* reporting of public opinion research he found "headlines to be misleading, the customary buttressing of story themes with clarifying facts to be frequently lacking, interpretation of facts to be in error, and if I'm not mistaken a supercilious approach to the field of public opinion research that raises questions as to the seriousness of the editors in their efforts to inform either

themselves or their readers regarding this area." To *The Times'* credit, it has since made some notable efforts to improve its coverage of opinion research and of the social sciences in general. It has subscribed to the Gallup Poll, and in 1970 it retained the Yankelovich organization to run a series of local election surveys. Gerhart D. Wiebe, "*The New York Times* and Public Opinion Research: A Criticism," *Journalism Quarterly*, Vol. 44, No. 4, Winter 1967, pp. 654–658.

30. No attempt has been made to review here the extensive research literature on voting behavior. Among the classic studies are Paul F. Lazarsfeld, Bernard Berelson, and Hazel Gaudet, *The People's Choice*, Duell Sloan and Pearce, New York, 1944; Bernard Berelson, Paul F. Lazarsfeld, and William N. McPhee, *Voting*, University of Chicago Press, Chicago, 1954; Angus Campbell, Gerald Gurin, and Warren E. Miller, *The Voter Decides*, Row, Peterson, Evanston, Ill., 1954; Angus Campbell, Philip E. Converse, Warren E. Miller, and Donald E. Stokes, *The American Voter*, Wiley, New York, 1960.

31. Fred Mosteller, Herbert Hyman, Philip J. McCarthy, Eli S. Marks, and David B. Truman, *The Pre-Election Polls of 1948: Report to the Committee on Analysis of Pre-Election Polls and Forecasts*, Social Science Research Council, New York, 1949. For a topical critique of polls see also Lindsay Rogers, *The Pollsters*, Knopf, New York, 1949.

32. In January of 1948, long before the election, Gallup found Truman leading Dewey, 49 to 44 percent. But by April, Truman had dropped to 42 percent while Dewey's share had risen to 52 percent. The gap remained at this level or greater until early October, by which time Dewey had dropped to 50 percent and Truman had risen back up to 45 percent. In the popular vote those proportions were exactly reversed, but the pollsters had stopped their surveys by the middle of October. Dramatic swings in voter sentiment can occur in a short period of time as an election campaign reaches its climax. A series of local polls made by Dorothy Corey before the Los Angeles mayoralty election of 1969 found the incumbent's support in one Councilmanic district going from 35 percent on April 12 to 73 percent on May 27 and in another district from 37 to 56 percent.

33. In spite of his public expressions of disdain for polls, Harry Truman, while President, commissioned one from Dun & Bradstreet to measure available coal stocks when he was faced with a strike threat from labor leader John L. Lewis.

34. Mark Abrams, "The Opinion Polls and the 1970 British General Election," *Public Opinion Quarterly*, Vol. 34, No. 3, Fall 1970, pp. 317–324.

35. Richard Rose, ed., *Polls and the 1970 Election*, University of Strathclyde, Strathclyde, 1970.

36. For an authoritative description of voter behavior see V. O. Key, Jr., *The Responsible Electorate: Rationality in Presidential Voting, 1936–60*, Belknap Press, Cambridge, 1966.

37. A 1964 survey by the Census Bureau showed that 76.6 million of the 110.6 million eligible voters *claimed* to have voted, but in fact only 70.6 million voters really did so. Of those who did not register in 1966, 8 percent were aliens, 19 percent did not meet state residency requirements, and 63 percent had other explanations. Among those with four years or less of elementary school, only 31 percent voted, compared with 71 percent of the college graduates. Among the college graduates who were not registered, 42 percent mentioned residency restrictions, reflecting the greater mobility of the better educated and well-to-do.

Except for people in the retirement years, the likelihood of voting increases steadily with age. Half of the unregistered people of voting age are under 30.

38. Irving Crespi points out that in the final, preelection Gallup survey in 1952, the candidate preferences broke down 47 percent for Eisenhower, 40 percent for Stevenson, and 13 percent undecided. If the pollster were to assume that the undecided voters would end up voting for Stevenson two to one, the final prediction would have been Eisenhower 51 percent, Stevenson 49 percent. If the undecided were allocated three to one, Eisenhower and Stevenson would each have had 50 percent. Harold Mendelsohn and Irving Crespi, *Polls, Television and the New Politics,* Chandler, San Francisco, 1970, pp. 82–83.

39. Among those originally undecided, however, the percentage that eventually voted varied substantially, from 63 percent in the 1964 Presidential election to 25 percent in the 1966 Congressional election.

Examining the data on Presidential and Congressional elections between 1950 and 1966, Paul K. Perry finds that in the average survey 16.4 percent of the sample of voting age first declared themselves undecided or with no preference. Each of the undecided respondents was then asked a follow-up question about the candidate he was leaning toward even if he had not made up his mind whom to vote for. After this question was asked, the "undecided" proportion fell almost by a half, to 8.6 percent. Among those individuals considered to be "likely voters," because of their answers to a series of questions on voting participation, the undecided dropped further to 6.7 percent. When the same voters were given a secret ballot which forced a choice on their part, the proportion undecided dropped down to 3.9 percent.

Among those ranked as most likely to vote on the voting participation scale, 56 percent were Republicans; among the group rated least likely to vote, 52 percent were Democrats.

In follow-up interviews with people polled before the elections between 1952 and 1966, the nonvoters numbered about 15 percent more Democrats (as a percentage of the Democratic-Republican preference) than the voters.

(Paul K. Perry and Irving Crespi, "The Measurement of Candidate Preferences and the Role of Issues in the 1968 Presidential Election," a paper delivered before the American Psychological Association, September 1, 1970.)

40. Archibald M. Crossley and Helen M. Crossley, "Polling in 1968," *Public Opinion Quarterly,* Vol. 33, No. 1, Spring 1969, pp. 1–16.

41. Of 45 senators and governors replying to a poll on the "Contemporary Use of Private Political Polling," 41 used polls in planning their election campaigns. The greatest use of polls reported by congressmen was among freshman Republicans. Of 46 questioned, 37 reported such use. (It seems probable that the convinced users of polls replied in disproportionate numbers to this poll on their practices.) Robert King and Martin Schnitzer, *Public Opinion Quarterly,* Vol. 32, No. 3, Fall 1968, pp. 431–436.

42. Kuchel, in turn, used a Don Muchmore state poll which showed that the Democratic favorite for the senate nomination, Alan Cranston, would defeat Rafferty but that Kuchel would defeat Cranston. In spite of this poll, Kuchel lost the Republican nomination to Rafferty, who lost the election.

43. *The New York Times,* October 30, 1970.

44. *Wall Street Journal,* March 8, 1968.

45. Thomas J. Fleming, "Selling the Product Named Hubert Humphrey," *The New York Times Magazine,* October 13, 1968.

46. *The New York Times,* November 7, 1966.

47. *The New York Times,* July 28, 1968.

48. By April 21 Gallup found that Nixon could beat all three Democrats. Kennedy ran behind McCarthy, though he was still ahead of Humphrey. Nixon led Humphrey 43 percent to 34 percent early in April, but in mid-June Humphrey led Nixon 42 percent to 37 percent. By late July Nixon and Humphrey were neck and neck, 40 percent to 38 percent.

49. To develop advertising themes Rockefeller's public opinion specialist, Lloyd Free, used a national Gallup sample to get people to indicate how much they worried about twenty-one problems identified from earlier research. (Earlier, Free, with his colleague, Hadley Cantril, had used a somewhat similar approach to compare prevailing attitudes and concerns in different countries.) The findings led him to recommend to Rockefeller that he not concern himself with seeking the votes of the poor or of Negroes, according to the account of Lewis Chester, Godfrey Hodgson, and Bruce Page, *An American Melodrama: The Presidential Campaign of 1968*, Viking, New York, 1969, p. 198.

50. In spite of the fact that a majority of voters identify themselves with the Democrats, the same survey showed that the lead was nearly two to one for the Republicans on the question of which political party "would be more likely to keep the United States out of World War III."

51. Theodore H. White, *The Making of the President, 1968*, Atheneum, New York, 1969, p. 327.

52. *Ibid.*, p. 313.

53. Sindlinger Poll: 42 percent approved of the nomination of Humphrey, and 38 percent did not; 52 percent reported watching Humphrey's acceptance speech, and 65 percent read about it in the paper; 26 percent said that Humphrey's speech was better than Nixon's, and 28 percent said it was not as good.

54. On September 3–7, Gallup found Nixon ahead 43 percent to 31 percent, but by September 20–22, Nixon's lead was 43 percent to 28 percent. Wallace moved forward from 19 percent to 21 percent in the same period. A significant moment in the campaign came when Humphrey announced that as President he would stop bombing in North Vietnam if the North Vietnamese agreed to neutralize the demilitarized zone. Sindlinger found that of those who knew of the speech (about three in ten), 37 percent favored Humphrey, and 30 percent were for Nixon, whereas among those who had not read, heard, or watched the speech, Nixon led 37 percent to 26 percent. (This is a classic case of chicken and egg; Humphrey supporters were more likely to expose themselves to the speech, but it also must have had a persuasive effect among some who were previously uncommitted or opposed to him.)

55. For an authoritative statement of Nixon's "Southern strategy," see Kevin P. Phillips, *The Emerging Republican Majority*, Arlington House, New Rochelle, New York, 1969.

56. In mid-September the Harris poll reported that 81 percent of the voters questioned in a national survey agreed with the statement, "Law and order has broken down in this country," while only 14 percent disagreed. Eighty-four percent also agreed that "A strong president can make a big difference in directly preserving law and order," and 63 percent agreed that "until there is justice for minorities there will not be law and order." Asked what caused a breakdown of law and order, 61 percent blamed organized crime, 56 percent named Communists, and 38 percent anti-Vietnam demonstrators. Only 22 percent agreed with the statement that "Demands for law and order are made by politicians who are against progress for Negroes."

In early October, Gallup reported that 25 percent of whites and 40 percent of Negroes were fearful of using the streets at night, and the proportion fearful of walking in some areas within a mile of home included 50 percent of all women (compared with 19 percent of men) and 49 percent of all metropolitan central city residents. (Gallup noted that Wallace, who stressed crime as a campaign issue, had least strength in the central cities where the fear was objectively greatest, and most strength in the rural areas where there was the least real fear.)

57. Warren Mitofsky, "Who Voted for Wallace?" paper delivered before the American Association for Public Opinion Research, 1969.

58. Philip E. Converse, Warren E. Miller, Jerrold G. Rusk, and Arthur G. Wolfe, "Continuity and Change in American Politics: Parties and Issues in the 1968 Election," paper delivered to the American Political Science Association, 1969. These authors conclude that a plurality of those Democrats who supported McCarthy before the convention gave Wallace their preference in the fall, and note that ten times as many Democrats shared Wallace's ideas as shared McCarthy's. However, their observations are based on extremely small subsamples of individuals who retrospectively acknowledged an early commitment to McCarthy.

59. Harris found that the proportion who said they admired George Wallace for "having the courage to say what he really thinks" rose from 77 percent in June to 86 percent in September. As many individuals (40 percent) disagreed with the proposition that Wallace was a racist as agreed that he was one.

60. Spokesmen for both Harris and Gallup indeed conjectured that those refusing to be interviewed might include a disproportionate number of Wallace supporters, since people who did not want to open the door might be generally anxious about security and therefore more sensitive on the issue of "law and order." This was not borne out by the results when Gallup compared a secret ballot with his regular open questioning. There was no difference. In Detroit, immediately after the assassination of Robert Kennedy, interview refusal rates had run up to 40 percent, perhaps reflecting jumpiness on the part of some people, as well as bitterness on the part of Negroes. Harris' field director, Richard Mack, said refusals "were just killing us," particularly in New York City, not a Wallace stronghold. When officials of the Census Bureau raised the question of whether the pollsters might be encountering a high rate of refusal to be interviewed or the problem of people who were not at home when an interviewer called, Mack replied that only between 10 and 15 percent of his sample was not fulfilled either because no one was home or because of refusals. The Gallup organization reported about 8 percent refusals, but did not report its "not at home" rate because it used a weighting procedure to compensate for this problem (giving greater weight to those people who reported that they were least often at home at the time of the interview). As Election Day loomed closer, the pollsters expressed increasing caution, and called attention to the possibility that last-minute switches might affect the final results.

61. Gallup's final projection was 42 percent for Nixon, 40 percent for Humphrey, and 14 percent for Wallace. Since 1948, Gallup has maintained his previously perfect record of calling the winner in Presidential elections. In 1952 Gallup showed Eisenhower leading Stevenson slightly, 51 percent to 49 percent in early September and again later that month. His final poll showed Eisenhower leading 52 percent to 48 percent. The actual vote turned out to be 55.4 percent to 44.6 percent.

In 1956 Gallup found Eisenhower leading Stevenson 56 percent to 44 percent through most of the campaign, ending up with a 60 percent to 41 percent lead. The actual vote was 58 percent to 42 percent.

In 1960 Gallup showed Kennedy and Nixon very closely matched, with Kennedy first leading in early September, 51 percent to 49 percent and then the two candidates' positions reversed by late September, returning in the final poll to a 51 percent to 49 percent split in Kennedy's favor. In the actual vote, Kennedy won by a mere 0.2 percent margin of the popular vote.

In 1964 Gallup showed Johnson leading Goldwater, 68 percent to 32 percent, early in September and maintaining his lead until the final poll, 64 percent to 36 percent. The actual vote was 61.3 percent to 38.7 percent.

62. Columbia Broadcasting System, Office of Social Research, *Bandwagon: A Review of the Literature,* New York, 1964, p. 18.

63. Charles K. Atkin, "The Impact of Political Poll Reports on Candidate and Issue Preferences," *Journalism Quarterly,* Vol. 46, No. 3, Autumn 1969.

64. "Some Thoughts About the Role of Public Opinion Polls in Today's Political and Social Processes," a talk delivered before the American Psychological Association, September 1, 1968.

Part II

1. This point may be illustrated by a study made during the Korean War, when the U.S. Army was moving to desegregate. Troops were asked how an imaginary soldier, "Joe Doakes," would and should react in two hypothetical instances in which Negroes were introduced into an all-white unit. In one case the commanding officer makes a speech favoring integration; in the other he urges his men to make things tough for the new recruits so that they will know they are not wanted. The proportion of Northern white soldiers who thought that Joe *would* make things tough for the Negroes or ignore them went up from 5 percent in the favorable situation to 14 percent when the Captain was unfriendly. When the Captain was favorable, 63 percent thought Joe should treat the Negroes like any other soldiers. The proportion dropped to 47 percent when the Captain was unfavorable. Although 26 percent said Joe should report the Captain to the Inspector General, only 12 percent thought he would actually do so. The point being made has nothing to do with the actual percentages, which would look quite different today. It is rather that in every instance the proportion giving a response favorable to integration is greater in the normative (or "should") question than in the projective (or "would") question. Within the coercive structure of military authority, the leader was able to modify behavior more readily than to change the opinions of his men. Leo Bogart, ed., *Social Research and the Desegregation of the U.S. Army,* Markham Publishing Co., Chicago, 1969.

2. Konrad Kellen, "Einstein: Personal Reminiscences," *Virginia Quarterly Review,* Vol. 42, Winter 1966, pp. 89–94.

3. Quoted by Arthur Blaustein, "Washington Report," *Harper's,* March 1969, p. 28.

4. *The New York Times,* October 14, 1969.

5. Quoted by Tom Wicker in the *New York Times,* April 27, 1971.

6. *The New York Times,* May 21, 1968.

7. *The New York Times,* October 10, 1969.

8. Jacques Ellul, *Propaganda,* Knopf, New York, 1965, p. 124.

9. Dean Rusk, "A Fresh Look at the Formulation of Foreign Policy," *U.S. Department of State Bulletin,* Vol. 44, March, 1961, p. 398.

10. Elliott Roosevelt, ed., *Franklin Delano Roosevelt: His Personal Letters,* Vol. 4, 1928–1945, 4 Vols., Duell, Sloan & Pearce, New York, 1947–1950, p. 968.

11. William L. Langer and S. Everett Gleason, *The Challenge to Isolation, 1937–1940,* Harper & Brothers, New York, 1952, p. 38.

12. Hadley Cantril, *The Human Dimension,* Rutgers University Press, New Brunswick, N.J., 1967, p. 42.

13. Robert E. Sherwood, *Roosevelt and Hopkins, An Intimate History,* Harper & Brothers, New York, 1950, p. 861. The author's attention was drawn to this by Sebastian de Grazia.

14. George Kennan, *Memoirs,* Little, Brown, Boston, 1967, p. 221.

15. Amitai Etzioni, "The Kennedy Experiment," *Western Political Quarterly,* Vol. 20, No. 2, Part I, June 1967, pp. 361–380.

16. Harris poll. As mentioned earlier, a telephone poll conducted by Gallup immediately after President Nixon's broadcast speech in defense of his Vietnam policy, on November 3, 1969, found that seven out of ten persons claimed to have heard the speech and of these, 77 percent approved the President's remarks. The viewers agreed six to one with the President's assertion that antiwar demonstrations were harmful to the cause of peace.

17. Elmer E. Cornwell, Jr., *Presidential Leadership of Public Opinion,* Indiana University Press, Bloomington, 1965, p. 184.

18. W. Phillips Davison cites the case of a public controversy in Israel over the use of radios in busses; when the authorities regulated them an editor called this "a triumph for public opinion," but the entire discussion had been conducted by three young men writing letters under a variety of fictitious names. (W. Phillips Davison, *International Political Communication,* Praeger, New York, 1965, p. 68.

19. Charles M. Winick, "Taste and the Censor in Television," a paper published by The Fund for the Republic, 1959, p. 32.

20. Manfred Landecker, *The President and Public Opinion: Leadership in Foreign Affairs,* Public Affairs Press, Washington, D.C., 1968, p. 48. See also Leila B. Sussmann, *Dear F.D.R.: A Study of Political Letter-Writing,* Bedminster Press, Totowa, N.J., 1963.

21. Letter to *The New York Times,* May 25, 1970, from Professor William A. Spurrier, Wesleyan University.

22. Senator Fulbright received 34,000 telegrams, 90,000 letters, and petitions signed by 100,000 names, within a month after the Cambodian move; 97 percent supported his position. In the same period, the White House got as many as 80,000 letters a day, with an "informed guess" saying 60 percent favored the President's position. (*The New York Times,* May 24, 1970).

23. This was perhaps no more than a survival from those Tsarist centuries of faith that the people's interests were close to the heart of the Little Father, surrounded though he was by obtuse and malevolent advisers.

24. James Q. Wilson, "The Urban Unease," *The Public Interest,* Summer 1968, p. 26.

25. A Harris survey in August 1969 attempted to get at the public's sense of priorities by asking people where they thought federal spending should be cut off first and last: 69 percent said spending should be cut first on foreign aid; 64 percent, on Vietnam; 51 percent, on the space program; 37 percent, on federal welfare; 26 percent, on other defense spending; 24 percent, on farm subsidies. In deciding what should be cut last, 60 percent said aid to education; 38 percent said pollution control; 34 percent named the federal poverty program; 26 percent, federal aid to cities; 24 percent federal highway financing.

26. Harris Poll, July 25, 1967.

27. Forty-one percent of the public say they least mind paying local taxes; 22 percent, federal taxes; and 14 percent, state taxes, while 23 percent are not sure. (Harris Poll, March 1969).

28. Norman R. Luttbeg, "The Structure of Beliefs Among Leaders and the Public," *Public Opinion Quarterly*, Vol. 32, No. 3, Fall 1968, pp. 398–409.

29. Robert L. Heilbroner, "Making a Rational Foreign Policy Now," *Harper's*, September 1968, p. 71.

30. Daniel P. Moynihan, *Maximum Feasible Misunderstanding—Community Action in the War on Poverty*, The Free Press of Glencoe, New York, 1969, p. 137.

31. Quoted in Edward Engberg, *The Spy in the Corporate Structure*, World, New York, 1967, p. 30.

32. The Gallup Poll (March 20, 1968) found a majority of members of labor union families favor compulsory arbitration of all labor disputes after a 21-day strike.

33. Richard M. Johnson, "The Public Schools and Confrontation Politics: The Views of Urban Blacks and Whites," unpublished paper, 1969.

34. Martin Mayer, *The Teachers' Strike, New York-1968*, Perennial Library, New York, 1969, p. 50.

35. *The New York Times*, October 10, 1968.

36. Mayer, *The Teacher's Strike*, p. 58.

37. Gallup Poll, *Newsweek*, June 30, 1969.

38. Angus Campbell and Howard Schuman, *Racial Attitudes in Fifteen American Cities: A Report Prepared for the National Advisory Commission on Civil Disorders*, University of Michigan Institute for Social Research, Ann Arbor, 1968. See also William Brink and Louis Harris, *Black and White*, Simon and Schuster, New York, 1966.

39. Letter to the (Negro-run) New York *Amsterdam News*. Although anti-Semitism among *young* Negroes runs 30 to 45 percent higher than among young whites, a nationwide survey shows that 68 percent of Negroes, compared to 51 percent of whites, said they would not be "disturbed if a Jew was nominated for president." (Gertrude J. Selznick and Steven Steinberg, *The Tenacity of Prejudice: Anti-Semitism in Contemporary America*, Harper and Row, New York, 1969.)

40. Letter to *The New York Times*, June 15, 1969.

Part III

1. Robert Hess and Judith Torney, *The Development of Political Attitudes in Children*, Anchor Books, Garden City, N.Y. 1968, p. 247. See also Fred I. Greenstein, *Children and Politics*, Yale University Press, New Haven, 1965; Richard E. Dawson and Kenneth Prewitt, *Political Socialization*, Little Brown, Boston, 1969; David Easton and Jack Dennis, *Children in the Political System: Origins of Political Legitimacy*, McGraw-Hill, New York, 1969.

2. Three out of four second graders think that the president makes the laws. By the eighth grade only 5 percent give this answer, and 85 percent say it is Congress. At the second-grade level, 14 percent believe that the United Nations does most to keep peace in the world, and 71 percent believe it is the United States. By the eighth grade, 10 percent mention the United States and 87 percent the United Nations. (*Ibid.*)

3. Jerald G. Bachman and Elizabeth Van Duinen, *Youth Look at National Problems*, Institute for Social Research, Survey Research Center, University of Michigan, Ann Arbor, 1971.

4. R. H. Bruskin Poll. The peace symbol was familiar to 34 percent of the total adult population.

5. 1971 survey by *Seventeen* magazine.

6. Gallup Poll data. The same phenomenon can be observed for a homogenous population. Of Harvard's alumni who graduated before 1930, 23 percent were Democrats; of those graduated between 1960 and 1967, 56 percent were Democrats. (From a study conducted for the Harvard Alumni Association by Cornelius DuBois.) Young people whose orientation may be described as cosmopolitan are less likely to share their fathers' political views than those with a more local perspective. Joel I. Nelson and Irving Tallman, "Political Attitudes of Youth," *American Journal of Sociology*, Vol. 75, No. 2, September 1969, pp. 193–207.

7. Gallup Poll, May 1970. (There is a long history behind the nonconformism of college students. Thomas Jefferson wrote in 1823, "The insubordination of our youth is now the greatest obstacle to their education.")

8. Gallup Poll.

9. CBS-Yankelovich Poll: 81 percent of the radicals reported that they had worked in a political campaign or taken part in a civil rights protest; among the conservatives the proportion was only 54 percent. Although two of every three students say they want a life different from that of their parents, they exhibit the characteristic American ambivalence between socialized idealism and personalized preoccupations. Among 2000 college seniors queried by Jeffrey K. Hadden in 1969, 85 percent said that the most important things in life could be understood only through involvement, but only a minority reported regular participation in any form of political activity. Eighty-nine percent said the problems of the cities were personally important to them, yet 78 percent expressed admiration for the life style of suburbia and gave "every indication that they will join the exodus." Three out of five said that protest leaders "give the rest of us a bad name." Among college students across the country, 54 percent thought that those who break laws while participating in campus demonstrations should be expelled. Louis Harris found that young people, by a two to one majority, favored a $15 tax to fight pollution, whereas their elders opposed it two to one.

10. In 1969, 2 percent of the students described themselves as extremely conservative; 19 percent moderately conservative; 24 percent middle-of-the-road; 41 percent, moderately liberal; and 12 percent extremely liberal. Two percent refused to classify themselves. Twenty-three percent of the students described themselves as Republicans; 33 percent as Democrats; and 44 percent as Independents; among the general public, 29 percent described themselves as Republicans; 42 percent as Democrats; and 29 percent as Independents.

11. Gallup Poll. Another study conducted in 1971 by Daniel Yankelovich with 872 college students at 35 universities found that three out of four preferred working with "the establishment" rather than through protest organizations. Sixteen percent thought the American two-party system offered no real political alternatives, and a majority agreed that Black Panthers, radicals, and hippies could not get a fair trial in the United States.

12. Survey by R. H. Goettler and Associates, Columbus, Ohio.

13. Steven H. Chaffee, L. Scott Ward, and Leonard P. Tipton, "Mass Communication and Political Socialization", *Journalism Quarterly*, Vol. 47, No. 4, Winter 1970, pp. 647–662.

14. Philip E. Converse, Warren E. Miller, Jerrold G. Rusk, and Arthur G. Wolfe,

"Continuity and Change in American Politics: The Parties and Issues in the 1968 Election," paper delivered to the American Political Science Association, 1969.

15. Among college students, nearly half said their main goal was to "benefit mankind." Gilbert Youth Research, February 1970.

16. 1971 Gilbert Youth Poll.

17. In 1960 twice as many Americans said life was getting "better" in terms of religion as said it was getting "worse." In 1968 the ratio was reversed, with opinion running two to one that religious life was getting worse. (Gallup Poll).

18. Similarly, the proportion of Koreans practicing contraception rose from 9 to 20 percent between 1964 and 1966. The percentage of women with an IUD (intra-uterine loop device) in place went from 0.4 to 9 percent in the same 2-year period. [From the KAP (Knowledge, Attitude, Practice) surveys sponsored by The Population Council.]

19. In 1937 the Gallup Poll found 46 percent of the electorate willing to vote for a Jewish presidential candidate. By 1965 the figure had risen to 80 percent. Yet not all such long-term opinion trends move consistently in the same direction. In 1937, about one out of every four Americans said anti-Jewish feeling was increasing in the United States (a revelation of their own feelings on the subject). By 1947 the proportion had risen to over half (now perhaps reflecting awareness of the Nazi atrocities). But by 1950 (after the establishment of Israel) the percentage dropped to 16.

When asked what groups were a menace to America, 17 percent named the Jews in 1940; 22 percent in 1946; but only 5 percent in 1950. In this same period, the nature of anti-Semitic stereotypes also changed. Jewish businessmen were less often seen as "dishonest" and more often described as "shrewd" or "tricky." The view of European Jewry as a weak, passive, and oppressed minority gave way to the view of Israel as an energetic, cocky, and even aggressive power. Charles Herbert Stember, *Jews in the Mind of America*, Basic Books, New York, 1966.

20. The proportion of Texans favoring integration of Negroes and whites at the university level went from 20 percent in 1948 to 36 percent in 1954. In April 1954, before the Supreme Court school integration decision, 74 percent of those queried by the Texas Poll said Negro children should not have the right to go to the same schools as white children. In September, after the Supreme Court decision, the proportion had changed only slightly, to 71 percent. By August 1958, the percentage had dropped to 59, and by 1961 a *majority* of whites (54 percent) favored school integration. Interestingly enough, the identical proportions (67 percent) of the Negroes and whites in 1958 answered affirmatively to the question, "Do you believe there will ever come a time when Negroes and whites will be going to the same school in all parts of Texas?"

21. Gallup Poll, *The New York Times*, May 3, 1970.

22. Southern youth became more pro-integration in the 1940s and 1950s, but those who grew up during school intergation were more negative than preceding age cohorts who knew it as a noble concept and were not exposed to the difficulties and clashes which attended its initiation. Herbert H. Hyman and Paul B. Sheatsley, "Attitudes Toward Desegregation," *Scientific American*, Vol. 211, No. 1, July 1964.

23. Angus Campbell and Howard Schuman, *Racial Attitudes in Fifteen American Cities: A Report Prepared for the National Advisory Commission on Civil Disorders*, University of Michigan Institute for Social Research, Ann Arbor, 1968.

24. Specific events may also accelerate changes of opinion which bear the unmistakable marks of a long-term trend. The proportion favoring an 18-year-old vote jumped

from 17 percent in June 1939 to 39 percent in January 1943, after the war had brought about a rise in teenage military service. It reached 63 percent in July 1953, after the Korean War; it dipped slightly in the following years, and rose again to 64 percent in 1967 and 1969. (Gallup Poll data.)

25. Anna J. Merritt and Richard L. Merritt, *Public Opinion in Occupied Germany,* University of Illinois Press, Urbana, 1970, pp. 16–17.

26. *Ibid.,* p. 33.

27. *Ibid.,* p. 39.

28. National Opinion Research Center and Gallup polls.

29. In July (before the invasion) 37 percent believed it impossible for the United States and the Soviet Union to reach a workable long-term agreement to control wars in the world. In late August (after the invasion) this proportion had risen to half the public. (Harris Poll.) Another example: In September, 1967, the proportion of Germans who felt threatened by the Soviet Union went from 58 to 67 percent in a single week, after French President de Gaulle visited Poland and proclaimed the permanence of the Oder-Neisse line. (Surveys by the Wickert Institute.)

30. Israel Institute for Social Research data, reported in a personal communication.

31. In the words of Paul Sheatsley and Jacob Feldman: "The assassination of their President did not seem to make them more or less anti-Communist, it did not affect their attitudes toward civil rights, and it did not erode their basic optimism about other people's motives. These attitudes are not inflexible; three of them, at least have shown substantial changes in the past." (Paul B. Sheatsley and Jacob J. Feldman, "A National Survey on Public Reactions and Behavior," in Bradley S. Greenberg and Edwin B. Parker, eds., *The Kennedy Assassination and the American Public,* Stanford University Press, Stanford, Calif., 1965, p. 175.)

32. Soon after the Kennedy assassination, the Harris Poll found that at least 39 percent of the people believed that Oswald had not acted alone. This belief persisted after publication of the Warren Commission report. The proportion actually rose to 44 percent after the appearance of books and articles which criticized the report. In May 1967, after James Garrison, the district attorney of New Orleans, announced his discovery of an assassination "plot," the conspiracy theory was accepted by 66 percent. Although Garrison's inquiry produced nothing, in September 60 percent still believed that Kennedy had been killed by a conspiracy.

33. James S. Coleman and Sidney Hollander, Jr., "Changes in Belief in the Weeks Following the Assassination," in Greenberg and Parker, *The Kennedy Assassination.*

34. Verba has described this effect as a "complex admixture of the rational institutions of politics with the more traditional religious and indeed somewhat magical aspects of political commitment. . . . The level of commitment to politics is both more intense than that revealed by the usual public opinion surveying techniques and of a somewhat different order." He likens it to "a primordial emotional attachment. It is not the rather fragile support that is based solely on a calculation of interest; it is support based on a longer run, less rational sort of attachment." (Sidney Verba, "The Kennedy Assassination and the Nature of Political Commitment," in Greenberg and Parker, *The Kennedy Assassination.*)

35. Opinion changed rapidly also on the occasion of yet another Kennedy family tragedy. A day or two after his accident at Chappaquidick in 1969, Senator Edward Kennedy went on television to defend his actions. A *Boston Globe* poll of the Massachusetts public showed that four out of five approved his handling of his Senate office and felt he should retain it. Only 6 percent thought he should resign. Kennedy's

speech changed the attitudes of a majority of the viewers, particularly among the Senator's supporters, who said they "felt better" after listening to him. But another similar poll by Oliver Quayle found a drop from 72 to 55 percent in the proportion who favored Kennedy for President (even though three out of four believed his statement that he had not been driving under the influence of alcohol) and Gallup found nationally that the proportion giving an "extremely favorable" rating to the Senator fell to 34 percent after the accident, from a level of 49 percent three months earlier. By May 1970, a national Harris survey found a two to one majority of the public who agreed that Senator Kennedy's driving contributed to the death of Mary Jo Kopechne. The proportion who said they had lost respect for the Senator grew from 28 percent after the accident to 43 percent nine months later, after the inquest. The Quayle poll and a nationwide Harris poll showed a majority who felt that many questions about the accident remained unanswered, but two out of three (according to Harris) felt that "the same thing could have happened to anybody." At the end of July, Kennedy was named as first choice for the Democratic Presidential nomination in 1972 by 30 percent, compared with 41 percent who named him in May. In the same period, Senator Muskie jumped from 19 to 28 percent. By July 1971, Harris found one-third of the public agreeing that "because of what happened at Chappaquidick," Senator Kennedy showed he does not deserve the presidency, although two-thirds believed he was a good Senator. From then on, both Harris and Gallup found Kennedy rating high compared with other leading Democrats in trial heats against Nixon. (See also Michael J. Robinson and Philip M. Burgess, "The Edward M. Kennedy Speech: The Impact of a Prime Time Television Appeal," *Television Quarterly,* Vol. IX, No. 1, Winter, 1970, pp. 29–39.)

36. Parallel to these trends was the changing proportion who predicted the United States would enter the war. A bare majority (51 percent) were convinced of this at the outset, but the proportion dropped to 31 percent within a few months as the government took measures to assure neutrality, and as strong anti-war sentiment began to mobilize. The proportion rose back to 50 percent when the "phony war" period ended with the German invasion of Holland and Belgium, but fell back to 29 percent when France fell and the war seemed almost over. (Hadley Cantril, "Opinion Trends in World War II: Some Guides to Interpretation," *Public Opinion Quarterly* Vol. 12, 1948, pp. 30–44.)

37. Gertrude J. Selznick and Stephen Steinberg warn, "An anti-Semitic candidate with a promised economic solution during a crisis period might gain the votes of all those susceptible to political anti-Semitism—the 25 percent who said they would vote for an anti-Semitic candidate, the more than one-third who said the candidate's anti-Semitism wouldn't matter, plus uncountable fellow travelers who made up the indifferent majority." Selznick and Steinberg report 37 percent of the population hold negative images of Jews; 25 percent defend the rights of social clubs to exclude Jews; another 29 percent, while opposed in principle, would not do anything to combat such practice; 36 percent are firmly opposed; and 10 percent have no opinion. Only 5 percent say they would vote for an anti-Semitic candidate, but over one-third say his views would make no difference to them. Only 16 percent represent "the small minority which can be described as principled and consistent opponents of anti-Semitism." (See *The Tenacity of Prejudice: Anti-Semitism in Contemporary America,* Harper and Row, New York, 1969.)

38. Gallup Poll, June 24, 1969.

39. Alienation was measured with items like, "Few people really understand how

it is to live like I live," "People running the country don't really care what happens to people like ourselves."

40. Perhaps this was because of differences in the questions asked, as well as because of the tragedies and racial turmoil of the time intervening. Eleven percent said they would join a riot (the proportion had been 15 percent in 1966); 18 percent felt Negroes had more to gain than to lose by resorting to violence; 21 percent said, Negroes could not win their rights without violence; 30 percent felt that riots had been justified; 10 percent approved of Negro students carrying guns on campus; 64 percent agreed that there would be riots in the future. (*Newsweek,* June 30, 1969, pp. 19–23.)

41. Gilbert Youth Research, February 1970.

42. Gary Marx, reviewing the evidence from surveys made in the late 1960s, concludes that between 5 and 20 percent of the Negro population "hold attitudes indicating a depth of estrangement and bitterness unique in American history." (Gary T. Marx, *Protest and Prejudice: A Study of Belief in the Black Community,* Harper and Row, New York, 1969.)

In 1968, 10 percent of Miami Negroes were described as "violent" or "ready for violence," and another 13 percent "leaning toward violence." Conventional (nonviolent) militancy increased with social privilege and with political knowledge and morale. Opposition to violence was highest among the college educated, next among those with the least education, and least among the high school and trade school educated. (*Miami Herald* Survey.) Another survey of 199 Negro Vietnam veterans in the Jacksonville, Florida, area found opinion evenly divided for and against the Black Panthers, and predominantly favorable to CORE and to SNCC. The same study showed a substantial distrust of white institutions and authorities. (James Fendrich and Michael Pearson, "Black Veterans Return," *Trans/Action,* Vol. 7, No. 8, March 1970, pp. 32–37.)

43. Harris Poll, March 1970.

44. *The New York Times,* May 26, 1971.

45. From published accounts of the survey, it appears that about 150 Negroes were included in the sample. How many, one must wonder, were in the teen-age group whose separate opinion was cited?

46. I have discussed this elsewhere in describing a study of the desegregation of the U.S. Army during the Korean War:

"The prevailing state of [troop and officer] opinion could no more than reflect the existing policy and organizational structure of the Army . . . opinion was subject to change along with that policy and structure . . . it was far more important to look into the differences in opinion from one set of conditions to the next than to tote up the numbers and arrive at generalizations. . . .

"Our approach to the data runs completely contrary to the popular concept of public opinion polling, as well as to much of the actual practice in survey research. The policymaker may be constrained by public opinion to modify the timing or direction of what he deems to be the proper course of action; if he merely charts that course to follow public opinion, he ceases to be a policymaker altogether. . . . The fact that our surveys showed only a minority favoring segregation might have appeared as an interesting or even surprising datum to the military leadership, but it could and should have had no relevance to the decision to desegregate. Our research concern was to establish the variability of this percentage under different circumstances which could be controlled.

"There were, at that time, troop units with comparable assignments but with every conceivable racial balance. Differences in the opinions held by the same kinds of people under varying circumstances provided a guide to the *processes* of opinion. The very susceptibility of opinion to change, as documented by the results, meant that the *overall* breakdown of opinion would have shown quite different percentages had the surveys been made a month sooner or a month later: the percentages themselves meant little. Our responsibility was to investigate the limits of opinion and its susceptibility to change as a result of change in policy." (Leo Bogart, *Social Research and the Desegregation of the U.S. Army*, Markham Publishing Co., Chicago, 1969, pp. 31–32.)

47. In an address March 12, 1969, before the Women's National Democratic Club, Washington, D.C.

48. The *New York Times*, March 7, 1969.

49. Sidney Verba, Richard A. Brody, Edwin B. Parker, Norman H. Nie, Nelson W. Polsby, Paul Ekman, and Gordon S. Black, "Public Opinion and the War in Vietnam," *American Political Science Review*, LXI, No. 2, June 1967, pp. 317–333.

50. In February 1965, of those who said they had been following developments in Vietnam, two out of three had supported retaliatory air strikes against the North. In April, 29 percent favored deescalation or withdrawal; 31 percent continuation or escalation of the action. In September 1966, 48 percent agreed that the United States was right in having sent troops to fight in Vietnam, but only 21 percent expected a United States military victory. In May 1967, the Harris Poll found that 45 percent favored total military victory and 41 percent wanted withdrawal under United Nations supervision.

51. Jeffrey Record, "Viet Cong: Image and Flesh", *Trans/Action*, Vol. 8 No. 3, January 1971, p. 51.

52. Sidney Verba and Richard A. Brody, "Participation, Policy Preferences and the War in Vietnam," *Public Opinion Quarterly*, Vol. 34, No. 3, Fall 1970, pp. 325–332.

53. Gallup pollster Irving Crespi observed, "The immediate reaction to Tet was to strike back hard, but apparently second thoughts as to the implication of further escalation led to a more Dovish climate of opinion." After Johnson withdrew from the presidential race, approval of his handling of the Vietnam War went to 57 percent, the same as the proportion in August 1965 and January 1966.

54. Harris Poll. In mid-September, Harris reported that Nixon held an 18-point lead over Humphrey, 39 to 21, among voters who wanted to use nuclear weapons in the war (8 percent of the total). Overall, more voters felt that Nixon would do a better job in handling the war in Vietnam than thought that Humphrey would, and this was obviously a factor in his victory. At this time, 18 percent of the voters wanted to win with conventional weapons; 17 percent wanted to keep military pressure on; 17 percent supported a policy of withdrawal to a few coastal enclaves; 18 percent favored gradual withdrawal of U.S. troops; 13 percent, total withdrawal. In all, 43 percent wanted to sustain or step up military pressure and 48 percent wanted to scale it down, with 9 percent unsure.

In March 1968, 35 percent of the public told Gallup that the war in Vietnam would be over in less than two years; 39 percent felt it would last more than two years. A year later, in March 1969, a smaller proportion, 27 percent, said the war would last under two years, and 40 percent said it would go on for over two years.

55. Two-thirds of the public at this time felt that the Paris peace talks were not making headway. In March 1969, following a three-week Vietcong offensive, 32 percent were in favor of going "all out"; 26 percent favored a pullout; 19 percent favored continuing the present policy of talking and fighting; and 19 percent were in favor of an end of the war "as soon as possible."

In April, Gallup showed Americans evenly divided in opinion as to whether Nixon was pursuing his own independent policy in Vietnam or Johnson's. In late June, after Nixon had ordered a withdrawal of 25,000 U.S. troops, 42 percent believed the rate of withdrawal should be faster; 16 percent, slower; 29 percent, no change; and 13 percent, no opinion. At this time 61 percent opposed immediate withdrawal of all troops from Vietnam, and 29 percent favored it.

By July, 53 percent approved Nixon's conduct of the war, and 28 percent acknowledged that they had not given thought to what the United States should do next in Vietnam. The solutions advocated ranged from escalation (11 percent) to immediate withdrawal (12 percent), with only 9 percent favoring the status quo and 43 percent favoring some form of deescalation. By September, Harris found that seven out of ten felt that it would take a long time to achieve a settlement, and only 35 percent expressed approval of Nixon's handling of the war.

The proportion favoring immediate withdrawal from Vietnam, according to Gallup, dropped from 29 percent in June 1969 to 21 percent in November, following the President's television appeal for more time. The proportion opposing withdrawal was not very different among people in their twenties (73 percent) than among the rest of the adult population (75 percent). Curiously enough (considering the strong vocal opposition to the war among intellectuals) the greatest support for immediate withdrawal came from the least educated sector of the public. This probably reflected the war's extreme unpopularity among Negroes.

56. In March 1970, 21 percent were in favor of immediate withdrawal, and 25 percent for withdrawal within 18 months; 39 percent favored slow withdrawal to permit Vietnamization; only 7 percent wanted to escalate with American troops.

57. A Gallup Poll a few weeks after the publication of the Pentagon Papers found that only 55 percent had heard of them; among these, opinion ran two to one that publication was "the right thing."

58. As a typical example, under the headline "Poll Finds More Back Escalation," *The New York Times* of May 17, 1967, refers to "rising public support for escalation of the American war effort in Vietnam." Forty-five percent of those polled said they favored "total military victory." The corresponding figure in February was 43 percent—not a significant difference.

59. Jerald G. Bachman and Elizabeth Van Duinen, *Youth Look at National Problems,* Institute for Social Research, Survey Research Center, University of Michigan, Ann Arbor, 1971.

60. By July 1970 two out of three people aged 14 to 25 were opposed to United States involvement in Vietnam, and one in four felt that a young man drafted to fight in Vietnam should refuse to serve. A survey conducted in the spring of 1970 by Kenneth and Mary Gergen among 5000 college students at 39 campuses found that over 40 percent reported that the war had changed their political loyalties, mostly in the direction of either the left or of dillusionment. One-third said that the war had decreased their interest in graduate study and their respect for college administrators. Brighter students in better schools were most affected by the war.

61. Philip Converse and Howard Schuman, " 'Silent Majorities' and the Vietnam War," *Scientific American,* Volume 222, Number 6, June 1970, pp. 17–25.

62. Irving Crespi, "Longitudinal versus Cross-sectional Measures of Public Opinion on Vietnam: A Methodological Note," an unpublished paper, May 1968.

63. Nelson Polsby, "Hawks, Doves, and the Press," *Trans/action,* April, 1967, pp. 35–40.

Part IV

1. Alfred Hero, "Public Reaction to Government Policy," in John P. Robinson, Jerrold G. Rusk, and Kendra B. Head, *Measures of Political Attitudes,* Survey Research Center, Ann Arbor, Mich., 1968.

2. Forty-one percent said that public education needed attention and change, and 28 percent said the same of the federal government, but only 10 percent said it of religion. Three out of five say they talk about "bringing up children"; half about family life and religion; two in five talk about public education; about a third each name the federal government, clothing and fashions, and professional sports; 18 percent about labor unions; 13 percent about big business; 11 percent about advertising. (Raymond A. Bauer and Stephen A. Greyser, *Advertising in America: The Consumer View,* Division of Research, Graduate School of Business Administration, Harvard University, Boston, 1968, pp. 86–87.)

3. Allen Parducci, "The Relativism of Absolute Judgment," *Scientific American,* December 1968, pp. 84–90.

4. For a somewhat outdated review of the psychological evidence, see Leon Festinger, "Behavioral Support for Opinion Change," *Public Opinion Quarterly,* Vol. XXVIII, No. 3, Fall 1964, pp. 404–17.

5. Howard Leventhal, "Fear For Your Health," *Psychology Today,* Vol. 1, No. 5, September 1967, pp. 55–58.

6. During World War II, the U.S. Army conducted expensive experiments to measure what "indoctrination" films accomplished upon captive audiences of troops, for example in raising their estimate of the British as allies. (Carl I. Hovland, Arthur A. Lumsdaine, and Fred D. Sheffield, *Experiments on Mass Communications,* Princeton University Press, Princeton, 1949. The American Association for the United Nations conducted a massive experiment in Cincinnati to improve the public regard for the U.N. (Shirley Star and Helen MacGill Hughes, "Report on an Educational Campaign: The Cincinnati Plan for the United Nations," *American Journal of Sociology,* Vol. LV, No. 4, January 1940, pp. 389–400.) The U.S. Information Agency ran newspaper advertisements ostensibly to familiarize the Greek public with the United Nations Declaration of Human Rights, but with the more subtle purpose of building Greek regard for the United States as the major guardian of those rights. (Leo Bogart, "Measuring the Effectiveness of an Overseas Information Campaign: A Case History," *Public Opinion Quarterly,* Vol. 21, No. 4, Winter 1957–1958, p. 475.)

7. R. H. Bruskin Poll.

8. For a summary of the literature and theory on this subject, see the chapter on "The Effects of Enforced Discrepant Behavior" in Arthur R. Cohen, *Attitude Change and Social Influence,* Basic Books, New York, 1964. See also Robert P. Abelson, Eliot Aronson, William J. McGuire, Theodore M. Newcomb, Milton J. Rosenberg, and Perry Tannenbaum, eds., *Theories of Cognitive Consistency: A Sourcebook,* Rand-McNally, Chicago, 1968.

9. Quoted in *Atlas,* February 1969.

10. Howard Leventhal, "Fear for Your Health," *Psychology Today,* Vol. 1, No. 5, September 1967, pp. 55–58. In another study, Stanley Lehmann found that messages which aroused a moderate level of anxiety were more persuasive than either those which were extremely threatening, or those which aroused little anxiety. "High self-esteem coupled with high anxiety would increase the resistance to threat but be susceptible to reassurance and vice versa. . . . Behavioral compliance was better pre-

dicted than opinion change." "Low-anxious, low-self esteem women were better motivated by threat, while high-anxious, high-self esteem women were better motivated
by reassurance." ("Personality and Compliance: A Study of Anxiety and Self-Esteem in
Opinion and Behavior Change," *Journal of Personality and Social Psychology*, Vol. 15,
No. 1, 1970, pp. 76–86.)

11. Viewers of a documentary public affairs television program not only become better informed on the subject and shift their attitudes in the direction advocated by
the program, they also become more certain of their opinions, because these now form
a system with its own established rationale. (Stephen J. Fitzsimmons and Hobart G.
Osburn, "The Impact of Social Issues and Public Affairs Documentaries," *Public Opinion Quarterly*, Vol. 32, No. 3, Fall 1968, pp. 379–397.)

12. Anthony G. Greenwald and Joseph S. Sakumura, "Attitudes and Selective
Learning: Where are the Phenomena of Yesteryear?" *Journal of Personality and
Social Psychology*, Vol. 7, No. 4., 1967, pp. 378–397.

13. Carolyn W. Sherif, Muzafer Sherif, and Roger E. Nebergall, *Attitude and Attitude Change*, W. B. Saunders, Philadelphia, 1965.

14. "The individual's commitments, dedications, and cherished positions on highly
involving matters (matters related to family, sex role, religion, school, politics, or profession) are ingredients of his self-picture . . . of the individual's very self-identity."
(*Ibid.*, p. 228.)

15. In an experiment by J. Allyn and Leon Festinger, two groups of teenagers were
presented with the same speech on the dangers of teenage driving. One group was told
in advance that they were to rate the personality of the "expert" speaker; the other
group was warned that the speaker thought teenage drivers were a menace and would
seek to persuade them. Overall, the two groups did not differ significantly in the degree
to which their opinions changed after the speech. However, among those students
(about one in three) who had strong opinions on the subject to begin with, there was
substantially more opinion change when the purpose of the experiment was disguised.
"The Effectiveness of Unanticipated Persuasive Communications," *Journal of Abnormal
and Social Psychology*, 1961–62, pp. 35–40.

16. Demetrios Papageorgis, "Warning and Persuasion," *Psychological Bulletin*, Vol.
70, No. 4, October 1968, pp. 471–482.

17. D. O. Sears, J. L. Freedman, and E. F. O'Connor, "The Effects of Anticipated
Debate and Commitment on the Polarization of Audience Opinion," *Public Opinion
Quarterly*, Vol. 28, 1964, pp. 617–627.

18. The concept of "relative deprivation" in psychology is analogous to "reference
group" theory in sociology; both elaborate the principle that people tend to position
their own judgments in terms of the standards of a group with which they identify.

19. Judson Mills and Jerald M. Jellison, "Effect on Opinion Change of Similarity
Between the Communicator and the Audience he Addressed," *Journal of Personality
and Social Psychology*, Vol. 9, No. 2, 1968, pp. 153–56.

20. That attitudes are modified to resemble the judgment of the group was demon-
strated first by Muzafer Sherif in "A Study of Some Social Factors in Perception,"
Archives of Psychology, Vol. 27, 1935, No. 187. See also Solomon E. Asch, "Effects of
Group Pressure Upon the Modification and Distortion of Judgments," in Eleanor
E. Maccoby, Theodore E. Newcomb, and Eugene L. Hartley, eds., *Readings in Social
Psychology*, Holt Rinehart and Winston, New York, 1958, pp. 174–183. More recent
literature on conformity is reviewed by V. L. Allen, "Situational factors in Conformity,"
in Leonard Berkowitz, ed., *Advances in Experimental Social Psychology*, Vol. 2, Academic Press, New York, 1965.

21. Kenneth Lenihan, "Perceived Climates as a Barrier to Housing Desegregation," Bureau of Applied Social Research, New York, 1965.

22. Gary I. Schulman, "The Popularity of Viewpoints and Resistance to Attitude Change," *Journalism Quarterly*, Vol. 45, No. 1, Spring 1968, pp. 86–90.

23. N. Pollis, "Relative Stability of Reference Scales Formed Under Individual, Togetherness, and Group Situations," Ph.D. dissertation, University of Oklahoma, 1964 (cited by Sherif and Nebergall, *Attitude and Attitude Change*).
In one series of experiments people were assigned to discussion groups, some with the expectation that they would continue with the group and some with the expectation that they would not. The experimenter gave everyone a fictitious "rating" of how attractive he supposedly was to the rest of the group. It was found that the less we think others like us, the less we like them. When we think others like us, we modify our opinions to resemble theirs. But if we think they do *not* like us, our response to their opinions depends on whether or not we consider ourselves permanent members of the group. If our membership is temporary, the less we like them the less their opinions are apt to influence us. If we are committed to staying with the group, their opinions will affect our own regardless of whether or not we think we are liked. (Charles A. Kiesler, "Conformity and Commitment," *Trans/Action*, June 1967, pp. 32–35.)

24. Serge Moscovici and Marisa Zavalloni, "The Group as a Polarizer of Attitudes," *Journal of Personality and Social Psychology*, Vol. 12, No. 2, 1969, pp. 125–135.

25. E. E. Maccoby, N. Maccoby, A. K. Romney, and J. S. Adams, "Social Reinforcement in Attitude Change," *Journal of Abnormal and Social Psychology*, Vol. 63, No. 1, 1961, pp. 109–115.

26. Bernard Berelson, Paul Lazarsfeld, and William McPhee, *Voting—A Study of Opinion Formation in a Presidential Campaign*, University of Chicago Press, Chicago, 1954, p. 355. Also see Paul Lazarsfeld, Hazel Gaudet, and Bernard Berelson, *The People's Choice*, Columbia University Press, New York, 1948.

27. V. O. Key, Jr., *The Responsible Electorate*, Random House, New York, 1968.

28. Sigmund Freud, "Dream Censorship," in John McCormick and Mairi MacInnes, *Versions of Censorship*, Aldine, Chicago, 1962.

29. William James, *The Varieties of Religious Experience*, Modern Library, New York, 1902, p. 193.

30. *Ibid.*, p. 251.

31. See W. I. Thomas and Florian Znaniecki, *The Polish Peasant in Europe and America*, Vol. 1, R. G. Badger, Boston, 1918.

32. Quoted and translated by Peter Gay, *Weimar Culture*, Harper and Row, New York, 1968, p. 27.

33. Leon Rappaport and George Cvetkovich, "Opinion on Vietnam," a paper presented to the American Psychological Association, 1968.

34. Arthur Koestler, *Darkness at Noon*, Modern Library, New York, 1946.

35. Writing in *Reporter* of Prague during the hiatus before the Russian invasion (reproduced in *Atlas*, Vol. 16, No. 3, September, 1968, pp. 18–24).

36. Quoted by David Halberstam, "Love, Life, and Selling Out in Poland," *Harper's*, July 1967, pp. 78–9.

37. Ithiel de Sola Pool, "Public Opinion in Czechoslovakia," *Public Opinion Quarterly*, Vol. 24, No. 1, Spring 1970, pp. 10–25.

38. *East Europe*, April 1966, p. 19, quoted by Zbigniew Brzezinski, *Between Two Ages: America's Role in the Technetronic Era*, Viking, New York, 1970.

39. Philip E. Converse, "The Nature of Belief Systems in Mass Publics," in David E. Apter, ed., *Ideology and Discontent,* Free Press of Glencoe, New York, 1964, pp. 206–261.

40. It should be noted that 80 percent of the experiments reported in psychological journals published in the United States use undergraduates as subjects.

41. Jack W. Brehm and Arthur R. Cohen, *Explorations in Cognitive Dissonance,* Wiley, New York, 1962, pp. 34, 40.

42. Irving L. Janis and B. T. King, "The Influence of Role Playing on Opinion Change," *Journal of Abnormal and Social Psychology,* Vol. 49, 1954, p. 218.

43. John Wallace, "Role Reward and Dissonance Reduction," *Journal of Personality and Social Psychology,* Vol. 3, No. 3, 1966, pp. 305–312.

44. A. O. Elbing, "An Experimental Investigation of the Influence of Reference Group Identification on Role Playing as Applied to Business," Ph.D. dissertation, 1962, University of Washington (quoted by Sherif and Nebergall, *Attitude and Attitude Change, op. cit.*)

Part V

1. Alexis de Tocqueville, *Democracy in America,* Vol. 2, Knopf, New York, 1945, p. 10.

2. Lloyd A. Free and Hadley Cantril, *The Political Beliefs of Americans,* Rutgers University Press, New Brunswick, N.J., 1968.

3. A Harris Poll conducted in November 1968 found that only 17 percent consider themselves "liberal"; 38 percent style themselves "conservative"; and 32 percent middle-of-the-road." Since a majority of voters describe themselves as Democrats, it is clear that only a minority of Democratic voters are self-conscious liberals.

4. Early in the 1968 election campaign, Gallup data showed that 61 percent of Humphrey supporters and 63 percent of McCarthy supporters felt that Negroes being treated in their home communities "the same as whites." In the case of Nixon supporters, the proportion was 74 percent, and among Wallace supporters 88 percent. Twenty percent of Wallace supporters felt that whites are "more to blame for the present conditions in which Negroes find themselves"; the proportion was 23 percent among the pro-Nixon group, 31 percent of those for McCarthy, and 33 percent of the Humphrey supporters. These differences are not nearly as striking as one might suppose.

However, on specific tactics (as opposed to generalizations), the adherents of Wallace expressed their racial opinions more distinctively. Eighty-three percent said that the Johnson administration was pushing integration too fast, compared with fewer than 30 percent of the Humphrey and McCarthy supporters.

To consider a more general subject, 51 percent of the Wallace supporters disagreed with the statement that America is a "sick society," but the proportion among supporters of Nixon, Humphrey, and McCarthy varied between 61 percent and 63 percent. As might be expected, 89 percent of Wallace supporters believed that "life today is getting worse in terms of morals"; 81 percent of the Nixon supporters agreed with this, but so did 70 percent of the Humphrey supporters and 71 percent of the McCarthy supporters.

On the subject of the Vietnam War, 46 percent of the Wallace supporters described themselves as Hawks and 33 percent as Doves. Among the Nixon supporters the proportions were evenly divided; 44 percent and 43 percent. Among the Humphrey supporters the proportions were 39 percent Hawks and 41 percent Doves, and among the McCarthy supporters, 37 percent described themselves as Hawks and 41 percent as Doves.

This was at the beginning of April 1968, before the polarization of the Humphrey and McCarthy forces. Not surprisingly, 38 percent of the McCarthy supporters felt at that time that it was *not* a mistake for the United States to have sent troops to fight in Vietnam.

5. Gallup Poll.

6. Philip E. Converse, Warren E. Miller, Jerrold G. Rusk, and Arthur G. Wolfe, "Continuity and Change in American Politics: Parties and Issues in the 1968 Election," paper delivered to the American Political Science Association, 1969, p. 29.

7. Anti-Semitism is lower among college graduates than in any other part of the population, but the college-educated with high income and high social status are the heaviest supporters of social club discrimination. This kind of anomaly may be accounted for in part by the presence of distinct subsegments within a larger social class, in part by the greater exposure to Jews (and hence the higher salience of opinions about them pro and con) at the upper reaches of the social scale, and in part by the sheer willingness of people to be inconsistent between what they think personally and what they do within the framework of their established institutions. (Gertrude J. Selznick and Stephen Steinberg, *The Tenacity of Prejudice: Anti-Semitism in Contemporary America,* Harper and Row, New York, 1969, pp. 33–39.)

8. Richard T. La Piere, "Attitudes vs. Actions," *Social Forces,* Vol. 13, 1939, pp. 230–237.

9. Lyle G. Warner and Melvin L. DeFleur, "Attitude as an Interactional Concept: Social Constraint and Social Distance as Intervening Variables Between Attitudes and Action," *American Sociological Review,* Vol. 34, No. 2, April 1969, pp. 153–169.

10. E. Q. Campbell and T. F. Pettigrew, "Racial and Moral Crisis: The Role of Little Rock Ministers," *American Journal of Sociology,* Vol. 64, No 5, March 1959, pp. 509–516.

11. Harold Nicolson, *Diaries and Letters, 1930–1939,* Atheneum, New York, 1966, p. 163.

12. Carolyn W. Sherif, Muzafer Sherif, and Roger E. Nebergall, *Attitude and Attitude Change,* W. B. Saunders, Philadelphia, 1965, p. 67.

13. Milton Rokeach, *Beliefs, Attitudes and Values,* Jossey-Bass, San Francisco, 1968. Rokeach had undergraduates rank their basic values (such as "equality") and then got them to state a position on civil rights demonstrations. The inconsistency, when it existed, was revealed in a "self-confrontation," which produced a markedly more favorable attitude toward civil rights, reflected months later in response to fundraising appeals from the NAACP. (*Behavior Today,* Vol. 2, January 11, 1971.)

14. *The New York Times,* May 14, 1967.

15. John H. Bunzel, *Anti-Politics in America,* Knopf, New York, 1967, p. 178.

16. Jean Stoetzel, *Théorie des Opinions,* Presses Universitaires de France, Paris, 1944.

17. Individual opinions (the kind measured in polls and surveys) are always formed first, writes social psychologist Gerhart Baumert, while public opinion emerges out of the subsequent discussion, as more general interest rises in the subject and in the people who hold opposing views.

18. During the feverish days of Prague's liberal Spring, Ithiel de Sola Pool reported on the development of "a Hyde Park corner in the old Town Hall Square of Prague." At the beginning the people assembling in the Square had no loudspeaker system. Then they acquired one, then the crowd got bigger, and they were even addressed by government officials. The crowd, according to Pool, "was extraordinarily disciplined

and well behaved. They listened; they asked questions; they showed no signs of ugliness." Questions were passed on slips of paper up to the speakers. A young, more activist group arrived later. They expressed their comments by applauding or whistling but remained completely in order. At one point Pool came upon a table with signs and a petition calling for the abolition of censorship and the People's Militia and for free elections. The young man manning the table had two buttons in his lapel; one a Czech flag and the other a Pepsi Cola button. ("Notes From Prague," unpublished, August 9, 1968.)

19. For a description of how this happens, see Alexander Solzhenitsyn's novels *The First Circle* and *The Cancer Ward*.

20. "The Art of Propagating Opinion," *Works of Samuel Butler,* Vol. 20, Henry Jones and A. T. Bartholomew, eds., Trusberg Publishing Co., London, 1926, pp. 163–164.

21. November 10, 1966.

22. *The New York Times,* February 7, 1967. See also Orrin E. Klapp, *Symbolic Leaders,* Aldine, Chicago, 1964.

23. Harold Lasswell has suggested that the politician's constant need to "simulate" or play a role builds up inner tensions which often express themselves in aberrant personal behavior. He cites a study conducted at the Elgin, Illinois, State Hospital, in which patients elected their own ward representatives. These "political leaders" were more self-assured "even to the point of paranoiac certainty" than their constituents, or than the defeated candidates, suggesting that the successful politician is someone who can project self-confidence.

24. Jerry Rubin, *Do It,* Simon and Schuster, New York, 1970, pp. 134–135.

25. *Ibid.,* p. 83.

26. *The New York Times,* September 15, 1955.

27. *The New York Times,* January 23, 1970.

28. John Toland, *The Last 100 Days,* Random House, New York, 1966, p. 415.

29. Neil Sheehan, *The New York Times,* November 29, 1967.

30. Alan F. Westin, *Privacy and Freedom,* Atheneum, New York, 1967, pp. 44–46.

31. Clinton Rossiter, ed., *The Federalist,* Number 1, New American Library, New York, 1961, p. 34.

Part VI

1. Quoted by Ernst Kris and Hans Speier, *German Radio Propaganda,* Oxford University Press, New York, 1944, pp. 197–198.

2. *Ibid.,* p. 135.

3. Carl Oglesby, "Report from Cuba," *Life,* February 14, 1969, pp. 62–68.

4. Hans Ulrich Kempski, "Greek Chorus in Rumania: 'Ceausescu!'" *Süddeutsche Zeitung,* reprinted in *Atlas,* September, 1969.

5. Nadezhda Mandelstam, *Hope Against Hope: A Memoir,* Atheneum, New York, 1970, p. 145.

6. She was awarded the title *die Päbstin* by *Der Spiegel,* the news magazine.

7. Elisabeth Noelle, *Meinung und Massenforschung in U.S.A.,* Verlag Moritz Diesterweg, Frankfurt am Main, 1940, p. 1. In recent correspondence Noelle has explained that the statement was not an expression of her real opinion.

8. Josef Goebbels, *Wesen und Gestalt des Nationalsozialismus,* Junker und Dünnhaupt, Berlin, 1935. (Quoted by Jacques Ellul, in *Propaganda,* Knopf, New York,

1965, p. 206.) See also Ladislas Farago, ed., *German Psychological Warfare*, G. P. Putnam's Sons, New York, 1941.

9. Hannah Arendt, "Reflections: Truth and Politics," *New Yorker*, February 25, 1967, pp. 49–88.

10. *The Economist*, April 17, 1971.

11. Quoted by W. Phillips Davison, "Some Observations on Vietcong Operations in the Villages," Memorandum RM 5267-2ISA/ARPA, July 1967, Rand Corporation, Santa Monica, Calif., p. 11.

12. *The New York Times*, March 30, 1968.

13. See Alex Inkeles, *Public Opinion in Soviet Russia*, Harvard University Press, Cambridge, 1958. See also Alex Simirenko, ed., *Soviet Sociology: Historical Antecedents and Current Appraisals*, Quadrangle, Chicago, 1966.

14. Thomas Ruikes, *Journal, 1831–1841*, Longman, Brown, Green, Longmans and Roberts, London, 1858, entry for February 25, 1834, p. 130. I am indebted to Frederick W. Williams for calling this book to my attention.

15. Otto Ohlendorf, an SS man executed after the war for his part in the slaying of Polish Jews, prepared regular reports on the state of German public opinion from information supplied by the *Sicherheitsdienst* (the SS Security Service).

16. Quoted by John Lear, "Opinion Polling in the U.S.S.R.," *Saturday Review*, October 5, 1968, pp. 55–56.

17. George Fischer, *Science and Ideology in Soviet Society*, Atherton Press, New York, 1968. See also Alex Simirenko, *Social Thought in the Soviet Union*, Quadrangle, Chicago, 1968.

18. *The New York Times*, January 8, 1970.

19. *The New York Times*, February 22, 1969.

20. When the United States released a group of North Vietnamese sailors in October 1967, Hanoi attributed the gesture to "the struggle of the Vietnamese and world public opinion." In the preliminary sparring over the peace negotiation site, Hanoi proclaimed, "World public opinion demands that the U.S. Government give a formal answer to the Government of the Democratic Republic of North Vietnam about the choice of Warsaw as the site for the preliminary contact."

On May 14, 1968, the first day of negotiations, a spokesman for the North said that if the bombing continued, "World public opinion and all men of good will everywhere would condemn the United States then." He announced that "World opinion and progressive American opinion are against the United States' position." As authority for this he cited statements by Charles de Gaulle, Martin Luther King, Robert Kennedy, and William Fulbright.

21. In an interview with Harrison Salisbury of *The New York Times*, May 21, 1969.

22. February 1, 1968.

23. Kosygin told Americans, "From this (Vietnam) war you have gained absolutely nothing, and in the eyes of public opinion you have lost very much. Absolutely nobody can say a good word about this dirty war—except a group of persons waxing rich on it. This group does not express public opinion, yet it is trying to use the mass media to support United States aggression. Everybody realizes what lies behind such propaganda—a craving to make money on human blood."

Further examples: In October 1967, a commentator for *Pravda*, Ivan Shchedrev, reported that, "Imperialistic circles in the United States were trying to maneuver and escape the condemnation of world public opinion" and that this was responsible for rumors of an impending bombing halt. After President Johnson's restriction of bombing in North Vietnam, Vikenty Matveyev, another Soviet commentator, said the decision to restrict the bombing "deceived public opinion." A year later the North Vietnamese Communist Party newspaper leveled the same charge at President Nixon.

24. Marchenko wrote, "I am ashamed for my country. . . . I would also be ashamed for my countrymen if I believed that they were truly unanimous in supporting the policy of the Central Committee and the government. . . . The unanimity of our citizens is a fiction artificially created through the violation of the very freedom of speech that is being upheld in the Czechoslovak Socialist Republic."

An appeal to "world public opinion" was also made in the summer of 1968 by a group of the Crimean Tartars who remained in exile a quarter-century after Stalin had deported them from their ancestral homeland. (*The Economist*, March 29, 1969.)

25. Quoted in *The New York Times*, December 13, 1968.

26. *The New York Times*, August 29, 1968.

27. Alexis de Tocqueville, *Democracy in America*, Vol. 2, Knopf, New York, p. 22.

28. For an optimistic (and outdated) view, see Th. Ruyssen, "Existe-t-il une Opinion Internationale?" *L'Esprit International*, No. 45, January 1938, pp. 71–89.

29. Gordian Troeller and Claude Deffarge, "Underground in Greece—On the Inside," *Atlas*, Vol. 15, No. 3, March 1968, pp. 29–32.

30. Camelot was widely denounced both in Latin America and in the United States. It was sponsored by the Army through the device of a special institute set up at George Washington University. A part of the current vogue of studies in "counterinsurgency," motivated in the early 1960s by fear of Castro, Camelot had the military intelligence objective of providing better understanding of the techniques of leftist insurrection in Latin America. Camelot was not planned *sub rosa* and had no secret aspect. The plan was to conduct surveys openly, using local research organizations. The congressional reaction to Camelot overcompensated for the furor in the left-wing and nationalist press of Latin America. The effect was to strengthen the hand of the know-nothing element in Washington which was distrustful of all social research. See Robert Nisbet, "Project Camelot and the Science of Man," in *Tradition and Revolt: Historical and Sociological Essays*, Random House, New York, 1968.

31. *Trans/Action*, June 1971.

32. Hadley Cantril, *The Human Dimension: Experiences in Policy Research*, Rutgers University Press, New Brunswick, N.J., 1967.

33. Western researchers going into underdeveloped areas sometimes put their questions directly, as they might to a cross section of Americans or Europeans. Anthropological observations may be more appropriate and valid in some cases than opinion polls. (In Indonesia, direct questioning is considered impolite, and the unexpected situation calls for evasive answers.) The pollster who is engaged in multinational research is apt to be especially sensitive to the subtle necessities of transcending his own national perspective. In constructing questionnaires, the professional researcher is trained to avoid terms which may be part of the working vocabulary of his own political environment: "the Free World," "the building of socialism," and the sinister epithets applied to the adversary. Yet the political naiveté implicit in such terms may well intrude into the overall concepts which shape the design and analysis of research.

34. An example of this is a thirteen-nation survey conducted by the Gallup organization in 1968 which found the United States to be the country least tolerant of marriage between whites and nonwhites, with 20 percent approving and 72 percent disapproving. This compares with 67 percent approving and 21 percent disapproving in Sweden and 35 percent approving and 47 percent disapproving in West Germany. (*The*

New York Times, November 10, 1968.) Such comparative data are fascinating and valuable but can only be interpreted in the light of a historical understanding of the tremendously different intergroup relationships in these countries.

35. Harry Stack Sullivan, *The Interpersonal Theory of Psychiatry,* W. W. Norton, New York, 1953.

36. Jacques Kayser, *One Week's News: A Comparative Study of Seventeen Major Dailies for a Seven-Day Period,* UNESCO, Paris, 1953. See also Wilbur Schramm, *One Day in the World's Press: Fourteen Great Newspapers on a Day of Crisis,* Stanford University Press, Stanford, 1959.

37. There is a substantial difference between being a member of a great linguistic culture, like English, Spanish, or Russian, and being a member of a small culture, like Danish, Dutch, or Iranian. Members of small linguistic cultures are forced to become multilingual if they are to lead any kind of intellectual life at all. But it is the rare individual who is completely at home in another language. The average person in a small culture is inevitably handicapped in his access to specialized knowledge and literature which can flourish in large cultures where there are substantial subsegments of society with common interests and a common language base.

38. *The Center Magazine,* March/April 1971, p. 5.

39. Don D. Smith, "America's Short-Wave Audience: Twenty-five Years Later," *Public Opinion Quarterly,* Volume 33, Number 4, Winter 1969–1970, p. 537.

40. I asked a girl in East Germany whether she ever watched the West Berlin programs she could receive on the family television set; the reception was good, she said, but she never watched them: "We have our own station."

41. Television broadcasting directly from satellites to home receivers may eventually be used to leap the barriers of dictatorship, though there are still serious technical and cost problems to overcome. The political implications of worldwide direct satellite-to-home broadcasting were readily perceived in the Soviet Union. Yuri Sheinin writes in *Literary Gazette* that "in the first half of the coming decade the free reception of any television program in the world and the automatic home recording of that program will become feasible. It is enough to imagine what the malicious use of the latest channels of information for reactionary purposes might lead to. To a certain degree it could impede social progress." He sees this as a result of Western television firms beaming propaganda to Soviet homes and opening up "a new propaganda front." He specifically cites American television as notoriously contaminated by horror films and broadcasts that "propagandize for violence. (This is not to mention the annoying television advertising which unifies not only the tastes but also the views of the mass consumer.) Classes and parties that are departing from the historical scene strive to use information and communications media to create a mass base, to mobilize an army of supporters. The removal of these media from the hands of the monopolies is a necessary condition for the victory of Socialism and the realization on this basis of the genuine unity of mankind."

Part VII

1. Quoted in John Morley's biography of Rousseau (London, 1915 Vol. II, p. 132), cited by Robert Nisbet, *The Sociological Tradition,* Basic Books, New York, 1966, p. 40.

2. Herbert Marcuse, *An Essay on Liberation,* Beacon Press, Boston, 1969, pp. 64–65. The publication of the "Pentagon Papers" was obviously incongruous with the Marxist thesis that the American media are simply the mouthpieces of the American power

structure. Moscow's *Literary Gazette* provided an explanation in a full-page article answering the question, "Why did The *New York Times* begin to talk?" It explained that there were rivalries among different sectors—military-industrial, civilian, and military-civilian. The war had cut the profits of the "civilian monopolies" and they were, therefore, eager to publish documents discrediting the war. Thus "the action by Sulzberger in no way can be regarded . . . as having anything to do with freedom of the press."

3. Norman Birnbaum, *The Crisis of Industrial Society,* Oxford University Press, New York, 1969, p. 72.

4. Alexis de Tocqueville, *Democracy in America,* Vol. 2, Knopf, New York, 1945, p. 7.

5. Ralph K. White, *Nobody Wanted War,* Doubleday, New York, 1968.

6. See Frantz Fanon, *The Wretched of the Earth,* Grove Press, New York, 1966.

7. For a selection of tactical papers, see William J. Pomeroy, ed. *Guerilla Warfare and Marxism,* International Publishers, New York, 1968; also see Tariq Ali, ed., *The New Revolutionaries: A Handbook of the International Radical New Left,* William Morrow, New York, 1969; Harry Eckstein, ed., *Internal War: Problems and Approaches,* Free Press Glencoe, New York, 1964.

8. W. Phillips Davison, *International Political Communications,* Praeger, New York, 1965, p. 69.

9. "Participatory democracy," substitutes the *ad hoc* discussion group (amorphous in form and structure and hence easily dominated by the most strident voices) for the formally constituted authorities and procedures of government. Since the legitimacy of the ordinary democratic electoral institutions can be discounted as a self-perpetuating device of the Establishment, new organic forms of political expression may be created and a new legitimacy claimed for them. [This in fact was the rationale used in setting up the Bolshevik-dominated workers' and soldiers' councils (Soviets) of the Russian Revolution that represented an alternative system of organized power outside of the normal political structure (the democratically elected, bourgeois-dominated Constitutional Assembly). There were earlier forerunners in the Jacobin Clubs of the French Revolution and the workers' associations that created the Paris commune.]

10. Peter Kropotkin, *Memoirs of a Revolutionist,* Houghton Mifflin, Boston, 1899, p. 406.

11. See Eugene Luttwak, *Coup d'Etat,* Knopf, New York, 1969.

12. George Rudé, *The Crowd in the French Revolution,* Clarendon Press, London, 1959.

13. Eyewitness account.

14. Pitirim Sorokin made this point in an address to the American Sociological Association, 1963.

15. West India Emancipation Speech, August 1857, quoted by Stokely Carmichael and Charles V. Hamilton, *Black Power; The Politics of Liberation in America,* Random House, New York, 1967, p. x.

16. Jerome H. Skolnick, *The Politics of Protest,* Simon and Schuster, New York, 1969, p. 145.

17. In today's revolutionary glossary, the systematic destruction of property.

18. For an interesting contrast see Julien Sorel, *Reflections on Violence,* Free Press of Glencoe, Glencoe, Ill., 1950, and Régis Debray, *Revolution in the Revolution,* Grove Press, New York, 1968. See also Massimo Teodori, *The New Left: A Documentary History,* Bobbs Merrill, Indianapolis, 1969.

19. The public at large does not take to the confrontation tactics of white rebels

any more kindly than it does to rioting in the Negro neighborhoods. A national Sindlinger telephone poll immediately after the Democratic convention of 1968 found that 48 percent thought the street demonstrations were organized to disrupt the convention, and 71 percent believed the security measures against the demonstrators were justified; 62 percent said Mayor Daley was doing a good job. Gallup also found that a majority (56 percent) of the public approved of the way the Chicago police handled the demonstrations, though a substantial minority (31 percent) disagreed. Among a cross section of the American public interviewed by the Michigan Survey Research Center, 12 percent were unaware of the confrontation between the police and the demonstrators at the Chicago Convention; 12 percent were aware but had no opinion; 19 percent thought the police had used too much force; 32 percent, the right amount; and 25 percent, not enough force. Older individuals sided most strongly with the police, but Negroes were critical of them.

People in their twenties are somewhat more inclined to be lenient toward college demonstrators than are older people, but the overwhelming majority are still inclined to treat them harshly. A Gallup Poll in March 1969 found that seven out of ten thought that demonstrators who broke laws should be expelled from college, and four out of five thought that Federal loans should be taken away from them. (See also John P. Robinson, "Public Reaction to Political Protest: Chicago, 1968," *Public Opinion Quarterly*, Vol. 24, No. 1, Spring 1970, p. 1–9.

20. Cleaver, himself, like George Jackson the "Soledad Brother," was the prototype of a new gun-toting convict hero. Jackson's fatal attempt at a jailbreak in San Quentin in August 1971, and the uprising in New York's Attica prison a month later, aroused widespread public concern over the nation's system of criminal justice and correction. For the Left these episodes demonstrated that jail inmates were the political prisoners of a racist society.

21. *Barron's*, September 15, 1969, p. 12.

22. *The New York Times*, March 15, 1970. The same kind of psychotic imagery occurs in a review of a musical group in the July 1967 issue of *Helix*, a Seattle underground newspaper: "Their style is early cunnilingual with overtones of the Massacre of the Innocents. An electrified sex slaughter. A musical bloodbath. . . . The Doors scream into the darkened auditorium what all of us in the underground are whispering more softly in our hearts: we want the world and we want it . . . NOW!" (Quoted by Theodore Roszak, *The Making of a Counter Culture*, Doubleday, New York, 1969.) See also Mark Gerzon, *The Whole World is Watching: A Young Man Looks at Youth's Dissent*, Viking, New York, 1969; Massimo Teodori, ed., *The New Left: A Documentary History*, Bobbs Merrill, Indianapolis, 1969; and Julian Foster and Durward Long, *Protest. Student Activism in America*, William Morrow, New York, 1970.

23. *U.S. News and World Report*, May 18, 1970.

24. For evidence of this, see an analysis of a national survey by Shirley Star cited by Jack Elinson, Elena Padilla, and Marvin Perkins in *Public Image of Mental Health Services*, Mental Health Materials Press, New York, 1967.

25. Quoted by Irving Howe, *The New York Times Magazine*, October 25, 1968, p. 138.

26. Sidney Hook, *Academic Freedom and Academic Anarchy*, Cowles, New York, 1970, p. 56.

27. Jerry Rubin, *Do It*, Simon and Schuster, New York, 1970, p. 105.

28. Allen H. Barton, "The Columbia Crisis: Campus, Vietnam and the Ghetto," *Public Opinion Quarterly*, Vol. 32, No. 3, Fall 1968, p. 337. At Columbia, about one-third of the students were on the campus on the night of the police "bust" against

the sit-ins. Of these, three out of five (61 percent) thought there was widespread police violence, but only a third (36 percent) who had not been on hand felt this was so. Obviously the confrontation with the police attracted a disproportionate number of those who were predisposed to be unsympathetic to them, but the sight of police and students in conflict must also have engaged the loyalties of many who might otherwise not have been on the side of the militants.

29. A study of events on 232 campuses in the first six months of 1969 was made by the Urban Research Corporation of Chicago. In this period there were 292 "major protests" on these campuses, which drew the active participation of about 10 percent of the students. Half of the protests involved demands by Negro students, 44 percent related to demands for more "student power," and only 22 percent related to war issues like ROTC, recruitment, military research, and the war itself. About a fifth of the incidents involved injuries and about a fifth involved damage to property.

In 1967, Students for a Democratic Society claimed a membership of 35,000, of whom only about 1000 were estimated to be "hard-core" dues payers. (See Gene E. Bradley, "What Businessmen Need to Know about the Student Left," *Harvard Business Review*, September-October, 1968, pp. 49–60.)

In the early stages of the Berkeley upheavals of 1964, there were fewer than 200 rebels, but the numbers grew steadily after the civil authorities moved in with countermeasures. When a police car entered the campus, its occupants were held captive for 24 hours. Later, 800 students moved to occupy a building. The atmosphere had been "radicalized." In the Spring 1968, student riots in Paris, about 800 activists at the University of Nanterre managed to paralyze a campus with a student body of over 11,000.

30. Surveys conducted among Negroes by white research organizations invariably face special problems in establishing proper rapport between interviewers and respondents. This was dramatized when George Gallup was forced to scrap a special Harlem poll commissioned by *The New York Times* before the election of 1968. The study plan called for 400 interviews between August 24, and October 3. Of the 26 Negro interviewers, 16 were regular Gallup staff members, and the others were especially recruited and trained. When the *Times* (in apparent disregard of normal polling precautions to secure respondent anonymity) sent a reporter and a photographer to get comments and "color" for the eventual story, they managed to talk with only three of 23 people reportedly interviewed and found the homes of eight others who were not available. There were no buildings at addresses listed for seven, and the remaining five persons could not be located. Further inquiries revealed that only 36 of the 309 interviews reported by 15 of the 16 staff interviewers could be confirmed by telephone checks. (*The New York Times*, November 1, 1968).

The cancellation of this survey reflected the good sense and high standards of both the *Times* and of the Gallup organization—but in how many other instances is research of this kind taken at face value, without a secondary check? And in how many instances are disturbing questions, and even disturbing evidence, about the field work swept under the rug?

31. Eric Josephson, "Resistance to Community Surveys," unpublished paper, 1969. See also Lee Rainwater and David Pittman, "Ethical Problems in Studying a Politically Sensitive and Deviant Community," *Social Problems*, Spring 1967, and Joan Moore, "Political and Ethical Problems in a Large Scale Study of a Minority Population," in Gideon Sjoberg, *Ethics, Politics, and Social Science*, Schenkman, Cambridge, 1967.

32. *Psychology Today*, September 1970, p. 52.

Part VIII

1. Henry L. Dursin, "Public Issues: Who Cares About What?" *Public Relations Journal,* June 1967.

2. Clinton Rossiter, ed. *The Federalist Papers,* Number 35, New American Library, New York, 1961, p. 214.

3. Firdus Dzinic, "Opinion Surveys in a Federal Republic," *Polls,* Vol. 3, No. 3, 1968, p. 9.

4. John P. Robinson, Jerrold G. Rusk, and Kendra B. Head, *Measures of Political Attitudes, op. cit.*

5. Verling C. Troldahl and Robert Van Dam, "Face-to-face Communication About Major Topics in the News," *Public Opinion Quarterly,* Vol. 29, No. 4, 1965, pp. 626–634.

6. People who ask for information and people who volunteer it in conversation have about the same amount of media exposure, but they are far less broadcast-oriented and more print-oriented than those who are comparatively inactive in exchanging information. The traditional way of looking at a mass media communication is to regard it as a stimulus which produces a direct response from the mass audience. By contrast, the "two-step flow" theory of mass communication, advanced by Elihu Katz and Paul Lazarsfeld (*Personal Influence,* The Free Press, Glencoe, Ill., 1955) argues that the media have their effects on a limited number of opinion leaders who absorb information and ideas and pass them on to others in direct personal conversation. There is, however, a difference between our willingness to learn new facts directly from the media and our susceptibility to persuasion by them. For example, a study of Dutch farmers by A. W. Vanden Ban concludes that media may play an important part in providing information on agricultural technology, but that personal influence is more important in determining actual decisions on farming methods.

Marten Brouwer argues that mass communication may really reflect what people are talking about rather than the other way around. He suggests that they may be the visible manifestation of ideas that flow more basically in informal conversation (which, in a delightful botanical metaphor, he compares to the mycelium or underground network from which mushrooms spring to the surface). ("Prologomena to a Theory of Mass Communication," in Lee Thayer, ed., *Communication—Concepts and Perspectives,* Spartan Books, Washington, D.C., 1967.)

7. Bibb Latané and John M. Darley, *The Unresponsive Bystander: Why Doesn't He Help?* Appleton-Century-Crofts, New York, 1970, p. 2.

8. *Ibid.*

9. *New York Review of Books,* November 3, 1966.

10. Leo Tolstoy, *War and Peace,* translated from the Russian by Constance Garnett, McGraw-Hill, New York, 1963, p. 909.

11. Ralph E. Lapp, *The Weapons Culture,* W. W. Norton & Co., New York, 1968.

12. Gallup Poll.

13. Bruno Bettelheim, *The Informed Heart,* Free Press, Glencoe, Ill., 1963, p. 18.

14. The use of appropriate euphemisms is of course part of the apparatus of denial. The SS referred to extermination as "resettlement," and to their victims as "pieces," denied of humanity. Similarly, a witness at the Calley trial recalled Calley's use of the term "waste 'em" in ordering his men to kill the women and children. "I asked him why he used the word 'waste.' I had never heard it before, and he said, 'We never use kill. . . . The word kill refers to our childhood teachings: "Thou shalt not kill."

We never use the word kill to the men. It causes a negative emotional reaction. So you use "waste" or "destroy." Never kill.' "

15. *Commentary*, November 1965, pp. 52–53.

16. For a brilliant discussion of this phenomenon, see Arthur Koestler, "On Disbelieving Atrocities," in *The Yogi and the Commissar*, Macmillan, New York, 1967.

17. Gertrude J. Selznick and Stephen Steinberg, *The Tenacity of Prejudice: Anti-Semitism in Contemporary America*, Harper and Row, New York, 1969, p. 63.

When Ida Kaminska, the Yiddish theater star, fled to the West, she observed that although there were only 20,000 Jews left in Poland in 1968, the Poles were warning that "hundreds of thousands" of them might seize the country. Her daughter recounted that when she applied for her exit papers, "I was filling out these papers, and the woman asked me, 'Why are you leaving?' I told her there is no one left to play for in Poland. She said, 'There are 500,000 Jews.' They can't admit there are so few Jews. It would make them seem ridiculous." (*The New York Times*, December 2, 1968.)

Another study of public opinion in Oakland, California, with regard to the Eichmann trial, found that "Despite a year of headlines and constant reiteration of the official estimate [of six million Jewish victims], 51 percent of the white respondents aware of the trial either underestimated or did not know the correct figure. After being told the correct figure, 55 percent of the white sample rejected it as inflated or refused to commit themselves on its accuracy." (Charles Y. Glock, Gertrude J. Selznick, and Joe L. Spaeth, *The Apathetic Majority*, Harper and Row, New York, 1966, p. 141.)

18. Harvey A. Tilker, "Socially Responsible Behavior as a Function of Observer Responsibility and Victim Feedback," *Journal of Personality and Social Psychology*, Vol. 14, No. 2, February 1970, pp. 95–100.

19. Melvin Lerner, "The Unjust Consequences of the Need to Believe in a Just World," unpublished paper delivered before the American Psychological Association, 1966.

20. M. J. Lerner and C. H. Simmons, "Observers' Reaction to the 'Innocent Victim': Compassion or Rejection?" *Journal of Personality and Social Psychology*, Vol. 4, No. 2, 1966, pp. 203–210.

21. Latané and Darley, *The Unresponsive Bystander*, p. 38.

INDEX

239